DIVERTICULITIS COOKBOOK FOR BEGINNERS

400+ Healthful Recipes. Clear Liquid, Low Residue, and High Fiber Content. Prevent
Flare-Ups, Revitalize your Digestive System and Gut Health Now
30-Day Meal Plan and Food List Included

Suzanne Scarrett

SUZANNESCARRETT.COM

TABLE OF CONTENT

SUZANNE SCARRETT

Hi, I'm *Suzanne Scarrett*.

Thank you for purchasing my book.

I invite you right now to visit my website that I run every day:

www.suzannescarrett.com

Every day I receive dozens of emails and many more personal requests for help.

I am genuinely pleased and proud of all that my team and I can do and provide for our customers.

Inside the site, you will find various recipes with pictures and articles related to diets and health. In addition, I am at your complete disposal to receive any advice or request you wish to make.

Finally, you will also find a section to contact me privately if you want.

It only remains to wish you much joy and serenity with the reading of this book.

INTRODUCTION

Diverticulitis is a condition in which a pouch or diverticulum forms in the wall of the bowel near an intestine's exit, allowing partially digested food to collect there. Over time, most cases of diverticulitis cause pain and discomfort as well as bleeding out the side (colon). It is similar to appendicitis, but with appendicitis, the inflammation affects the appendix, while with diverticulitis, it affects parts of the large intestine. There is no cure for diverticulitis, and the symptoms will usually go away within six weeks. Jodie Wilson, a nurse at Sutter Roseville Medical Center in California, states, "[Diverticulitis] is a condition that cannot be prevented. But it can be managed by watching what a person eats, getting good nutrition, and doing regular physical activity."

Although the exact cause of diverticulitis is unknown, some things can increase your chances of developing it. These include:

Bending the body's small colon. Bending the small colon can put pressure on the small intestine and lead to diverticulitis. This is called an "aspiration," in which bits of food from your meal travel into your abdomen.

Having high levels of body fat (adiposity). Obesity is also associated with an increased risk for diverticulitis as well as many other health conditions. Obesity decreases the number of skin folds between the bowels, increasing pressure in a small intestine.

Not receiving enough fluid. Normally, the bowel absorbs enough fluid to keep up with body needs. If not enough fluid is absorbed, it can put pressure on the intestines. This can lead to inflammation and diverticulitis.

Taking NSAIDs (non-steroidal anti-inflammatory drugs). NSAIDs reduce pain by damaging blood vessels and causing them to leak fluids into surrounding tissues. This can increase the chances of developing diverticulitis.

There are 35 million Americans at risk of developing this illness every year, according to a study done at Wake Forest Baptist Medical Center in North Carolina (North Carolina, United States). Researchers found that chronic constipation is a major risk factor for diverticulitis. They also found that a lean body mass index, more than 52 years old, and lack of physical activity are also predictors of this disease.

People who suffer from diverticulitis include former U.S. President Theodore Roosevelt and American actor, director, and producer Clint Eastwood. A lot of celebrities, including singers Bobby Brown and David Cassidy as well as actor Eric Roberts, have also dealt with this disease.

All cases of diverticulitis are considered an emergency because they can lead to the development of perforations in the intestines or abscesses if left untreated.

The condition can manifest itself as a complication of inflammatory bowel diseases (IBD), such as Crohn's disease or ulcerative colitis, or it may be caused by fecal matter that lodges in a small pouch in the intestine wall and causes irritation and inflammation. The risk of diverticular disease may be influenced by dietary fiber intake; those who eat more fiber have a reduced risk. There are also some other pieces of evidence showing that low levels of vitamin D increase the likelihood of diverticulitis. Studies show that vitamin D may not only help you absorb calcium for healthier bones and muscles, but it may also help your body maintain a healthy immune system. Other studies suggest that a low level of vitamin D can increase your risk for colon cancer. When you have low levels of vitamin D, you are more likely to have high levels of C-reactive protein (CRP), which is a marker for inflammation in the body.

Complications from diverticulitis include abscesses and bacterial peritonitis. Other complications include diverticulitis-associated right lower quadrant (RLQ) abdominal pain, bowel obstruction, abscess formation, and ileus.

Diverticulitis is a common condition in the United States. In the US, diverticulitis affects approximately 1% of the population, or roughly six million people each year. Of those affected by the diverticular disease, 60% are women; 20% are men. The average age of onset is 52 years old but can start at any age. More common in people over 50 years of age, it occurs even more frequently in African Americans and Hispanics than Caucasians. It is four times more prevalent among females than males in all races.

The American College of Gastroenterology (ACG) estimates that more than one million people in the United States are affected by diverticulitis, resulting in almost $3 billion per year in direct medical costs. This comes out to an estimated cost of $2600 per patient during their lifetime.

DIVERTICULITIS A GENERAL OVERVIEW

Diverticulitis

Diverticulitis is a disease of the gastrointestinal tract or digestive system, most specifically colonic diverticulitis.

Diverticulitis occurs when your diverticula become inflamed. Diverticula are aberrant pouches that can form in the large intestine's walls.

Diverticulitis is characterized by acute aches in the lower abdomen, though the pain may last for several days. Pain is frequently felt on the sigmoid colon (the left bottom side of the abdomen) in Europeans and Northern Americans. On the other hand, Asians have pain in the ascending colon. You may also have constipation, diarrhea, or nausea if you have diverticulitis. When you notice blood in your poop or have a fever, the sickness is thought to have progressed to a more difficult stage. Attacks on a regular basis are widespread.

The majority of patients develop abscesses that are sealed off or sinus tracts and fistulas that are confined. Fistulas most commonly affect the colon, urinary bladder, vaginal canal, and anterior abdominal wall.

Diverticulosis

Diverticulosis is a condition in which the colon has several pouches (diverticula) that are not inflamed. These are out pockets of the colonic mucosa and sub mucosa caused by muscle layer weaknesses in the colon wall, and may be caused in part by a low-fiber diet that causes alterations in intestinal micro biota and low-grade inflammation. In most cases, diverticula do not cause symptoms. Diverticular disease develops when the diverticula become inflamed clinically, which is known as diverticulitis.

Diverticulosis is most commonly found in the sigmoid colon, which is prone to high pressure. In the United States, the left side of the colon is more usually impacted, whereas in Asia, the right side is more commonly affected. Typically, the diagnosis is made during a routine colonoscopy or as a result of an unintentional detection during a CT scan.

It is widespread in Western countries, with about half of people over 60 in Canada and the United States suffering from it. Diverticulosis is uncommon before the age of 40 and become more common after that. Africa has lower rates; the reasons for this are unknown, but it could be due to a higher prevalence of a high-fiber diet, as opposed to the lower-fiber diet typical of many Western populations. Most people with diverticulosis are completely unaware that they have it until their colon is inspected for another reason and the pouches are discovered. However, some people may have bloating, minor cramps, or constipation.

The following symptoms will appear if your diverticulosis progresses to diverticulitis:

- Fever
- Nausea
- Pain in the abdomen
- Chills
- Diarrhea or constipation
- Vomiting

Diverticulitis and diverticulosis have symptoms that are similar to those of other diseases, such as;

- Appendicitis.
- Ulcerative colitis
- Cyst in the ovaries

- Irritable bowel syndrome (IBS) with Cohn's disease

To make an accurate diagnosis, your doctor may request tests such as ultrasonography, endoscopy, or x-rays.

Relation Between Diverticulosis and Diverticulitis

The terms diverticulosis and diverticulitis are often confused with each other. People confuse themselves to have diverticulitis when all they have is common diverticulosis. Diverticulosis is a common infection while diverticulitis is a more serious condition and is caused due to acute inflammation of the bowel wall. It is not easy to cure diverticulitis and it often calls for treatment through antibiotics.

In extreme situations, the patient may also be required to undergo surgery and has to be kept under prolonged medical supervision. Diverticulosis on the other hand is the condition where people have large intestinal pockets known as diverticula. This condition is sufficiently common and does pose serious consequences. It can be treated with normal dietary and lifestyle changes.

The convenient way to differentiate between the two terms is to remember the term "itis." Any disease ending with this term generally represents some kind of inflammation. The common medical precaution is to minimize the chances of the inflammation bursting. In case it bursts, it can be severely life-threatening.

Diverticulitis is generally observed in the colon or large bowel as holes or multiple pockets. They are named holes but have a very thin lining that prevents the stool and bacteria to pass out to the wall of the colon. The lining is excessively thin and any unwanted pressure on it causes the diverticulum to break. The breakage of this lining is responsible for the spread of bacteria and stool onto the wall of the colon thus infecting it severely. Such breakage may also lead to a walled-off infection that gets filled with bacteria and pus. This formation is known as an abscess. The infection does not remain confined to the colon wall but is likely to spread to the other adjacent organs like ovaries, bladder, uterus, etc. The bladder often suffers a condition of holes' formation known as a fistula. Another commonly reported situation is the passing of air while the patient urinates. Curing the abscess is very difficult and complicated since other organs are involved and are prone to damage.

Diverticulosis has a common occurrence and no significant symptoms. It is known to adopt progression and cannot be cured completely. The only way to control it is early detection and adopting preventive measures. Diverticulosis is the presence of pockets in the colon which are not harmful. The real problem is the high-pressured zones created due to thickened muscles known as mycosis. This thickening generates in the sigmoid colon in the left lower abdomen. This condition may cause austere narrowing and muscle buildup leading to muscle contractions. These contractions cause excruciating pain. They may also lead to extremely high pressures that can pressurize the colon walls, causing them to burst and spread infection in and around the colon wall. This is the condition which in severe cases leads to the formation of diverticulitis. A high fiber diet and plenty of liquid intakes are the only ways through which diverticulosis can be kept under check.

GENERAL CAUSES

A majority of the time, diverticulitis is caused by a large amount of waste in the lower part of your bowel due to disease, bacterial infection, physical trauma, or major change in diet. The enlarged pouch becomes inflamed and this can cause inflammation and bleeding into other organs within your abdomen. Diverticulitis can occur anywhere in the large intestine but causes symptoms such as gas pain under the ribs, fever, diarrhea that lasts for more than two weeks without improvement, and abdominal tenderness.

Causes of Diverticulitis

Diet and Intestinal Bacteria
About 90% of people with diverticulitis suffer from chronic constipation. For otherwise healthy patients, it is nearly always caused by a diet low in fiber, which can make the stool too large for the intestine to handle. Also, it's important to know that a large number of people have developed diverticulosis-like symptoms on an all-meat diet. This condition is known as "rabbit starvation" and has been documented throughout history in areas where rabbits are the primary food source.

Past Medical History
People who have had an intestinal perforation or surgery for colorectal cancer are also at a higher risk of developing diverticulosis and diverticulitis.

Age
People under the age of 60 have a higher risk of developing diverticulitis than people over the age of 60.

Hemorrhoids and Clogged Pouches
The development of the condition is in part caused by hemorrhoids, also known as piles, which are enlarged veins in the bottom chamber of your rectum. People with these conditions may have lower levels of internal pressure that can lead to pouching or squeezing off small sacs from within the large intestine. It's also possible for a blockage to form when blood collects inside a small blood vein or artery and leaks into that sac and causes it to swell.

Family History
If your family has been affected by diverticulosis or diverticulitis, you're at a higher risk for developing it than someone who doesn't have this history. It is important to mention that most people with this condition will never develop diverticulitis.

Pregnancy
During pregnancy, a woman's body releases a hormone that causes the colon to relax and allows even small particles to travel more easily through it. This can cause a pouching effect within the large intestine, which can lead to diverticulitis.

Physical Trauma
Fecal matter can become trapped in partial obstruction and this can cause an inflammatory reaction.

Symptoms of Diverticulitis

Abdominal Pain
Diverticulitis pain is often located near the belly button and can sometimes move to either side of the belly. It may resemble a tummy ache, but unlike an upset stomach, it comes and goes.

Fever

You may also experience a fever, which can be mild or high. Your doctor will need to understand if you have ever been diagnosed with diverticulitis, as this condition requires immediate medical attention.

Bleeding

Diverticula can rupture and bleed into neighboring organs like the colon or bladder, or into the abdominal cavity itself. It's not uncommon for some people to pass blood in their stools without knowing that it came from their intestines. Throbbing pain, fever, and nausea can point to an intestinal rupture.

Diarrhea

Diverticulitis can cause diarrhea that is sometimes watery with mucus or blood, according to the National Digestive Diseases Information Clearinghouse (NDDIC). You should see your doctor if you have diarrhea that lasts for more than two weeks without improvement.

Weight Loss

Weight loss and eating a low-fiber diet can lead to diverticulosis and many people may not know until there's a complication like diverticulitis. You need to bring any of these symptoms to your doctor's attention as soon as you notice them because they may be pointing to another serious disease.

Stool Changes

You may notice fluctuations in your stools, such as more than usual mucus, which may indicate a buildup of bacteria or inflammatory material. It is also possible to have a blockage in your intestines that can lead to constipation and cause this extra mucus.

Other symptoms include abdominal swelling that persists after you've passed stool, difficulty breathing or swallowing, the urge to defecate but not being able to do so, and blood in your stool.

How to Know If You Have Diverticulitis

Diverticulitis is a condition of swelling and inflammation of the pouches in the large intestine, which causes pockets to form and can be painful. There are methods for testing to know if you have diverticulitis. Some of these include anorectal manometry, computerized tomography (CT) scan, barium enema, colonoscopy, sigmoidoscopy with biopsy.

If your doctor recommends any of these tests or procedures then you may want to talk about what options you would like and how much they will cost. Let us talk about each of these in detail:

Anorectal Manometry

Anorectal manometry is a test used to measure the function of your muscles around the anus. It measures how well you empty your bowels and if the muscles are working properly. The test involves inserting a thin, flexible tube into your anus and rectum. The tube has no sharp edges or wires, so it shouldn't hurt to insert the tube, but your doctor may give you an anesthetic gel to put on the tip before inserting it.

Computerized Tomography (CT) Scan

A CT scan is a diagnostic imaging procedure that uses X-rays and computer technology to produce highly detailed images of one or more specific areas of an object. You may get a CT scan before or after certain tests such as colonoscopy or sigmoidoscopy. This test is very important because it can detect any abnormalities in the areas that your doctor suspects are infected.

Barium Enema

A barium enema is an X-ray exam of the large intestine and rectum. It's usually performed to see if you have some type of infection or injury in these areas and also to see if there are any problems with your intestines and rectum. Barium is a white, chalky substance that coats the inside of the intestine. When barium is swallowed, it shows up on an X-ray image.

Colonoscopy

A colonoscopy is a procedure used to look at the inside of your colon and rectum through a narrow tube with a camera on the end to see if there are any abnormal growths or infections there. During this procedure, your doctor will insert the tube into your large intestine through your anus and take pictures as they pass along. This test can help doctors determine if you have diverticulitis or another type of infection in the intestines; usually, your doctor won't know for sure until they actually see it during this test. If you're healthy, your doctor may recommend this test if you have high fevers or pain with your movements that lasts for more than 3 days.

This procedure is also done if the doctor suspects polyps (small growths) in your colon or rectum. Polyps are usually harmless but can increase the risk of developing cancer. But, if you have diverticulitis, there's a chance that IBD (Inflammatory Bowel Disease) could develop after the diagnosis of diverticulitis.

Sometimes your doctor may recommend a colonoscopy even if they don't suspect something is wrong because it can help them find out what is making you sick. But, if you already have diverticulitis, then this is not recommended.

Sigmoidoscopy

Sigmoidoscopy with biopsy is the most frequent test that doctors recommend to people who have pain with bowel movements or any other symptoms of diverticulitis. This test involves passing a thin flexible tube into the colon through the anus and turning it so its tip points towards your rectum.

The doctor will look at the walls of your colon with a special instrument called a sigmoidoscope, which can show abnormalities in the lining of your colon. This test can detect signs of diverticulitis, polyps, inflammation, scar tissue, or cancer.

Many people with diverticulitis may be recommended to get this test because it's the most useful to know what is causing the problem if you can have it done by a doctor who has special training in treating IBD.

But if you have diverticulitis then your doctor will just recommend this test without needing to know any other information about you other than that you have diverticulitis. The doctor might also recommend this test if you have had an appendectomy or an abdominal operation in the last 6 months.

Sigmoidoscopy With Biopsy

This is the same test as sigmoidoscopy with a biopsy but it also involves taking small samples of tissue (biopsies) from certain parts of your colon to check for any abnormalities. Colonoscopy is usually recommended first to investigate diverticulitis, but if you have severe symptoms or if you are not able to pass a large amount of stool, then sigmoidoscopy may be recommended before endoscopic examination because this procedure can induce spasms and cause more pain.

Bowel Capsule (H Capsule)

The H-capsule test is done after you take a laxative, and then your doctor will insert an X-ray camera into the anus and rectum to take X-rays of your digestive system while it's working. It's usually performed to see if you have any problems with your large intestine such as ulcers or diverticulitis.

This test is more used for gathering information on constipation than diverticulitis. But if you do have diverticulitis, then the doctor might report having extra pressure in the colon or inflammation in the lining of the colon.

Endoscopy

Endoscopy, or gastroscopy, lets the doctor look at the inside of your digestive tract. This test can be done after you have had a biopsy or after you have had an exploratory procedure such as sigmoidoscopy. Endoscopy is usually done in a hospital to allow intravenous sedation and to provide oxygen, fluids, antibiotics, and other medications for the patient. They may also give you medicine to prevent nausea in the operating room. An endoscope is a thin flexible tube with a camera at one end that can be inserted into your rectum or anus.

WHAT TO EAT AND WHAT NOT

Food to eat

"On the other hand, when you have diverticulitis, your polyps become irritated, inflamed, and possibly infected. Taylor explains, "We aim to lessen traffic in your GI tract so that nothing else disturbs them." "Reducing the amount of fiber in your diet can assist."

During a flare-up of diverticulitis, your doctor may advise rest, antibiotics, and a clear liquid or low-fiber diet.

Clear liquid diet for diverticulitis

A clear liquid diet may be recommended if a diverticulitis flare-up is severe or necessitates surgery. "You graduate from clear liquids to a low-fiber diet after a day or two," Taylor explains. "Even if your pain does not go away, you continue to eat usual foods." You can't stay on a liquid diet for an extended period of time because you'll get malnourished."

You can eat the following foods on a clear liquid diet:

- Broths that are clear (not soup).
- Juices that are clear and pulp-free (such as apple and cranberry juice)
- Popsicles
- Water

Low-fiber diet for diverticulitis

Eat a low-fiber, or GI soft, diet for milder forms of diverticulitis. Depending on the severity of the flare-up, a low-fiber diet restricts fiber consumption to 8 to 1/2 grams per day.

Low-fiber foods to consider include:

Grains: Lover's of white spaghetti and white bread, delight! Low-fiber alternatives include these, as well as white rice and white crackers.

Starches with low fiber content: Remove your peeler from the drawer. Skinless potatoes are one alternative. You can mash, roast, or bake them. Low-fiber cereals like corn flakes and puffed rice cereal receive a thumbs up.

Protein can be found in eggs and egg whites, tofu, beef, and seafood. "The best options are shredded chicken, lean ground beef, and soft baked salmon."

Fruits: Fruits contain a lot of fiber, so be cautious when eating them. Soft, ripe cantaloupe and honeydew, as well as canned fruits like peaches and pears, applesauce, ripe bananas, and soft, ripe cantaloupe and honeydew, are also wonderful options. "Because you don't eat the skin, there isn't a lot of fiber." The skins contain insoluble fiber, which can irritate irritated polyps."

"Cottage cheese and Greek yogurt are major winners if you're recovering from a flare-up: They're high in protein, calcium, and other minerals, but they're also deficient in fiber." "If you're unwell, they're also soft, wet, and easier to swallow." There's also milk and cheese to choose from.

Food to avoid

Foods high in FODMAPs

Some persons with irritable bowel syndrome benefit from following a low FODMAP diet (IBS). Some persons with diverticulitis may benefit from it as well.

FODMAPs are carbohydrate types. Fermentable oligosaccharides, disaccharides, monosaccharide's, and polyols are all included.

People who follow this diet avoid foods that are rich in FODMAPS. This includes, for example, the following foods:

- Apples, pears, and plums are examples of fruits.
- Fermented foods, such as sauerkraut or kimchi beans dairy foods, such as milk, yogurt, and ice cream
- Legumes
- Meals with a lot of Trans fats
- Cabbage with soy sauce
- Brussels sprouts (Brussels sprouts)
- Garlic and onions

Meats that have been red and processed

Eating a diet strong in red and processed meats may raise your chance of having diverticulitis. A diet rich in fruits, vegetables, and whole grains may help to lower the risk of heart disease.

High-sugar and high-fat foods

The typical Western diet is high in fat, sugar, and fiber, but low in fiber. As a result, a person's risk of having diverticulitis may increase.

According to a 2017 study with over 46,000 male participants, avoiding the following foods may help prevent or lessen the symptoms of diverticulitis:

Fried food, red meat, refined carbohydrates, full fat dairy.

Shopping list

Your doctor will most likely recommend that you gradually start shopping for solid foods after your symptoms have subsided. Begin by consuming low-fiber, readily digestible foods like dairy, eggs, low-fiber cereal and bread, pasta, white rice, and canned or soft fruits and vegetables with no seeds or skin. Gradually increase your fiber intake by 5 to 15 grams per day until you are able to eat a high-fiber diet once more.

Supplements and probiotics

Diverticular disease has no recognized etiology, but a lack of dietary fiber is a contributing factor. Probiotics are used to maintain intestinal health and boost the number of good bacteria in the gut in order to prevent diverticular disease and its symptoms.

1st step

Get a physical exam to determine which form of diverticular illness you have. Consult your doctor about your symptoms and obtain the testing you need to find out if you have diverticular illness. According to the National Digestive Diseases Information Clearinghouse, you may need a digital rectal exam or colonoscopy in addition to blood testing, depending on the severity of your symptoms. Once you've been diagnosed with diverticular disease, talk to your doctor about adding probiotics to your diet. Probiotics will not be able to heal the ailment. Probiotics, in addition to following your doctor's dietary advice, can help maintain gut integrity and avoid additional damage.

2nd Step

Supplements of Lactobacillus acidophilus should be purchased in large quantities. Lactobacillus acidophilus, popularly known as "good bacteria," is a common probiotic. This type of bacteria already presents in your body, but diverticular illness can reduce the amount of healthy bacteria in your gut, causing digestive problems. This probiotic aids in the reduction of diverticular disease-related diarrhea, intestinal infections, and pouch inflammation. At your local health food store, look for L. acidophilus in tablet or pill form.

3rd step

Take probiotic supplements as directed on a daily basis. According to the University of Maryland Medical Center, the usual daily capsule dose of probiotics such as L. acidophilus or bifid bacteria for treating diverticular illness is 250mg given in between meals.

4th step

Instead than taking pills, eat meals with added probiotics. In the grocery store, you can get probiotic-enriched dairy products like cultured yogurt or milk, soy beverages, and even juices. Look for words like "probiotic" or "active and living cultures" on product labels. MayoClinic.com recommends eating eight ounces of probiotic-rich foods every day. For the specific dose required to treat diverticular disease, consult your doctor.

5th step

Increase the probiotic benefits in your intestines by eating fermentable fiber. Prebiotics are non-digestible fermented fibers that function in tandem with probiotics to boost intestinal health. Natural prebiotics can be found in fiber foods like legumes, wheat, and vegetables. To gain the best outcomes for preventing diverticular disease, eat plenty of fiber-rich foods in addition to your probiotic-enhanced foods. Make an effort to eat five to eight servings of fiber-rich foods every day.

TIP

Before using probiotics to treat active diverticular disease, talk to your doctor.

TREATMENT FOR DIVERTICULITIS

If your diverticulitis is mild, your doctor may prescribe an antibiotic like metronidazole (Flagyl®), ciprofloxacin (Cipro®), trimethoprim-sulfamethoxazole (Bactrim®), or clavulanic acid (Augmentin®) or amoxicillin. Rest, over-the-counter pain relievers, and a low-fiber or liquid diet may be advised until the symptoms improve. Once your symptoms have improved, you can gradually return to soft foods, followed by a more normal diet containing plenty of high-fiber foods. The specifics of the treatment plan will be discussed between you and the healthcare provider. You could be admitted to the hospital for intravenous (IV) antibiotics, IV fluids, or surgery if the diverticulitis is severe, you have rectal bleeding, or you are having a repeat bout of diverticulitis.

Diet plan

A low residue diet may be prescribed. A low-fiber diet was formerly assumed to allow the colon enough time to heal. Evidence contradicts this, with a 2011 analysis showing no evidence for the efficacy of low residue diets in the treatment of diverticular disease and suggesting that a high-fiber diet may help avoid the condition. Although no high-quality research was discovered in a systematic review published in 201/2, various studies and guidelines favored a high-fiber diet for the treatment of symptomatic illness.

A Diet for Diverticulitis Recovery

It's critical to help your digestive tract clean itself out and mend during a diverticulitis flare-up, or at the onset of symptoms. Use my beef bone broth recipe as a starting point.

Eating bone broths prepared from cattle, chicken, lamb, and fish aids in the healing of leaky gut syndrome, improves joint health, strengthens the immune system, and even helps to reduce cellulite, all while aiding in the healing of the digestive tract.

Bone broths, when combined with cooked vegetables and a small amount of meat, offer your body critical minerals such as calcium, magnesium, phosphorus, silicon, sulphur, and more, in an easily digestible form.

Vegetables such as carrots, celery, and garlic, as well as an egg poached in the soup, can be added to your bone broth. Lover's of white spaghetti and white bread, delight! These are a couple of Drink two to three cups of warm ginger tea each day to aid with inflammation and digestion. Ginger is a nutrient-dense spice that helps your immune and digestive systems work better.

Low-fiber options include white rice and white crackers, which break down the collagen in cattle and chicken bones into gelatin in around 48 hours and 24 hours, respectively. Although you may prepare broth in less time, I recommend cooking it in a crock pot for at least 48 hours to extract the most flavor out of the bones.

Gelatin has incredible healing powers, and it can even help people with food sensitivities and allergies handle these foods better. It also helps to maintain a healthy probiotic balance by breaking down proteins to make them easier to digest. The truth about probiotics is that they aid in the creation of a healthy gut environment.

Only clear bone broths, clear fresh juices (no pulp), and soothing ginger tea should be consumed during the first phase of the diverticulitis diet.

Start adding fiber-rich foods like fresh fruits and vegetables, as well as unprocessed grains like quinoa, black rice, fermented grains, or sprouted lentils, once your body has adjusted to these foods.

Whole nuts and seeds should be avoided since they can easily become trapped in the diverticula and cause more harm.

Fiber, according to University of Oxford experts, lowers the incidence of diverticular illness. Fiber from fruits, vegetables, grains, and potatoes was studied.

So, gradually introduce high-fiber foods throughout the first several days, introducing one new food every 3-4 days.

As your body adjusts, start taking about 25-35 grams of fiber per day to help prevent any potential flare-ups whiles your digestive tract repairs. Begin with potatoes, sweet potatoes, and root vegetables, and then gradually include non-processed grains and beans like oats and lentils.

The distinction between soluble and insoluble fiber is one of the most significant distinctions to make. Soluble fiber absorbs water and transforms into a gel as it passes through the digestive system. The gel aids digestion by slowing it down, enabling more critical nutrients to be absorbed. Insoluble fiber, on the other hand, thickens stools, allowing food to travel more quickly through your system.

Soluble fiber is abundant in oat bran, nuts, seeds, beans, lentils, barley, and peas.

Insoluble fiber is abundant in whole grains, wheat bran, and vegetables.

Insoluble fiber reduces the risk of developing diverticular disease, according to Harvard Medical School's Department of Nutrition researchers.. But don't let this deter you from maintaining a healthy diet. You don't need to, and you shouldn't, avoid soluble fiber.

Diverticulitis can flare up if a proper balance of protein, fiber, and fresh fruits and vegetables is not maintained.

For millennia, Native Americans have used slippery elm both topically and internally to ease stomach disorders, coughs, and sore throats.

It is now recommended for the treatment of GERD, Crohn's disease, IBS, and other digestive problems. For the length of the diverticulitis diet, start with 500 milligrams three times a day. Before taking this supplement, drink a full glass of water or another clear beverage.

Aloe juice assists digestion, normalizes pH levels, regulates intestinal function, and promotes the growth of good digestive bacteria.

Aloe juice in the amount of 1/2 to 16 ounces per day is advised; any more than that will irritate your system.

It's in the organics area of your local grocery store, as well as many Asian stores.

Licorice Root reduces stomach acid, relieves heartburn, and acts as a mild laxative to aid in the elimination of waste from the colon. This root aids digestion by increasing bile production and decreasing cholesterol levels. When you possess symptoms of diverticulitis, take 100 milligrams every day.

The ultimate purpose of the diverticulitis diet, vitamins, and lifestyle adjustments is to encourage your digestive tract to work efficiently, in addition to repairing your colon from diverticulitis.

Digestive enzymes aid in the breakdown of foods, allowing nutrients to be absorbed. Individuals with digestive issues might take digestive supplements containing vital enzymes to help with digestion.

Live probiotics should be included in one's diet to help with food sensitivities and digestive issues such as constipation, gas, and bloating. Probiotics are beneficial bacteria that line the lining of the digestive tract and aid in infection resistance. If you have diverticulitis, you will need an infusion of these bacteria to help repair your colon and avoid recurrence of the disease.

Diverticulitis necessitates more than just a diverticulitis diet and supplements to keep the digestive tract healthy. The mouth is where digestion begins. It is critical to chew each bite of food thoroughly until it is virtually liquefied. The more nutrients are accessible for absorption before food enters the stomach, the better.

Diverticular illness can be prevented by combining physical exercise and a high-fiber diet, according to medical studies. On a daily basis, running or using a rebounder can help relieve symptoms and flare-ups. Even moderate-intensity exercise can help with bowel function, stress relief, and weight loss.

Your psychological and physical well-being are connected; stress management and the development of effective coping mechanisms are essential. Both the mind and the body are affected by stress.

When you strain on the toilet, you put too much pressure on your colon, which causes minor tears.

Choose a stool that allows you to elevate your feet slightly to decrease strain.

Antibiotics

Diverticulitis can cause infection, which usually clears itself after a few days of antibiotic treatment. An abscess in the colon wall may occur if the infection worsens.

An abscess is a collection of pus in a specific area that can cause swelling and tissue destruction. If the abscess is minor and remains in the colon's wall, antibiotic treatment may be enough to clear it out. If antibiotics do not clear up the abscess, the doctor may need to drain it with a catheter, which is a thin tube that is inserted into the abscess through the skin. The doctor inserts the needle through the skin until it reaches the abscess and then drains the fluid through the catheter after giving the patient numbing drugs. Sonography or x-ray may be used to guide this approach.

Percutaneous Drainage Using A CT Scan

CT scans are routinely used to examine people who have the symptoms listed above.

The use of a CT scan to diagnose diverticulitis is extremely accurate (98 percent). Thin section (5 mm) transverse pictures are taken through the entire belly and pelvis after the patient has been given oral and intravascular contrast to extract as much information as possible regarding the patient's health.

The images show localized thickening of the colon wall, as well as inflammation that has spread to the fat around the colon. When the affected segment contains diverticula, an accurate diagnosis of acute diverticulitis can be obtained. Patients with more serious diverticulitis, such as those who have an accompanying abscess, may be identified using CT scans. It might even allow for radio logically guided abscess draining, avoiding the need for emergency surgery.

The doctor will ask about your medical history, perform a physical exam, and maybe order one or more diagnostic tests to determine whether you have diverticular disease. Diverticulosis is frequently discovered through testing requested for a different condition because most patients have no symptoms. Diverticulosis, for example, is frequently discovered during a colonoscopy, which is performed to check for cancer or polyps, as well as to assess complaints of pain or rectal bleeding.

Doctors may inquire about bowel habits, discomfort, other symptoms, nutrition, and medications when collecting a medical history. A digital rectal exam is typically part of the physical examination. The doctor uses a gloved, lubricated finger to detect pain, obstruction, or blood in the rectum. The doctor may check for evidence of bleeding in the stool and perform a blood test to look for signs of infection.

The following radiologic tests may be ordered if diverticulitis is suspected:

A CT scan is a type of imaging that uses a computer to create a three-dimensional image of the body. A CT scan is a noninvasive x-ray that generates cross-section images of the body. The doctor may inject dye into a vein and administer a comparable combination for the patient to drink. The person is lying on a table that slips inside a machine that looks like a donut.

The dye aids in the detection of problems like perforations and abscesses that might occur as a result of diverticulitis.

Surgery

A hospital stay will almost certainly be required in severe cases of diverticulitis with intense pain and consequences. Surgery may be required if a patient develops problems or fails to respond to therapy.

Perforations can form in infected diverticula. Peritonitis is a disorder that occurs when perforations in the colon allow pus to flow out and build a big abscess in the abdominal cavity. Nausea, vomiting, fever, and acute abdominal discomfort are common symptoms of peritonitis. The situation necessitates prompt surgery to clear the abdominal cavity and remove the colon section that has been injured. Peritonitis can be lethal if not treated promptly.

Diverticula-related rectal bleeding is a rather uncommon side effect. The bleeding is thought to be triggered by a weakening and then bursting of a tiny blood artery in a diverticulum. Blood can occur in the toilet or in the stool when the diverticula bleed. Bleeding can be significant, but it often stops on its own and does not require medical attention. Any rectum bleeding, no matter how minor, should be seen by a doctor as soon as possible. Colonoscopy is frequently performed to locate and control bleeding in the colon. To identify and treat diverticular bleeding, the doctor may inject dye into an artery, a procedure known as angiography. If the bleeding persists, surgery to remove the affected part of the colon may be required.

A fistula between the bladder and the colon is the most common type of fistula. Men are more likely than women to have this sort of fistula. It can cause a serious, long-term urinary tract infection. Surgery to remove the fistula and the damaged portion of the colon can be used to repair the condition.

Infection-related scarring can result in intestinal obstruction, which is a partial or complete blockage of the intestine. The colon is unable to transport bowel contents normally when the gut becomes clogged. Emergency surgery may be required if the intestine is fully obstructed. The operation to correct a partial blockage is not an emergency, thus it can be scheduled.

Surgery's Risks

There are risks and potential consequences associated with every procedure. You should talk to your doctor about all of the possible hazards.

After the Surgery: What to Expect

There are risks and potential consequences associated with every procedure. All dangers and healing should be discussed with your physician.

Expectations and Requirements after Discharge

There are risks and potential consequences associated with every procedure. All dangers and healing should be discussed with your doctor.

PREVENTING DIVERTICULOSIS

How can you protect yourself from getting diverticulitis? As with any condition, especially those that are chronic, prevention is key! The most significant things you can do to prevent diverticulitis is to eat a healthy diet, maintain an active lifestyle, manage your weight, and reduce stress. When your stomach muscles are strong enough to support your colon, they will work together to keep food moving through your colon at a healthy pace. This is why it is so important for you to consume fiber rich foods on a daily basis. If you're not already, start eating foods like fruits and vegetables, whole grains, beans and legumes, nuts and seeds, and even more fiber if it's available. Eating more fiber will help you lose weight, prevent constipation, make stools easier to pass (which can prevent diverticular disease), and it can also be very helpful for your overall health including your heart!

Exercise: Your muscles need to be strong enough to support the colon during everyday activities. Some of the most effective ways that you can strengthen your muscles is through exercise. Although exercise won't prevent diverticulitis 100%, it can definitely help reduce your chances of getting diverticulitis.

Stress has been linked to diverticulitis because stress weakens your muscles, which increases the likelihood that you will get the condition. There are many other physical reactions that occur when you are under stress, all of which make it more tough for you to fight off infection or disease.

Maintaining a healthy weight is very important. If you are overweight your colon muscles will have to work harder to push things through your colon, which can weaken them. Being overweight also leads to many other problems that are related to obesity including high blood pressure, high cholesterol, strokes, heart disease, diabetes, and cancer.

Preserving an active routine is another great means to reduce the chances of getting diverticulitis. Even if it's just walking briskly throughout the day or playing golf, exercise has many health benefits including reducing arthritis pain during and after an attack of diverticulitis.

Diverticulitis may cause a variety of health issues and consequences, including:

- bloody bowel movements
- nausea
- fever
- severe abdominal pain
- fistula
- an abscess or a tissue pocket irritated

Foods To Avoid With Diverticulitis

During diverticulitis flare-ups, doctors used to suggest a low-fiber, clear liquid diet.

However, some doctors now think that if you have diverticulosis or diverticulitis, you don't have to avoid specific foods.

Diverticulitis treatment, on the other hand, is dependent on the individual. Some individuals may find that eliminating particular foods is beneficial.

During minor flare-ups, some physicians still suggest a clear liquid diet. They may suggest switching to a low-fiber diet until symptoms subside, gradually increasing to a high-fiber diet.

The sections that follow examine the evidence behind certain foods that you should avoid if you have diverticulosis or diverticulitis.

High FODMAP foods

Some patients with irritable bowel syndrome benefit from following a low FODMAP diet (IBS). Some people with diverticulitis may benefit from it as well.

FODMAPs are carbohydrate types. The list includes fermentable oligosaccharides, disaccharides, monosaccharides, and polyols.

According to some studies, a low FODMAP diet may help individuals avoid or treat diverticulitis by preventing excessive pressure in the colon.

People who follow this diet avoid foods that are rich in FODMAPS. This includes, for example, the following foods:

- Certain fruits, such as apples, pears, and plums
- legumes
- Dairy foods, such as milk, yogurt, and ice cream
- foods high in trans fats
- onions and garlic
- soy
- fermented foods, such as sauerkraut or kimchi
- cabbage

- beans
- Brussels sprouts

Red and processed meat

A diet rich in red and processed meats may raise your chance of getting diverticulitis, according to a 2018 study. A diet rich in fruits, vegetables, and whole grains may help lower the risk of heart disease.

Foods high in sugar and fat

The typical Western diet is rich in fat, sugar, and fiber but low in fiber. As a result, a person's chance of getting diverticulitis may rise.

According to a 2017 research including over 46,000 male participants.

the following foods may help prevent or decrease the symptoms of diverticulitis:

- full-fat dairy
- red meat
- refined grains
- fried food

Should I Avoid High Fiber Foods?

Fiber's impact on diverticulitis varies from person to person. In the past, physicians advised a low-fiber or clear liquid diet for patients with diverticulitis. Some physicians nowadays are no longer following this advice.

According to a 2018 study, dietary fiber may decrease the symptoms of diverticular illness and improve gastrointestinal function. According to the researchers, fiber may enhance colon health by allowing for improved stomach motility and stool bulk.

Poor fiber diets, coupled with excessive meat consumption, low physical activity, and smoking, have been linked to an increased incidence of diverticulitis in certain studies.

High fiber foods include:

- fruits
- navy beans, chickpeas, lentils, and kidney beans are examples of beans and legumes.
- vegetables
- Brown rice, quinoa, oatmeal, maize, spelled, and bulgur are examples of whole grains.

While some studies have connected a high-fiber diet to a lower incidence of diverticulitis, this may not be appropriate for someone suffering from a flare-up.

Fiber bulks up the stool and may cause painful colon spasms during a flare-up. During an acute flare, your doctor may advise you to avoid fiber.

Each individual is unique. Before making major dietary changes, it's usually a good idea to get medical advice.

Drink lots of water while adding fiber to your diet to prevent constipation.

1. Unit conversation table

Volume

Imperial	Metric		Imperial	Metric
1 tbsp	15ml		1 pint	570 ml
2 fl oz	55 ml		1 ¼ pints	725 ml
3 fl oz	75 ml		1 ¾ pints	1 litre
5 fl oz (¼ pint)	150 ml		2 pints	1.2 litres
10 fl oz (½ pint)	275 ml		2½ pints	1.5 litres
			4 pints	2.25 litres

Weight

Imperial	Metric		Imperial	Metric		Imperial	Metric
½ oz	10 g		4 oz	110 g		10 oz	275 g
¾ oz	20 g		4½ oz	125 g		12 oz	350 g
1 oz	25 g		5 oz	150 g		1 lb	450 g
1½ oz	40 g		6 oz	175 g		1 lb 8 oz	700 g
2 oz	50 g		7 oz	200 g		2 lb	900 g
2½ oz	60 g		8 oz	225 g		3 lb	1.35 kg
3 oz	75 g		9 oz	250 g			

Metric cups conversion

Cups	Imperial	Metric
1 cup flour	5oz	150g
1 cup caster or granulated sugar	8oz	225g
1 cup soft brown sugar	6oz	175g
1 cup soft butter/margarine	8oz	225g

1 cup sultanas/raisins	7oz	200g
1 cup currants	5oz	150g
1 cup ground almonds	4oz	110g
1 cup oats	4oz	110g
1 cup golden syrup/honey	12oz	350g
1 cup uncooked rice	7oz	200g
1 cup grated cheese	4oz	110g
1 stick butter	4oz	110g
¼ cup liquid (water, milk, oil etc.)	4 tablespoons	60ml
½ cup liquid (water, milk, oil etc.)	¼ pint	125ml
1 cup liquid (water, milk, oil etc.)	½ pint	250ml

Oven temperatures

Gas Mark	Fahrenheit	Celsius	Gas Mark	Fahrenheit	Celsius
1/4	225	110	4	350	180
1/2	250	130	5	375	190
1	275	140	6	400	200
2	300	150	7	425	220
3	325	170	8	450	230
			9	475	240

Oven temperatures

Gas Mark	Fahrenheit	Celsius	Gas Mark	Fahrenheit	Celsius
1/4	225	110	4	350	180
1/2	250	130	5	375	190
1	275	140	6	400	200
2	300	150	7	425	220
3	325	170	8	450	230
			9	475	240

Weight

Imperial	Metric		Imperial	Metric
½ oz	10 g		6 oz	175 g
¾ oz	20 g		7 oz	200 g
1 oz	25 g		8 oz	225 g
1½ oz	40 g		9 oz	250 g
2 oz	50 g		10 oz	275 g
2½ oz	60 g		12 oz	350 g
3 oz	75 g		1 lb	450 g
4 oz	110 g		1 lb 8 oz	700 g
4½ oz	125 g		2 lb	900 g
5 oz	150 g		3 lb	1.35 kg

DIVERTICULITIS
LOW RESIDUE/FIBER RECIPES

1. Creamy Cherry Smoothie

Preparation time: 5 minutes | **Serving:** 4
Ingredients:

- Avocado – ¼, ripe
- Dark cherry juice – 100ml
- Tahini – one tsp, hulled
- Lecithin granules – one tsp
- Unsweetened oat milk – 150ml
- Coconut crème – one tbsp
- Cherry – one

Instructions:

1. Add all ingredients into the blender and blend until smooth.
2. Pour smoothie into the glass.
3. Serve and enjoy!

Nutrition: Calories; 271, Carbs; 61g, Fats; 10g Proteins; 1g

2. Lemon Baked Eggs

Preparation time: 5 minutes | **Cooking time:** 10 minutes | **Serving:** 1
Ingredients:

- Eggs – 2g
- Cheddar cheese – 2 slices, low-fat
- Salt – to taste
- Lemon – 1 tsp, julienned
- Parsley – 2 tbsp, chopped
- Crusty white roll – one

Instructions:

1. Preheat the oven to 180 degrees C.
2. Spray the dish with olive oil.
3. Slice the cheddar cheese into three strips.
4. Line the edges of the dish with cheese. Break the eggs in the middle.
5. Place julienned lemon over the egg and sprinkle with fresh parsley.
6. Place dish into the oven and cook for 8 to 10 minutes.
7. Serve with crusty white bread rolls.

Nutrition: Calories;233, Carbs; 0.6g, Fats; 16.8g Proteins; 21.3g; Fiber; 2g

3. Banana Pancakes

Preparation time: 10 minutes | **Cooking time:** 5-10 minutes | **Serving:** 4
Ingredients:

- Firm silken tofu – 349g
- Dairy-free milk – 400ml
- Grapeseed oil – 4 tbsp
- Vanilla extract – 1 tbsp
- Flour – 250g, gluten-free
- Cinnamon powder – 2 tsp
- Baking powder – 1 tbsp
- Sugar – 4 tbsp
- Peanut butter – 4 tbsp. smooth
- Banana – 2, peeled, sliced
- Maple syrup, to serve

Instructions:

1. Add tofu, vanilla, cinnamon, and half of the dairy-free milk into the blender and blend until smooth.
2. Add remaining dairy-free milk to the mixture.
3. Pour baking powder and flour into another bowl. Make a hole in the centre of the dry mixture and pour the wet mixture in it and blend until smooth.
4. Add 2 tsp of oil into the pan and place it over medium flame.
5. Pour batter into the pan and cook for two minutes.
6. Flip and cook for two minutes more.
7. Spread peanut butter onto the pancakes.
8. Garnish with sliced banana.
9. Drizzle with maple syrup.

Nutrition: Calories; 193, Carbs; 29.2g, Fats; 6.6g Proteins; 5g; Fiber; 2g

4. Deviled egg

Preparation time: 10 minutes | **Cooking time:** 5 minutes | **Serving:** 12
Ingredients:

- Whole egg mayonnaise – 3 tbsp

- Eggs – six
- Turmeric powder – one pinch
- Mustard powder – one pinch
- Salt and pepper, to taste
- Paprika – one pinch
- Water cracker – one packet

Instruction:

1. Add eggs into the saucepan and cover with water. Place it over medium flame. Bring to a boil. When boiled, cook the eggs for four and a half minutes.
2. Remove from the flame. Add eggs into the cold water for one minute.
3. Then, peel and slice them in half, lengthwise.
4. Scoop out the yolks and add them into the bowl. Let mash with pepper, salt, mustard, mayonnaise, and turmeric.
5. Slice a little piece of the rounded bottom of the egg white halves. Place onto the cracker or plate.
6. Place yolk mixture into the white egg halves.
7. Sprinkle with paprika.

Nutrition: Calories; 125, Carbs; 7g, Fats; 10.5g Proteins; 6.4g; Fiber; 2g

5. Basil Zoodle Frittata

Preparation time: 10 minutes | **Cooking time:** 30 minutes | **Serving:** 4

Ingredients:

- Bread crumbs – ½ cup
- Chives – ¼ cup, chopped
- Zucchini – two spiralized
- Eggs – six
- Cottage cheese – ½ cup
- Salt – one pinch
- Olive oil – 1 tbsp
- Basil leaves – ¼ cup

Instructions:

1. Preheat the oven to 180 degrees C.
2. Press breadcrumbs down onto the dish.
3. Put it into the oven and bake for ten minutes until golden.

4. Press it again. Blanch zucchini in boiled water and sprinkle with salt, and drain it onto the paper towel.
5. Add bay leaves, garlic powder, cottage cheese, chives, olive oil, and zucchini into the bowl and combine it well. Place onto the dish and press it down.
6. Beat the eggs and pour over the mixture.
7. Place it into the oven and bake for 20 to 30 minutes until golden.

Nutrition: Calories; 152, Carbs; 3.7g, Fats; 11.2g Proteins; 9.2g; Fiber; 3g

6. Pear and Muesli Muffins

Preparation time: 5 minutes | **Cooking time:** 20 minutes | **Serving:** 10

Ingredients:

- Wholemeal self-rising flour – 200g
- Muesli – 150g
- Brown sugar – ½ cup
- Pears – two, thinly sliced
- Walnuts – 75g
- Milk – one cup
- Butter – 50g, melted
- Egg – one

Instructions:

1. Preheat the oven to 180 degrees C.
2. Combine the walnuts, pears, sugar, flour, and muesli into the bowl.
3. Make a well in the middle of the mixture.
4. Pour butter, egg, and milk into the well and combine it well.
5. Divide the mixture into the greased muffin tray.
6. Sprinkle with muesli and bake for 18 to 20 minutes.

Nutrition: Calories; 372kcal, Carbohydrates; 47g, Fats; 18g Proteins; 6g, fibre; 5g

7. Green Omelet with Portobello fries

Preparation time: 10 minutes | **Cooking time:** 10 to 15 minutes | **Serving:** 2

Ingredients:

Omelet:
- Zucchini – ½ cup, grated
- Fresh spinach – one cup
- Green onion – 1 tsp, green part only
- Chives – one tbsp, chopped
- Extra-virgin olive oil – 20ml
- Eggs – four
- Avocado – ½
- Lemon rind – 1 tsp
- Feta cheese – optional
- Pepper and salt – to taste

Portobello Fries:
- Portobello mushrooms – four, thickly sliced
- White breadcrumbs – 1 ½ cups
- Lemon rind – one tsp
- Parmesan cheese – one tbsp
- Eggs – two, beaten

Instructions:

Portobello fries:
1. Add parmesan cheese, lemon rind, and breadcrumbs into the bowl.
2. Let coat the mushroom slices in the beaten egg and then immerse in the breadcrumb mixture.
3. Spray the olive oil onto the baking paper. Place mushrooms onto the baking paper. Place it into the oven and bake for ten to fifteen minutes.

Omelet:
4. Add lemon rind and avocado into the bowl and keep it aside.
5. Add olive oil into the pan and heat it. Add green onion (green part only) and fry for two to three minutes. Then, add spinach and zucchini and cook for one minute until wilted.
6. Add eggs and sprinkle with chives.
7. Cook until firm.
8. Add feta cheese and turn the heat off.
9. Cut omelet in two and top with Portobello fries and sliced avocado.

Nutrition: Calories; 259, Carbs; 12g, Fats; 12g Proteins; 28g; Fiber; 3g

8. Shakshuka

Preparation time: 10 minutes | **Cooking time:** 10 to 15 minutes | **Serving:** 2

Ingredients:
- Red pepper 100g, drained, chopped
- Tomatoes – 800g, diced and cooked
- Tomato paste – 2 tbsp
- Green onion ½, minced, green part only
- Paprika – 1 ½ tsp
- Cumin – 1 tsp
- Stevia powder – ¼ tsp
- Salt and pepper to taste
- Olive oil spray
- Eggs – six
- Parsley – 1 tbsp, chopped

Instructions:
1. Place a pot over medium flame. Sprinkle with olive oil.
2. Add green onion and cook until translucent.
3. Then, add tomato paste, red pepper, and tomatoes and combine them well. Then, add stevia and spices and add them into the sauce.
4. Sprinkle with pepper. Lower the heat. Break eggs over the sauce.
5. Cover the pot with a lid and simmer for 10 to 15 minutes.
6. Garnish with fresh parsley leaves.

Nutrition: Calories; 146, Carbs; 10g, Fats; 9g Proteins; 7g; Fiber; 3g

9. Salmon Fritter

Preparation time: 10 minutes | 10 minutes | **Serving:** 4

Ingredients:
- Tuna or salmon – 350g, drained
- Olive oil – 2 tbsp
- Tomato paste – 50g
- Cooked white rice – 400g
- Paprika – ½ tsp
- Oats – ½ cup
- Wholemeal flour – ¼ cup

- Egg – one

Instructions:
1. Preheat the oven to 100 degrees C.
2. Add rice, paprika, salmon, and oats into the bowl. Make a well and pour beaten egg and tomato paste, and blend until smooth.
3. Add white flour and shape the mixture into eight patties.
4. Place onto the baking dish and cook for five minutes.
5. Flip and cook for five minutes more.
6. Serve with tomato sauce.

Nutrition: Calories; 304,Carbs; 23.8g, Fats; 10g Proteins; 30g; Fiber; 3g

10. Vanilla Almond Hot Chocolate

Preparation time: 10 minutes | **Serving:** 2

- **Ingredients:**
- Vanilla almond milk – 600ml
- Full fat coconut cream – 30g
- Dark chocolate – 60g
- Cocoa – 1 tsp
- Stevia – to taste

Instructions:
- Add vanilla almond milk into the pan and place it over medium flame.
- Add stevia, cocoa powder, and chopped chocolate and heat it.
- Top with coconut cream and chocolate shavings.

Nutrition: Calories; 195, Carbs; 33g, Fats; 4g Proteins; 8g; Fiber; 1g

11. Banana and Pear Pita Pockets

Preparation Time: 10 minutes | **Cooking Time:** 0 minutes | **Servings:** 1

Ingredients:
- 1/2 small banana, peeled and sliced
- 1 round pita bread, made with refined white flour
- 1/2 small pear, peeled, seedless, cored, cooked and sliced
- 1/4 cup low-fat Cottage cheese

Instructions:
1. Combine the banana, pear, and Cottage cheese in a small bowl. Slice the pita bread to make a pocket.
2. Fill it with the mixture.
3. Serve.

Nutrition: Calories 402, Fat 2g, Carbs 87g, Fiber 11g, Protein 14g.

12. Ripe Plantain Bran Muffins

Preparation Time: 10 minutes | **Cooking Time:** 20 minutes | **Servings:** 12

Ingredients:
- 1 ½ cup refined cereal
- 2/3 cup low-fat milk
- 4 large eggs, lightly beaten
- 1/4 cup canola oil
- 2 medium ripe plantains, mashed
- 1/2 cup brown sugar
- 1 cup refined white flour
- 2 teaspoons baking powder
- 1/2 teaspoon salt

Instructions:
1. Preheat the oven to 400°F. In a bowl, combine the bran cereal and milk; set aside.
2. Add eggs and oil; stir in brown sugar and mashed ripe plantain. In another bowl, combine salt, flour, and baking powder.
3. Dissolve the dry ingredients into the ripe plantain mixture, stir until combined.
4. Pour the batter evenly into paper-lined muffin tins; bake for 18 minutes or until golden brown and firm. Allow cooling before serving.

Nutrition: Calories 325, Fat 19g, Carbs 37g, Fiber 2g, Protein 3g.

13. Easy Breakfast Bran Muffins

Preparation Time: 10 minutes | **Cooking Time:** 20 minutes | **Servings:** 10

Ingredients:
- 2 cups refined cereal

- 1 cup boiling water
- 1/2 cup brown sugar
- 1/2 cup butter
- 2 eggs
- 1/2-quart buttermilk
- 2 ½ cups refined white flour
- 2 ½ teaspoons baking soda
- 1/2 teaspoon salt

Instructions:

1. Preheat the oven to 400°F. Soak 1 cup of cereal in 1 cup of boiling water and set aside.
2. In a mixer, merge the brown sugar and butter until it is fully mixed. Add each egg separately and beat until fluffy. Then, stir in the buttermilk and the soaked cereal mixture.
3. In another bowl, combine salt, flour and baking soda. Add the flour mixture into the batter and ensure not to over mix.
4. Add in the remaining cup of cereal. Set the batter evenly into 10 greased or paper-lined muffin tins. Bake for 15-20 minutes. Allow cooling before serving.

Nutrition: Calories: 440, Fat: 20g, Carbs: 57g, Fiber: 3g, Protein: 9g

14. Apple Oatmeal

Preparation Time: 10 minutes | **Cooking Time:** 1-2 minutes | **Servings:** 1

Ingredients:

- 1/2 cup instant oatmeal
- 3/4 cup milk or water
- 1/2 cup apples, peeled and cooked pureed
- 1 teaspoon brown sugar

Instructions:

1. In a microwave-safe bowl, mix oats, milk or water and apples. Cook in a microwave on high.
2. Stir and cook for another 30 seconds. Sprinkle with brown sugar and add a splash of milk.

Nutrition: Calories: 295, Fat: 7g, Carbs: 47g, Fiber: 5g, Protein: 13

15. Breakfast Burrito Wrap

Preparation Time: 15 minutes | **Cooking Time:** 15 minutes | **Servings:** 1

Ingredients:

- 1 tablespoon extra-virgin olive oil
- 2 slices turkey bacon
- 1/4 cup green bell peppers, seeded and chopped
- 2 eggs, beaten
- 2 tablespoons milk
- 1/4 teaspoon salt
- 2 tablespoons low-fat Monterrey Jack cheese, grated
- 1 white tortilla

Instructions:

1. In a small non-stick pan, warm olive oil on medium heat and cook the turkey for about 2 minutes until slightly crispy.
2. Attach bell peppers and continue to cook until warmed through. In a small bowl beat the eggs with milk and salt.
3. Gently, stir in your eggs until almost cooked through. Turn the heat down then add the cheese.
4. Cover and continue cooking until cheese has completely melted. Place the mixture on the tortilla and roll it into a burrito.

Nutrition: Calories: 355, Fat: 2g, Carbs: 14g, Fiber: 4g, Protein: 23g

16. Zucchini Omelet

Preparation Time: 15 minutes | **Cooking Time:** 15 minutes | **Servings:** 4

Ingredients:

- 2 tablespoons extra-virgin olive oil
- 1 medium zucchini, seeded and cubed
- 1/2 medium tomato, seeded and chopped
- 4 large eggs
- 1/4 cup milk
- 1 teaspoon salt
- 4 whole-wheat English muffins

Instructions

1. In a large non-stick pan, warm olive oil over moderate heat. Add the zucchini and tomato.
2. Cook vegetables for 5-10 minutes or until they are soft.
3. In a separate bowl, merge the eggs, milk and salt.
4. Attach the egg mixture to the pan and stir to cook through. Set with white English muffins.

Nutrition: Calories: 160, Fat: 10g, Carbs: 14g, Fiber: 2g, Protein: 6g

17. Coconut Chia Seed Pudding

Preparation Time: 15 minutes | **Cooking Time:** 0 minutes | **Servings:** 2

Ingredients:
- 6 tablespoons Chia seeds
- 2 cups coconut milk, unsweetened)
- Blueberries for topping

Instructions:
1. Merge the chia seeds and milk; mix well. Refrigerate overnight.
2. Stir in the berries and serve.

Nutrition: Calories: 223, Fat: 12g, Carbs: 18g, Fiber: 2g, Protein: 10g

18. Spiced Oatmeal

Preparation Time: 2 minutes | **Cooking Time:** 2 minutes | **Servings:** 2

Ingredients:
- 1/3 cup quick oats
- 1/4 teaspoon ground ginger
- 1/8 teaspoon ground cinnamon
- A dash of ground nutmeg
- A dash of ground clove
- 1 tablespoon almond butter
- 1 cup Water

Instructions:
1. Combine the oats and water.
2. Microwave for 45 seconds, then stir and cook for another 30-45 seconds.
3. Add in the spices and drizzle on the almond butter before serving.

Nutrition: Calories: 467, Fat: 11g, Carbs: 33g, Fiber: 4g, Protein: 6g

19. Breakfast Cereal

Preparation Time: 5 minutes | **Cooking Time:** 5 minutes | **Servings:** 4

Ingredients:
- 3 cups cooked old fashioned oatmeal
- 3 cups cooked quinoa
- 4 cups bananas, peeled and chopped

Instructions:
1. Combine the oatmeal and quinoa; mix well.
2. Evenly, divide into 4 bowls and top with the bananas before serving.

Nutrition: Calories: 228, Fat: 3g, Carbs: 43g, Fiber: 6g, Protein: 12g

20. Sweet Potato Hash with Sausage and Spinach

Preparation Time: 5 minutes | **Cooking Time:** 15 minutes | **Servings:** 4

Ingredients:
- 4 small chopped sweet potatoes
- 2 apples, cored and chopped
- 1 garlic clove, minced
- 1 pound ground sausage
- 10 ounces chopped spinach
- Salt and pepper

Instructions:
1. Brown the sausage until no pink remains. Add the remaining ingredients.
2. Cook until the spinach and apples are tender. Season to taste and serve hot.

Nutrition: Calories: 544, Fat: 2g, Carbs: 65g, Fiber: 2g, Protein: 11g

21. Cajun Omelet

Preparation Time: 5 minutes | **Cooking Time:** 8 minutes | **Servings:** 2

Ingredients:
- 1/4-pound spicy sausage
- 1/3 cup sliced mushrooms
- 1/2 diced onion

- 4 large eggs
- 1/2 medium bell pepper, chopped
- 2 tablespoons water
- A pinch of cayenne pepper (optional)
- Sea salt and fresh pepper to taste
- 1 tbsp. Mustard

Instructions:
1. Brown the sausage in a saucepan until cooked through. Add the mushrooms, onion and bell pepper. Cook for another 3-5 minutes, or until tender.
2. Meanwhile, whisk together the eggs, water, mustard and spices. Season with salt and pepper.
3. Top with your eggs over then reduce to low heat. Cook until the top is nearly set and then fold the omelet in half and cover.
4. Cook for another minute before serving hot.

Nutrition: Calories: 467, Fat: 14g, Carbs: 11g, Fiber: 2g, Protein: 16g

22. Strawberry Cashew Chia Pudding

Preparation Time: 10 minutes | **Cooking Time:** 0 minutes | **Servings:** 2

Ingredients:
- 6 tablespoon chia seeds
- 2 cups cashew milk, unsweetened
- Strawberries, for topping

Instructions:
1. Merge the chia seeds and milk; mix well. Refrigerate overnight.
2. Stir in the berries and serve.

Nutrition: Calories: 223, Fat: 12g, Carbs: 18g, Fiber: 2g, Protein: 10g

23. Peanut Butter Banana Oatmeal

Preparation Time: 5 minutes | **Cooking Time:** 0 minutes | **Servings:** 1

Ingredients:
- 1/3 cup quick oats
- 1/4 teaspoon cinnamon (optional)
- 1/2 sliced banana

- 1 tablespoon peanut butter, unsweetened

Instructions:
1. Merge all ingredients in a bowl with a lid.
2. Refrigerate.

Nutrition: Calories: 645, Fat: 32g, Carbs: 65g, Fiber: 5g, Protein: 26g

24. Overnight Peach Oatmeal

Preparation Time: 10 minutes | **Cooking Time:** 0 minutes | **Servings:** 2

Ingredients:
- 1/2 cup old fashioned oats
- 2/3 cup skim milk
- 1/2 cup plain Greek yogurt
- 1 tablespoon chia seeds
- 1/2 teaspoon Vanilla
- 1/2 cup peach, peeled and diced
- 1 medium banana, peeled and chopped

Instructions:
1. Combine the oats, milk, yogurt, chia seeds and vanilla in a bowl with a lid.
2. Refrigerate for 12 hours.
3. Top with the fruits before serving.

Nutrition: Calories: 282, Fat: 6g, Carbs: 48g, Fiber: 2g, Protein: 10g

25. Mediterranean Salmon and Potato Salad

Preparation Time: 15 minutes | **Cooking Time:** 18 minutes | **Servings:** 4

Ingredients:
- 1-pound red potatoes, peeled and cut into wedges
- 1/2 cup plus 2 tablespoons more extra-virgin olive oil
- 2 tablespoons balsamic vinegar
- 1 tablespoon fresh rosemary, minced
- 2 cups peas, cooked and drained
- 4 (4 ounces each) salmon fillets
- 2 tablespoons lemon juice
- 1/4 teaspoon salt
- 2 cups English cucumber, sliced and seedless

Instructions:

1. In a saucepan, set water to a boil and cook potatoes until tender, about 10 minutes.
2. Drain and set potatoes back into the pan. To make the dressing, in a bowl, set together 1/2 cup of olive oil, vinegar and rosemary.
3. Combine potatoes and peas with the dressing. Set aside. In a separate medium pan, warm the remaining 2 tablespoons of olive oil over medium heat.
4. Attach salmon fillets and set with lemon juice and salt.
5. Cook on both sides or until fish flakes easily. To serve, place cucumber slices on a serving plate top with potato salad and fish fillets.

Nutrition: Calories: 463, Fat: 4g, Carbs: 75g, Fiber: 18g, Protein: 34g

26. Celery Soup

Preparation Time: 8 minutes | **Cooking Time:** 10 minutes | **Servings:** 2

Ingredients:

- 1 tablespoon olive oil
- 3 garlic cloves, minced
- 2 pounds fresh celery, chopped into 1-inch pieces
- 6 cups vegetable stock
- 1 teaspoon salt

Instructions:

1. Reserve celery tops for later use. Warmth up the oil over medium heat in a soup pot.
2. Cook the garlic until softened, about 3-5 minutes. Add celery stalks, salt and vegetable stock then bring to a boil.
3. Cover and reduce the heat to low and simmer until the celery softens. Let the soup cool for a bit then puree with a hand blender.
4. Add and cook the celery tops on medium heat for 5 minutes.

Nutrition: Calories: 51, Fat: 3g, Carbs: 4g, Fiber: 2g, Protein: 2g

27. Pea Tuna Salad

Preparation Time: 15 minutes | **Cooking Time:** 0 minutes | **Servings:** 4

Ingredients:

- 3 pounds cooked peas
- 1/2 cup low-fat mayonnaise
- 1/3 cup tarragon vinegar
- 1 teaspoon honey Dijon mustard
- 2 small shallots, thinly sliced
- 2 (6 ounces) cans tuna fish, drained
- 2 small sprigs fresh tarragon, finely chopped

Instructions:

1. In a large bowl, merge mayonnaise, vinegar and mustard. Add tuna fish, shallots and peas; toss to coat with dressing.
2. Secure and refrigerate for 1 hour before serving. Set with fresh tarragon and serve.

Nutrition: Calories: 246, Fat: 13g, Carbs: 11g, Fiber: 1g, Protein: 22g

28. Vegetable Soup

Preparation Time: 15 minutes | **Cooking Time:** 1 hour 20 minutes | **Servings:** 2

Ingredients:

- 2 tablespoons extra-virgin olive oil
- 4 garlic cloves, finely chopped
- 2 celery stalks, finely sliced
- 2 carrots, finely sliced
- 6 cups water or chicken broth
- 1/4 teaspoon thyme
- 1/4 teaspoon rosemary
- 1 bay leaf
- 1 can (14 ounces) peas
- 1/2 teaspoon salt

Instructions:

1. Warmth up the oil over medium heat in a soup pot. Add garlic, celery, and carrots and continue to cook for 5 minutes, stirring occasionally.
2. Add water or chicken broth, thyme, rosemary and bay leaf. Cook until it comes to a boil.

3. Set the heat and simmer gently for about 45-60 minutes. Add peas and season with salt.
4. Let soup cool slightly, remove the bay leaf and puree with a hand blender, until creamy.
5. Serve in warmed soup bowls.

Nutrition: Calories: 242, Fat: 8g, Carbs: 34g, Fiber: 13g, Protein: 12g

29. Carrot and Turkey Soup

Preparation Time: 15 minutes | **Cooking Time:** 40 minutes | **Servings:** 4

Ingredients:
- 1/2-pound lean ground turkey
- 1/2 bag frozen carrot
- 1/4 cup green peas
- 1 can (32 ounces) chicken broth
- 2 medium tomatoes, seeded and roughly chopped
- 1 teaspoon garlic powder
- 1 teaspoon paprika
- 1 teaspoon oregano
- 1 bay leaf

Instructions:
1. Over medium heat, set the ground turkey in a soup pot. Add peas, frozen carrot, paprika, tomatoes, garlic powder, bay leaf, oregano, and broth.
2. Set the pot to a boil, lower heat, cover, and simmer for 30 minutes.

Nutrition: Calories: 436, Fat: 12g, Carbs: 20g, Fiber: 6g, Protein: 59g

30. Creamy Pumpkin Soup

Preparation Time: 15 minutes | **Cooking Time:** 1 hour 10 minutes | **Servings:** 4

Ingredients:
- 1 pumpkin, cut lengthwise, seeds removed and peeled
- 1 sweet potato, cut lengthwise and peeled
- 2 tablespoons olive oil
- 4 garlic cloves, unpeeled
- 4 cups vegetable stock

- 1/4 cup light cream
- Salt
- 1 tbsp. chopped Shallots

Instructions:
1. Preheat the oven to 375ºF. Cut all the sides of the pumpkin, shallots and sweet potato with oil.
2. Transfer your vegetables with the garlic to a roasting pan. Set to roast for about 40 minutes or until tender.
3. Let the vegetables cool for a time and scoop out the flesh of the sweet potato and pumpkin.
4. In a soup pot, place the flesh of roasted vegetables, shallots and peeled garlic. Add the broth and set to a boil.
5. Set the heat, and let it simmer, covered for 30 minutes, stirring occasionally. Let the soup cool.
6. Set the soup with a hand blender, until smooth. Add the cream.
7. Season to taste and simmer until warmed through, about 5 minutes. Serve in warm soup bowls.

Nutrition: Calories: 332, Fat: 18g, Carbs: 32gg, Fiber: 9g, Protein: 12g

31. Chicken Pea Soup

Preparation Time: 15 minutes | **Cooking Time:** 55 minutes | **Servings:** 4

Ingredients:
- 1 pound chicken breast, skinless, boneless and cubed
- 2 tablespoons olive oil
- 3 garlic cloves, minced
- 3 carrots, grated
- 1 bay leaf
- 1 teaspoon salt
- 1 teaspoon poultry seasoning
- 8 cups chicken broth
- 1/2 cup dried split peas, washed and drained
- 1 cup green peas

Instructions:

1. Warmth up the olive oil over medium heat in a soup pot. Add the chicken and cook for 5 minutes, until lightly browned.
2. Attach the garlic, bay leaf, carrots, salt and seasoning. Cook until vegetables soften, stirring occasionally.
3. Pour the broth and split peas into the pot; bring to a boil. Set the heat, cover and simmer on low heat for 30-45 minutes.
4. Stir in green peas to the soup and heat for 5 minutes, stirring to combine all ingredients.

Nutrition: Calories: 176, Fat: 5g, Carbs: 18g, Fiber: 6g, Protein: 15g

32. Mixed Bean Salad

Preparation time: 10 minutes | **Cooking Time:** 30 minutes | **Servings:** 6

Ingredients:

- Drained and rinsed green beans, 15 Ounces
- Drained and rinsed wax beans, 15 Ounces
- Drained and rinsed kidney beans, 15 Ounces
- Drained and rinsed garbanzo beans, 15 Ounces
- Chopped red onion, 1/4 Cup
- Chopped & marinated artichokes, 8 Ounces
- Fresh orange juice, 1/4 Cup
- Cider vinegar, 1/2 cup
- Olive oil, 1/2 Cup

Instructions:

1. Combine all the onion, artichokes & beans in the big serving bowl.
2. Combine the vinegar, olive oil & juice in a separate small bowl.
3. Put the dressing on a bean combination. Whisk to coat. Let it marinate for thirty minutes in the refrigerator before serving.

Nutrition: Calories: 98, Fat: 2g, Carbs: 48g, Fiber: 16g, Protein: 22g

33. Spinach Frittata

Preparation Time: 10 minutes | **Cooking Time:** 30 minutes | **Servings:** 4

Ingredients:

- 2 teaspoons olive oil
- 1 cup red pepper, seeded and chopped
- 1 garlic clove, minced
- 3 cups spinach leaves, chopped
- 4 large eggs, beaten
- 1/2 teaspoon salt
- 1/4 cup Parmesan cheese, freshly grated

Instructions:

1. Preheat the oven to 350°F. In a non-stick oven pan, heat 1 teaspoon of olive oil over medium heat.
2. Cook red peppers and garlic until vegetables are soft (about 10 minutes). In a medium bowl, combine the eggs, spinach and salt; set aside.
3. Add remaining 1 teaspoon of olive oil into the pan with vegetables and add in the egg mixture.
4. Set the heat and cook for 15 minutes. Sprinkle Parmesan cheese over the mixture and broil for an additional 4 minutes.

Nutrition: Calories: 106 Fat: 8 g Carbs: 7 g Fiber: 2 g Protein: 3 g

34. Fruit & Yogurt Smoothie

Preparation time: 5 minutes | **Cooking Time:** 5 minutes | **Servings:** 1

Ingredients:

- Plain yogurt, 3/4 cup
- Pure fruit juice, 1/2 cup
- Frozen fruit, like raspberries, blueberries, pineapple/peaches, 1 1/2 cups

Instructions:

1. In the blender, Puree yogurt with juice till smooth.
2. Put the fruit thru the hole in the lid while the motor blender is running & process till smooth.

Nutrition: Calories 279, Protein 11g, Carbs 56g, Fat 2g

35. Pear Pancakes

Preparation Time: 10 minutes | **Cooking Time:** 15 minutes | **Servings:** 4

Ingredients:

- 2 eggs
- 1 cup pear, peeled mashed
- 1 teaspoon cinnamon
- 2 teaspoons sugar
- 1 ½ cup refined white flour
- 1/2 cup flour, whole-wheat
- 2 teaspoons baking powder
- 2 teaspoons vanilla
- Non-stick cooking spray

Instructions:

1. In a bowl, beat the eggs until fluffy. Add baking powder, cinnamon, vanilla, sugar, flours, and pear, then continue to stir just until smooth.
2. Sprinkle with non-stick cooking spray. Pour a sizeable amount of the batter that you want your pancake to be into the hot pan.
3. Cook the pancakes until puffy and dry around the edges. Turn and cook another side until golden.
4. Serve pancakes with additional pear if desired.

Nutrition: Calories: 174 Fat: 2 g Carbs: 34 g Fiber: 2 g Protein: 5 g

36. Lentil Tomato Salad

Preparation time: 5 minutes | **Cooking Time:** 10 minutes | **Servings:** 4

Ingredients:

- Can Lentils, 15 Ounces
- Cherry Tomatoes, 3/2 Cups
- White Wine Vinegar, 1/4 Cup
- Chives, 1/8 Cup

Instructions:

1. The lentils should be drained and rinsed. Cherry tomatoes should be cut in half. Optional chives, sliced
2. in a mixing bowl, put all of the ingredients together. Season with salt and vinegar to taste.
3. Serve it or put it in the refrigerator in an airtight container to allow flavors to get more delicious.

Nutrition: Calories 190, Protein 1g, Carbs 3g, Fat 1g

37. Tropical Fruit Smoothie

Preparation time: 5 minutes | **Cooking Time:** 5 minutes | **Servings:** 2

Ingredients:

- Combination of pineapples, mangoes, & bananas, 1 Cup
- Vanilla yogurt, 1 Cup
- All-Bran cereal, 1/2 Cup
- Vanilla, 1 Teaspoon
- Honey, 1 Tablespoon
- Almond, 1 Cup
- Avocado, 1/2
- Ice, 1 Cup

Instructions:

1. In the blender, mix all the ingredients & mix on high speed till smooth & creamy.

Nutrition: Calories 112, Protein 2g, Carbs 5g, Fat 3g.

38. Creamy Blueberry-Pecan Overnight Oatmeal

Preparation time: 10 minutes | **Cooking Time:** 8 hours | **Servings:** 1

Ingredients:

- Rolled oats (old-fashioned), ½ cup
- Water, ½ cup
- Salt pinch
- Thawed blueberries, ½ cup
- Plain Greek yogurt, 2 tablespoons
- Toasted minced pecans, 1 tablespoon
- Pure maple syrup, 2 teaspoons

Instructions:

1. In the jar/bowl, combine water, salt & oats.
2. Cover & put it in the refrigerator for a night.
3. If required, in the morning, heat it & garnish with yogurt, blueberries, syrup & pecans.

Nutrition: Calories 291, Protein 9g, Carbs 48g, Fat 8g

39. Baked Egg, Parm, and Spinach Cup

Preparation Time: 10 minutes | **Cooking Time:** 10 minutes | **Servings:** 1

Ingredients:

- Nonstick cooking spray
- ¼ cup chopped fresh spinach
- 1 large egg
- 1 tablespoon nonfat milk
- ½ tomato, diced
- 1 tablespoon grated Parmesan cheese
- Freshly ground black pepper

Instructions:

1. Preheat the oven to 400°F. Coat a 6-ounce ramekin with cooking spray.
2. Place the spinach in the ramekin; then crack the egg over the top.
3. Add the milk, tomato, and Parmesan cheese. Season with pepper to taste.
4. Bake for 10 minutes, or until set. Enjoy warm.
5. STORAGE TIP: Double or triple the recipe and make several egg cups at once. Let the egg cups cool; then tightly cover with plastic wrap and refrigerate for up 3 days.
6. You can also cook several at once in a muffin tin (for 10 to 15 minutes until set), cool, and then refrigerate each in a sealed plastic zip-top bag for up to 3 days.

Nutrition: Protein: 9g; Calories: 112; Fat: 7g; Carbohydrates: 5g; Fiber: 1g; Total sugar: 3g; Added sugar: 0g; Sodium: 183g

40. Greek Yogurt, Granola, and Berry Parfait

Preparation Time: 10 minutes | **Cooking Time:** 15 minutes or Less | **Servings:** 1

Ingredients:

- ½ cup nonfat plain Greek yogurt
- 1 tablespoon rolled oats
- ¼ cup fresh blueberries
- ¼ cup fresh raspberries
- 1 tablespoon chopped walnuts
- 1 tablespoon chopped pecans
- 1 teaspoon honey

Instructions:

1. Place the yogurt in a 6-ounce glass.
2. Top with the oats, blueberries, raspberries, walnuts, and pecans. Drizzle the honey on top. Enjoy immediately.
3. STORAGE TIP: You can prepare your own granola with rolled oats and your favorite nuts, as well as additional goodies such as coconut flakes, dried fruit, or fruit chips.
4. Store it in an airtight container in a dry, dark place for up to 3 months.
5. Use it in this parfait, a smoothie, or as a snack on its own.

Nutrition:(8 ounces): Protein: 16g; Calories: 245; Fat: 11g; Carbohydrates: 25g; Fiber: 5g; Total sugar: 21g; Added sugar: 6g; Sodium: 46g

41. Protein-Packed Breakfast Bars

Preparation Time: 10 minutes | **Cooking Time:** 15 minutes | **Servings:** 1

Ingredients:

- cup porridge oats
- 1 tbsp. smooth nut butter
- 1 tbsp. coconut oil, melted
- 1 tbsp. agave/maple syrup
- tbsp. whey/soy vanilla protein powder
- 1 tsp. ground cinnamon

Instructions:

1. Heat the oven to 160°F.

2. Grease and line the base of an 18 x 25cm tin with a little cooking spray.
3. Mix the oats and nut butter in the tin.
4. Place in the oven for 5-10 minutes to toast.
5. Meanwhile, warm the coconut oil in a pan over low heat.
6. Add the oat mix, syrup, protein powder, and cinnamon to the pan.
7. Mix everything together until all the oats are well-coated.
8. Tip into the tin, press down lightly, then bake for 30 minutes.
9. Cool in the tin and cut into 6 bars.

Nutrition: Calories: 121 Protein: 6g Carbs: 16g Fiber: 2g Sugar: 6g Fat: 4g

LUNCH

42. Shrimp and Mango Salsa Lettuce Wraps

Preparation Time: 15 minutes | **Cooking Time:** 3 minutes | **Servings:** 6

Ingredients:
For the Salsa:
- 1 mango, peeled, pitted and chopped
- 1/4 cup red onion, finely chopped
- 1/2 cup red bell pepper
- 1/4 cup fresh cilantro, chopped
- 1 jalapeño pepper, seeded and finely chopped
- 2 tablespoons fresh lime juice
- Salt and freshly ground black pepper

For the Shrimp Wraps:
- 1 teaspoon organic olive oil
- 2 pounds large shrimp, peeled, deveined and chopped
- 1/2 teaspoon ground cumin
- 1 tablespoon red chili powder
- Salt and freshly ground black pepper
- 2 heads butter lettuce, leaves separated

Instructions:
For the salsa:
1. In a large bowl, mix all ingredients. Keep aside.

For the Shrimp Wraps:
2. In a skillet, heat oil on medium heat.
3. Add the shrimp and seasoning. Cook for approximately 2-3 minutes.

4. Remove from the heat and cool slightly.
5. Divide the shrimp mixture over lettuce leaves lightly.
6. Top with mango salsa evenly and serve.

Nutrition: Calories: 463, Fat: 4g, Carbs: 75g, Fiber: 18g, Protein: 34g

43. Bacon-Wrapped Asparagus

Preparation Time: 25 minutes | **Cooking Time:** 30 minutes | **Servings:** 6

Ingredients:
- 10 bacon slices cut in half
- 1-pound fresh asparagus, trimmed
- 1 tablespoon extra-virgin olive oil
- 1 tablespoon balsamic vinegar
- Freshly ground black pepper, to taste
- 1 lemon, sliced

Instructions:
1. Heat the oven to 400°F. Line a substantial baking dish with foil paper.
2. Wrap 1 bacon slice around each asparagus piece.
3. Arrange asparagus in the prepared baking dish.
4. Set with oil and vinegar. Sprinkle with black pepper.
5. Bake for approximately 15 minutes. Change the inside and bake for 10-15 minutes more.
6. Serve immediately with lemon slices.

Nutrition: Calories: 645, Fat: 32g, Carbs: 65g, Fiber: 5g, Protein: 26g

44. Zucchini Pasta with Shrimp

Preparation Time: 15 minutes | **Cooking Time:** 21 minutes | **Servings:** 4

Ingredients:

- 2 tablespoons ghee or coconut oil
- 1 tablespoon extra-virgin olive oil
- 3 garlic cloves, minced
- 1 pound shrimp, peeled and deveined
- 4 large zucchinis, spiralized with blade C
- Salt and freshly ground black pepper
- 4-6 fresh basil leaves, chopped

Instructions:

1. In a big skillet, heat the ghee and essential olive oil on medium heat.
2. Add garlic and sauté for approximately 1 minute.
3. Set the shrimp and cook for approximately 2-3 minutes.
4. Add the zucchini, tossing occasionally and cook for approximately 2-3 minutes.
5. Stir in salt and black pepper and take off from the heat.
6. Serve while using the garnishing of basil leaves.

Nutrition: Calories: 59, Fat: 1g, Carbs: 14g, Fiber: 1g, Protein: 1g, Sodium: 304 mg

45. Sweet Potato Buns Sandwich

Preparation Time: 25 minutes | **Cooking Time:** 25 minutes | **Servings:** 1

Ingredients:

For Sweet Potato Buns:

- 1 ½ tablespoon extra-virgin olive oil, divided
- 1 large, sweet potato, peeled and spiralized with blade C
- 2 teaspoons garlic powder
- Salt and freshly ground black pepper
- 1 large organic egg
- 1 organic egg white

For the Sandwich:

- 1 (1/2 ounce) salmon piece
- Salt and freshly ground black pepper
- 1 teaspoon fresh lime juice
- 1 tomato, sliced
- 1 onion, sliced
- 1/2 avocado, peeled, pitted and chopped
- 2 teaspoons fresh cilantro, chopped
- 1 large bit fresh kale
- 1 bacon piece

Instructions:

For the buns:

- In a sizable skillet, heat 1/2 tablespoon of oil on medium heat.
- Add the sweet potato and sprinkle with garlic powder, salt and black pepper.
- Cook for 5-7 minutes. Transfer the sweet potato mixture to a bowl.
- Add the egg and egg white; mix well. Now, transfer a combination into 2 (6 ounces) ramekins, midway full.
- Cover the ramekins with wax paper. Now, place them over noodles to press firmly down. Refrigerate for about 15-20 minutes.

For the Sandwich:

1. Preheat the grill to medium heat. Grease it.
2. In another bowl, add salmon, salt, black pepper and lime juice. Toss to coat well.
3. In a substantial skillet, heat the remaining oil on medium-low heat.
4. Carefully, transfer the sweet potato patties to the skillet.
5. Cook for 3-4 minutes. Change the medial side and cook for 2-3 minutes more.
6. Place the salmon, onion and tomato slices over the grill.
7. Grill the tomato slice for 1 minute. Grate the onion slice for approximately 2 minutes.
8. Cook the salmon for approximately 4-5 minutes or till the desired doneness.
9. In a bowl, add the avocado and cilantro, mash well.

10. On a plate, place the onion slice, salmon, tomato, bacon and kale over the bun.
11. Spread the avocado mash around the bottom side of another bun. Place the bun, avocado mash side downwards over the kale.
12. Secure having a toothpick and serve.

Nutrition: Calories: 75, Carbs: 0.1g, Protein: 13.4g, Fat: 1.7g, Sugar: 0g, Sodium: 253 mg

46. Shrimp, Sausage and Veggie Skillet

Preparation Time: 15 minutes | **Cooking Time:** 13 minutes | **Servings:** 3

Ingredients:
- 3 tablespoons organic olive oil, divided
- 1 pound shrimp, peeled and deveined
- 1/2 medium yellow onion, chopped
- 3/4 cup green peppers, seeded and chopped
- 3/4 cup green peppers, seeded and chopped
- 1 zucchini, chopped
- 6 ounces cooked sausage, chopped
- 2 garlic cloves, minced
- 1/4 cup chicken broth
- A pinch of red pepper flakes, crushed
- Salt and freshly ground black pepper

Instructions:
1. In a sizable skillet, heat 1 tablespoon of oil on medium-high heat.
2. Attach the shrimp and cook for around 3-4 minutes. Transfer it to a bowl.
3. In the same skillet, heat the remaining oil on medium heat.
4. Add the onion and sweet peppers. Sauté for about 4-5 minutes.
5. Stir in the zucchini and sausage. Cook for approximately 2 minutes.
6. Add the garlic and cooled shrimp. Cook for approximately 1 minute.
7. Pour the broth and mix to combine well. Stir in red pepper flakes, salt and black pepper. Cook for approximately 1 minute.
8. Serve hot.

Nutrition: Calories: 332, Fat: 18g, Carbs: 32g, Fiber: 9g, Protein: 12g

47. Sea Scallops with Spinach and Bacon

Preparation Time: 25 minutes | **Cooking Time:** 25 minutes | **Servings:** 4

Ingredients:
- 3 bacon slices
- 1 ½ pound jumbo sea scallops
- Salt and freshly ground black pepper
- 1 cup onion, chopped
- 6 garlic cloves, minced
- 12 ounces fresh baby spinach

Instructions:
1. Heat a sizable non-stick skillet on medium-high heat.
2. Add the bacon and cook for approximately 8-10 minutes.
3. Transfer the bacon into a bowl, reserving 1 tablespoon of bacon fat within the skillet.
4. Chop the bacon and keep it aside.
5. Attach the scallops and sprinkle with salt and black pepper.
6. Immediately, boost the heat to high heat.
7. Cook for about 5 minutes, turning once after 2 ½ minutes.
8. Transfer the scallops into another bowl. Cover having foil paper to ensure that they're warm.
9. In the same skillet, add the onion and garlic minimizing the temperature to medium-high.
10. Sauté them for around 3 minutes.
11. Add the spinach and cook for approximately 2-3 minutes. Season with salt and black pepper. Remove from the heat.
12. Divide the spinach among serving plates. Top with scallops and bacon evenly. Serve immediately.

Nutrition: Calories: 246, Fat: 13g, Carbs: 11g, Fiber: 1g, Protein: 22g

48. Liver with Onion and Parsley One

Preparation Time: 10 minutes | **Cooking Time:** 26 minutes | **Servings:** 4

Ingredients:

- 3 tablespoons coconut oil, divided
- 2 large onions, sliced
- Salt to taste
- 1-pound grass-fed beef liver, cut into 1/2-inch-thick slices
- Freshly ground black pepper, to taste
- 1/2 cup fresh parsley
- 2 tablespoons freshly squeezed lemon juice

Instructions:

1. In a sizable skillet, heat 1 tablespoon of oil on high heat.
2. Attach the onions plus some salt and sauté for about 5 minutes.
3. Set the heat to medium. Sauté them for 10-15 minutes more.
4. Place the onion right into a plate.
5. In the same skillet, heat another 1 tablespoon of oil on medium-high heat.
6. Add the liver and sprinkle with salt and black pepper.
7. Cook for approximately 1-2 minutes or till browned.
8. Flip alongside it and cook for approximately 1-2 minutes till browned. Set the liver right into a plate.
9. In the skillet, heat the remaining oil on medium heat.
10. Attach the cooked onion, parsley and lemon juice; stir well. Cook for about 2-3 minutes.
11. Set the onion mixture over the liver and serve immediately.

Nutrition: Calories: 228, Fat: 3g, Carbs: 43g, Fiber: 6g, Protein: 12g

49. Egg and Avocado Wraps

Preparation Time: 10 minutes | **Cooking Time:** 26 minutes | **Servings:** 5

Ingredients:

- 1 ripe avocado, peeled, pitted and chopped
- 1 tablespoon freshly squeezed lemon juice
- 1 tablespoon fresh parsley, chopped
- 2 tablespoons celery stalk, chopped
- 4 organic hard-boiled eggs, peeled and finely chopped
- Salt and freshly ground black pepper
- 4-5 endive bulbs
- 2 cooked bacon slices, chopped

Instructions:

1. In a bowl, add the avocado and freshly squeezed lemon juice and mash till smooth and creamy.
2. Add parsley, celery, eggs, salt and black pepper. Stir to mix well.
3. Separate the endive leaves. Divide the avocado mixture over endive leaves evenly.
4. Top with bacon and serve immediately.

Nutrition: Calories: 404, Fat: 7g, Carbs: 47g, Fiber: 6g, Protein: 15g

50. Creamy Sweet Potato Pasta with Pancetta

Preparation Time: 10 minutes | **Cooking Time:** 28 minutes | **Servings:** 4

Ingredients:

For the Creamy Sauce:
- 4-5 cups cauliflower florets
- 1 small shallot, minced
- 1 large garlic herb, chopped
- A pinch of red pepper flakes, crushed
- 1 cup chicken broth
- 1 tablespoon nutritional yeast
- Salt to taste

For the Pancetta:
- 8 pancetta slices, cubed

For the Sweet Potato Pasta:
- 1 tablespoon extra-virgin olive oil
- 3 medium sweet potatoes, peeled and spiralized with blade C
- 3 cups leeks
- Salt and freshly ground black pepper
- 1 tablespoon fresh parsley, chopped

Instructions:

1. In a pan of salted boiling water, attach cauliflower florets and cook for around 7-8 minutes. Drain well.
2. Meanwhile, heat a large non-stick skillet on medium heat.
3. Add pancetta slices and cook for approximately 5-7 minutes.
4. Transfer the pancetta into a bowl.
5. In the same skillet, add shallot, garlic and red pepper flakes. Sauté for around 2 minutes.
6. Transfer the shallot mixture into a higher speed blender.
7. Add the cauliflower and the remaining sauce ingredients. Pulse till smooth and creamy.
8. In the identical skillet, heat extra-virgin olive oil on medium heat.
9. Add sweet potatoes and leeks. Cook, tossing occasionally for approximately 8-10 minutes.
10. Stir in the sauce and cook for about 1 minute.
11. Serve this creamy pasta with all the topping of the pancetta and parsley.

Nutrition: Calories: 33, Carbs: 8.1g, Protein: 0.2g, Fat: 0.1g, Sugar: 7.6g, Sodium: 130 mg, Fiber: 0.1g

51. Roasted Beet Pasta with Kale and Pesto

Preparation Time: 10 minutes | **Cooking Time:** 15 minutes | **Servings:** 3

Ingredients:
For the Pesto:
- 3 cups fresh basil leaves
- 1 large garlic oil
- 1/4 cup organic olive oil
- 1/4 cup pine nuts
- Salt and freshly ground black pepper

For the Beet Pasta:
- 2 medium beets, trimmed, peeled and spiralized with blade C
- Olive oil cooking spray, as required

- Salt and freshly ground black pepper

For the Kale:
- 2 cups fresh baby kale

Instructions:
1. Heat the oven to 425°F. Lightly, grease a large baking sheet.
2. In a mixer, add all pesto ingredients and pulse till smooth. Keep aside.
3. Place the beet pasta in the prepared baking sheet.
4. Drizzle with cooking spray and sprinkle with salt and black pepper. Gently, toss to coat well.
5. Roast for around 5-10 minutes or till the desired doneness.
6. Transfer the pasta to a sizable bowl.
7. Add the kale and pesto. Gently, toss to coat well.

Nutrition: Calories: 37, Fat: 1g, Carbs: 3g, Fiber: 0g, Protein: 4g, Sodium: 58 mg

52. Veggies and Apple with Orange Sauce

Preparation Time: 30 minutes | **Cooking Time:** 16 minutes | **Servings:** 4

Ingredients:
For the Sauce:
- 1 (1 inch) fresh ginger, minced
- 2 garlic cloves, minced
- 1 tablespoon fresh orange zest, grated finely
- 1/2 cup fresh orange juice
- 2 tablespoons white wine vinegar
- 2 tablespoons coconut aminos
- 1 tablespoon red boat fish sauce

For the Veggies and Apple:
- 1 tablespoon extra-virgin olive oil
- 1 cup carrot, peeled and julienned
- 1 cup celery, chopped
- 1 cup onion, chopped
- 2 apples, cored and sliced

Instructions:
1. In a sizable bowl, mix all sauce ingredients. Keep aside.

2. In a big skillet, set the oil on medium-high heat.
3. Add the carrot and stir fry for about 4-5 minutes.
4. Attach celery and onion. Stir fry for approximately 4-5 minutes.
5. Pour the sauce and stir to combine. Cook approximately 2-3 minutes.
6. Stir in apple slices and cook for about 2-3 minutes more.
7. Serve hot.

Nutrition: Calories: 29, Fat: 1g, Carbs: 2g, Fiber: 1g, Protein: 1g

53. Cauliflower Rice with Prawns and Veggies

Preparation Time: 15 minutes | **Cooking Time:** 21 minutes | **Servings:** 4

Ingredients:
- 2 tablespoons coconut oil, divided
- 14 prawns, peeled and deveined
- 2 organic eggs, beaten
- 1 brown onion, chopped
- 1 garlic clove, minced
- 1 small fresh red chili, chopped
- 1/2-pound grass-fed ground chicken
- 1 cauliflower head, cut into florets, processed like rice consistency
- 1/4 red cabbage, chopped
- 1/2 cup green peas, shelled
- 1 head small broccoli
- 1 large carrot, peeled and finely chopped
- 1 small red bell pepper
- 2 bok choy, sliced thinly
- 3 tablespoons coconut aminos
- Salt and freshly ground black pepper

Instructions:
1. In a substantial skillet, heat 1/2 tablespoon of oil on medium-high heat.
2. Add the prawns and cook for approximately 3-4 minutes. Transfer to a large bowl.
3. In the same skillet, heat 1/2 tablespoon of oil on medium heat.
4. Add the beaten eggs and with the back of a spoon, spread the eggs. Cook for around 2 minutes.
5. Remove the eggs from the skillet and cut them into strips.
6. In the identical skillet, heat the remaining oil on high heat. Add the onion, garlic and red chili. Sauté for about 4-5 minutes.
7. Add the chicken and cook for about 4-5 minutes.
8. Add the cauliflower rice and remaining veggies except for the bok choy and coconut aminos and cook for around 2-3 minutes.
9. Add the bok choy, coconut aminos, cooked eggs, prawns, salt and black pepper. Cook for 2 minutes more.

Nutrition: Calories: 75, Carbs: 0.1g, Protein: 13.4g, Fat: 1.7g, Sugar: 0g, Sodium: 253 mg

54. Lentils with Tomatoes and Turmeric

Preparation Time: 15 minutes | **Cooking Time:** 10 minutes | **Servings:** 2

Ingredients:
- 1/2 onion, finely chopped
- 1/2 teaspoon garlic powder
- 1/2 (14 ounces) can chopped tomatoes, drained
- 1/8 teaspoon ground black pepper
- 1 tablespoon extra-virgin olive oil, plus extra for garnishing
- 1/2 tablespoon ground turmeric
- 1/2 (14 ounces) can lentils, drained
- 1/4 teaspoon sea salt

Instructions:
1. Heat the olive oil in a pot over medium-high heat until it starts shimmering.
2. Cook, stirring regularly, for around 5 minutes until the onion and turmeric are tender.
3. Add the garlic powder, salt, tomatoes, lentils, and pepper.
4. Cook, stirring regularly, for 5 minutes

Nutrition: Calories: 248, Fat: 8g, Carbs: 34g, Sugar: 5g, Fiber: 15g, Protein: 12g, Sodium: 243 mg

55. Fried Rice with Kale

Preparation Time: 10 minutes | **Cooking Time:** 12 minutes | **Servings:** 2

Ingredients:

- 4 ounces tofu chopped
- 1 cup kale, stemmed and chopped
- 2 tablespoons stir-fry sauce
- 1 tablespoon extra-virgin olive oil
- 3 sliced scallions
- 1 ½ cup cooked brown rice

Instructions:

1. Heat the olive oil in a big skillet or pan over medium-high heat until it starts shimmering.
2. Add the scallions, tofu, and kale. Cook until the vegetables are tender.
3. Combine the stir-fry sauce and brown rice in a mixing bowl. Cook, stirring regularly until thoroughly heated.

Nutrition: Calories: 301, Fat: 11g, Carbs: 36g, Sugar: 1g, Fiber: 3g, Protein: 16g, Sodium: 2.535 mg

56. Tofu and Red Pepper Stir-Fry

Preparation Time: 10 minutes | **Cooking Time:** 12 minutes | **Servings:** 2

Ingredients:

- 1 chopped red bell peppers
- 1 tablespoon extra-virgin olive oil
- 1/2 chopped onion
- 1/4 cup ginger teriyaki sauce
- 4 ounces chopped tofu

Instructions:

1. Heat the olive oil in a skillet or pan over medium-high heat until it starts shimmering.
2. Add the onion, red bell peppers, and tofu. Cook, stirring regularly.
3. Apply the teriyaki sauce to the skillet or pan after whisking it together. Cook, stirring

occasionally for 3-4 minutes, or until it thickens.

Nutrition: Calories: 166, Fat: 10g, Carbs: 17g, Sugar: 12g, Fiber: 2g, Protein: 7g, Sodium: 892mg

57. Sweet Potato and Bell Pepper Hash with a Fried Egg

Preparation Time: 10 minutes | **Cooking Time:** 25 minutes | **Servings:** 2

Ingredients:

- 1/2 chopped onion
- 2 cups peeled and cubed potatoes
- 2 tablespoons extra-virgin olive oil
- 1/2 chopped red bell pepper
- 1/2 teaspoon sea salt
- 2 eggs
- A pinch of freshly ground black pepper

Instructions:

1. Heat olive oil in a big non-stick pan over medium-high heat until it starts shimmering.
2. Add the red bell pepper, onion, and sweet potato. Season with salt and a pinch of black pepper. Cook, stirring regularly until the potatoes are soft and browned.
3. Serve the potatoes in 4 bowls.
4. Return the skillet or pan to heat, turn the heat down to medium-low, and swirl to secure the bottom of the pan with the remaining olive oil.
5. Scatter some salt over the eggs and carefully smash them into the tray. Cook until the whites are set, around 3-4 minutes.
6. Flip the eggs gently and remove them from the heat. Allow to rest for 1 minute in the hot skillet or pan. 1 egg should be placed on top of each serving of hash.

Nutrition: Calories: 384, Fat: 19g, Carbs: 47g, Sugar: 16g, Fiber: 8g, Protein: 10g, Sodium: 603 mg

58. Quinoa Florentine

Preparation Time: 5 minutes | **Cooking Time:** 25 minutes | **Servings:** 2

Ingredients:

- 1/2 chopped onion
- 2 minced garlic cloves
- 2 cups no-salt-added vegetable broth
- A pinch of freshly ground black pepper
- 1 tablespoon extra-virgin olive oil
- 1 ½ cup fresh baby spinach
- 1 cup quinoa, rinsed well
- 1/4 teaspoon sea salt

Instructions:

1. Heat the olive oil over medium-high heat until it starts shimmering.
2. Add the spinach and onion. Cook, stirring regularly, for 3 minutes.
3. Cook, stirring continuously, for 30 seconds after adding the garlic.
4. Combine the vegetable broth, salt, quinoa, and pepper in a mixing bowl. Set to a simmer, then reduce to low heat. Cook, covered, for 15-20 minutes, or until the liquid has been absorbed.
5. Using a fork, fluff the mixture.

Nutrition: Calories: 403, Fat: 12g, Carbs: 62g, Sugar: 4g, Fiber: 7g, Protein: 13g, Sodium: 278mg

59. Tomato Asparagus Frittata

Preparation Time: 5 minutes | **Cooking Time:** 20 minutes | **Servings:** 2

Ingredients:

- 5 trimmed asparagus spears
- 3 eggs
- 1 tablespoon extra-virgin olive oil
- 5 cherry tomatoes
- 1/2 tablespoon chopped fresh thyme
- A pinch of freshly ground black pepper
- 1/4 teaspoon sea salt

Instructions:

1. Preheat the broiler to the highest setting.
2. Heat the olive oil in a big ovenproof skillet or pan over medium-high heat until it starts shimmering.
3. Toss in the asparagus. Cook, stirring regularly, for 5 minutes.

4. Add in the tomatoes. Cook for 3 minutes, stirring once in a while.
5. Whisk together the thyme, salt, eggs, and pepper in a medium mixing cup. Carefully, spill over the tomatoes and asparagus, turning them about in the pan to ensure that they are equally distributed.
6. Turn the heat down to medium. Cook for 3 minutes, or until the eggs are hardened around the outside
7. Place the pan under the broiler and cook for 3-5 minutes, or until puffed and brown. To eat, cut into wedges.

Nutrition: Calories: 224, Fat: 14g, Carbs: 15g, Sugar: 10g, Fiber: 5g, Protein: 12g, Sodium: 343 mg

60. Tofu Sloppy Joes

Preparation Time: 5 minutes | **Cooking Time:** 15 minutes | **Servings:** 2

Ingredients:

- 1/2 chopped onion
- 1 (14 ounces) can crushed tomatoes
- 1/2 tablespoon chili powder
- 1 tablespoon extra-virgin olive oil
- 5 ounces chopped tofu
- 2 tablespoons apple cider vinegar
- 1/2 teaspoon garlic powder
- a pinch of freshly ground black pepper
- 1/4 teaspoon sea salt

Instructions:

1. Heat the olive oil in a big pot over medium-high heat until it starts shimmering.
2. Combine the tofu and onion in a mixing bowl. Cook, stirring regularly until the onion is tender.
3. Add the tomatoes, apple cider vinegar, salt, garlic powder, chili powder, and pepper in a large mixing bowl. Simmer for 10 minutes, stirring regularly, to enable the flavors to meld.

Nutrition: Calories: 209, Fat: 10g, Carbs: 21g, Sugar: 13g, Fiber: 8g, Protein: 11g, Sodium: 644 mg

61. Broccoli and Egg "Muffins"

Preparation Time: 5 minutes | **Cooking Time:** 10 minutes | **Servings:** 2

Ingredients:

- 1 tablespoon extra-virgin olive oil
- 1/2 cup chopped broccoli florets
- 1/2 teaspoon garlic powder
- 2 tablespoons freshly ground black pepper
- Non-stick cooking spray
- 1/2 chopped onion
- 4 beaten eggs
- 1/4 teaspoon sea salt

Instructions:

1. Preheat the oven to 350°F.
2. Using non-stick cooking oil, coat a muffin pan.
3. Heat the olive oil in a big non-stick skillet or pan over medium-high heat until it starts shimmering.
4. Add the broccoli and onion. Let it be for 3 minutes in the oven. Divide the vegetables equally among the four muffin cups.
5. Add the eggs, salt, garlic powder, and pepper. They can be poured over the vegetables in the muffin tins.
6. Bake for 15-17 minutes, or until the eggs are cooked through.

Nutrition: Calories: 207, Fat: 16g, Carbs: 5g, Sugar: 2g, Fiber: 1g, Protein: 12g, Sodium: 366 mg

62. Shrimp Scampi

Preparation Time: 10 minutes | **Cooking Time:** 15 minutes | **Servings:** 2

Ingredients:

- 1/2 finely chopped onion
- 1 pound shrimp, peeled and tails removed
- 1 lemon juice
- 2 tablespoons extra-virgin olive oil
- 1/2 chopped red bell pepper
- 3 minced garlic cloves
- 1 lemon zest
- A pinch of freshly ground black pepper
- 1/4 teaspoon sea salt

Instructions:

1. Heat the olive oil in a big non-stick pan over medium-high heat until it starts shimmering.
2. Add the red bell pepper and onion. Cook, stirring regularly, for around 6 minutes, or until tender.
3. Cook for around 5 minutes, or until the shrimp are yellow.
4. Add the garlic. Cook for 30 seconds while continuously stirring.
5. Stir in the zest and lemon juice, as well as the pepper and salt. Cook for 3 minutes on low heat.

Nutrition: Calories: 345, Fat: 16g, Carbs: 10g, Sugar: 3g, Fiber: 1g, Protein: 40g, Sodium: 424mg

63. Shrimp with Cinnamon Sauce

Preparation Time: 5 minutes | **Cooking Time:** 10 minutes | **Servings:** 2

Ingredients:

- 1 pound shrimp, peeled
- 1/2 cup no-salt-added chicken broth
- 1/2 teaspoon onion powder
- 1/8 teaspoon ground black pepper
- 1 tablespoon extra-virgin olive oil
- 1 tablespoon Dijon Mustard
- 1/2 teaspoon ground cinnamon
- 1/4 teaspoon sea salt

Instructions:

1. Heat the olive oil in a big non-stick skillet or pan over medium-high heat until it starts shimmering.
2. Toss in the shrimp. Cook, stirring regularly, for around 4 minutes, or until it is opaque.
3. Whisk together the chicken broth, mustard, onion powder, salt, cinnamon, and pepper in a shallow cup. Pour this into the skillet or pan and fry, stirring regularly, for another 3 minutes.

Nutrition: Calories: 270, Fat: 11g, Carbs: 4g, Sugar: 1g, Fiber: 1g, Protein: 39g, Sodium: 664mg

64. Veggie Bowl

Preparation time: 10 minutes | **Cooking time:** 0 minutes | **Serving:** 2

Ingredients:

- White basmati rice – 100g
- Green beans – six
- Red pepper, peeled, diced, and roasted
- Ripe avocado – ¼, sliced lengthways
- Cucumber – half cup, sliced
- Asparagus – six stems
- Tuna – one slice
- Pumpkin chunks – ½ cup, peeled and roasted
- Lemon – half, cut into quarters
- Ginger – 2 tsp, pickled
- Dressing:
- Orange juice – ½ cup, freshly squeezed
- Sesame oil – four tbsp
- Salt and pepper, one pinch

Instructions:

1. Cook the rice and drain it well.
2. Blanche green beans.
3. Grill red pepper and remove skin and then dice it.
4. Thinly slice the avocado lengthways.
5. Cut the cucumber thinly.
6. Drain six stems of asparagus.
7. Drain tuna slices of oil.
8. Boil the pumpkin chunks.
9. Place the red pepper in a mound in the middle of the plates.
10. Arrange all ingredients on the plates.
11. Pour sesame oil over it. Sprinkle with pepper and salt.
12. 1Pour dressing over the bowl.

Nutrition: Calories; 519, Carbs; 59.2g, Fats; 28.4g Proteins; 13.2g, fiber; 5g

65. Chicken Saffron Rice Pilaf

Preparation time: 15 minutes | **Cooking time:** 30 minutes | **Serving:** 6

Ingredients:

- Saffron – one pinch
- Ghee or olive oil – one tbsp
- Carrot – one, peeled, chopped
- Celery – one stalk, outside parts peeled, chopped
- Basmati rice or jasmine rice – 1 ½ cups
- Chicken broth – three cups, low-sodium
- Chicken breast – 1 ¼ cups, roasted, shredded
- Lemon – one
- Fresh parsley – chopped, to garnish

Instructions:

1. Add saffron and water into the bowl and soak it.
2. Add ghee into the skillet and heat it. Then, add celery and carrots and sauté for three to four minutes until softened. Add rice and sauté until toasted.
3. Add saffron and chicken broth to the skillet, bring to a boil, lower the heat, and cook for twenty-five to thirty minutes.
4. Add shredded chicken to the rice and toss to combine.
5. Let sit for five minutes.
6. When ready to serve, add lemon juice over the rice.
7. Garnish with chopped parsley leaves.

Nutrition: Calories; 269, Carbs; 41g, Fats; 5g Proteins; 13g

66. Pulao Rice Prawns

Preparation time: 5 minutes | **Cooking time:** 10 minutes | **Serving:** 4

Ingredients:

- Prawns – 20, deveined, shelled
- Extra virgin olive oil – three tbsp
- Water – 500ml
- Coconut milk – 200ml
- Cardamoms – three
- Bay leaves – two
- Red chili powder – one pinch
- Turmeric powder – ½ tsp
- Fresh coriander – ¼ cup, chopped
- Black pepper and pepper – to taste
- Garam masala powder – one pinch

- Asafoetida powder – one pinch

Instructions:

1. Add olive oil into the pan. Heat it.
2. Then, add black pepper, cardamoms, bay leaves, and spices clove and cook for one to two minutes until fragrant, about one to two minutes.
3. Add cardamom, bay leaves, and cloves into the tea leaf ball.
4. Add asafoetida powder, turmeric, garam masala, chili powder, salt, and prawns and combine well.
5. Drain and add rice to the pan and cover with 500ml water and 200ml coconut milk.
6. Lower the heat and simmer until cooked thoroughly.
7. Garnish with fresh coriander leaves.

Nutrition: Calories; 424kcal, Carbohydrates; 62g, Fats; 11g Proteins; 19g, fiber; 2g

67.Stewed Lamb

Preparation time: 5 minutes | **Cooking time:** 8 hours | **Serving:** 6

Ingredients:

- Lamb leg – 1 1/2kg, boneless
- Extra-virgin olive oil – 2 tbsp
- Beef or vegetable broth – 400ml
- Red wine – 300ml
- Whole meal flour – 80g
- Button mushrooms – 400g, sliced in half
- Fresh rosemary leaves – 1 tsp
- Potatoes – 1kg, cut into quarters, red-skinned
- Celery sticks – two chopped
- Carrots – two, cut into large chunks
- Parsley – 1 cup, chopped

Instructions:

1. Add olive oil into the saucepan and place it over medium flame.
2. Cook until browned. Add stock to the slow cooker, place the lamb with all ingredients into the slow cooker, and cook on low flame for eight hours.

3. After eight hours, turn off the slow cooker and add cooled stock to the bowl to make a paste with whole meal flour. Stir well.
4. Add flour paste and sprinkle with pepper and salt.
5. Sprinkle with fresh parsley leaves.

Nutrition: Calories; 481, Carbs; 22g, Fats; 27g Proteins; 28g, fiber; 4g

68.Lemongrass Beef

Preparation time: 5 minutes | **Cooking time:** 5-10 minutes | **Serving:** 4

Ingredients:

- Sesame oil – 2 tbsp
- Fish sauce – 1 tbsp
- Sweet chili sauce – 2 tbsp
- Basmati rice – 2 packets, microwave
- Coconut – 2 tsp, shredded
- Lemongrass paste – 1 tbsp
- Beef – 500g, minced, grass-fed
- Thai seasoning – 1 tbsp
- Cucumber – 100g, peeled and cut into chunks
- Carrots – two, peeled and julienned
- Basil – ¼ cup, chopped
- Lime – one, cut into four wedges

Instructions:

1. Add sesame oil, lemongrass paste, fish sauce, and Thai seasoning into the wok and heat it.
2. Add the minced beef and stir well and cook for three to four minutes until browned.
3. Cook the rice according to the instructions.
4. Add one tsp shredded coconut and stir well.
5. Add carrots, cucumber, rice, and minced beef into the bowl.
6. Sprinkle with Thai basil.
7. Pour sweet chili sauce and lime wedges over it.

Nutrition: Calories; 450, Carbs; 50g, Fats; 19g Proteins; 21g, fiber; 3g

69. Pulled Chicken Salad

Preparation time: 5 minutes | **Cooking time:** 5 minutes | **Serving:** 4

Ingredients:

- Pulled BBQ chicken – 200g, cooked
- Apricots – 1/3 cup, drained, thinly sliced
- Orzo pasta – 100g
- Spinach – 150g, stalks removed
- Cheddar cheese, 70g, cut into small cubes
- Parmesan cheese – 30g
- Parsley – ¼ cup, chopped
- Noodles – 1/3 cup
- Olive oil – five tbsp
- Red wine vinegar – three tbsp
- Salt and pepper, to taste

Instructions

1. Shred cooked and cooled chicken with a fork.
2. Add cooked and cooled orzo pasta into the microwave dish. Top with parmesan cheese and microwave for one to two minutes.
3. Add apricots, chicken, parsley, and spinach into the bowl and mix it well.
4. Add red wine vinegar and olive oil, sprinkle with pepper and salt, and pour over the salad.
5. Combine it well.
6. Add crispy noodles before serving.

Nutrition: Calories; 352, Carbs; 14g, Fats; 19g Proteins; 29g, fiber; 3g

70. Grilled Fish Steaks

Preparation time: 10 minutes | **Cooking time:** 10 minutes | **Additional time:** 1 hour 10 minutes | **Servings:** 2

Ingredients:

- Garlic, one clove, minced
- Olive oil – six tbsp
- Dried basil – one tsp
- Salt – one tsp

- Ground black pepper – one tsp
- Lemon juice – one tbsp
- Fresh parsley – one tbsp, chopped
- Halibut fillets – six ounces

Instructions:

1. Mix the parsley, lemon juice, pepper, salt, basil, olive oil, and garlic into the bowl.
2. Add halibut fillets into the glass dish and place marinade over it.
3. Place it into the refrigerator for one hour.
4. Oil the grate and preheat the grill on high heat.
5. Discard marinade and place halibut fillets onto the grill and cook for five minutes per side.
6. When done, serve and enjoy!

Nutrition: Calories; 554, Carbs; 2.2g, protein; 36.3g, fat; 43.7g

71. Apple Pudding

Preparation time: 10 minutes | **Cooking time:** 30 minutes | **Servings:** 6

Ingredients:

- Butter – half cup, melted
- White sugar – one cup
- All-purpose flour – one cup
- Baking powder – two tsp
- Salt – ¼ tsp
- Milk – one cup
- Apple – two cups, chopped and peeled
- Ground cinnamon – one tsp

Instructions:

1. Preheat the oven to 375 degrees Fahrenheit.
2. Mix the milk, salt, baking powder, flour, sugar, and butter into the baking dish.
3. Mix the cinnamon and apples into the bowl and microwave it for two to five minutes. Place apple into the middle of the batter.
4. Place it into the oven and bake for a half-hour.
5. Serve and enjoy!

Nutrition: Calories; 384l, carbs; 57.5g, protein; 3.8g, fat; 16g

72. Smoky Rice

Preparation time: 10 minutes | **Cooking time:** 20 minutes | **Serving:** 4

Ingredients:

- White basmati rice – 400g
- Pasta – 200ml
- Green onion – half, peeled and chopped, green part only
- Red capsicum – ¼, chopped
- Extra-virgin olive oil – 4 tbsp
- Tomato puree – 70g
- Bay leaves – three
- Paprika – one tsp
- Cumin – one tsp
- Black pepper – one pinch
- Chili – one pinch
- Coconut oil – four tbsp
- Banana – peeled and chopped
- Salt – to taste

Instructions:

Rice:

1. Rinse rice and soak for twenty minutes.
2. Let boil it for five minutes. Then, drain it.
3. Add black pepper, paprika, cumin, chili, half green onion (green part only), pasta, and red capsicum into the blender and blend until smooth.
4. Add oil into the saucepan and place it over medium flame.
5. Add capsicum mixture to the pan and sprinkle with salt and cook for few minutes until fragrant. Then, add tomato puree and bay leaves and cook for five minutes.
6. Add drained rice and one cup of water and simmer for eight minutes until the rice is soft.
7. Discard bay leaves. Keep it aside.

Banana:

1. Add coconut oil and banana into the pan and cook until golden.
2. Add banana over the rice.
3. Serve!

Nutrition: Calories; 447, Carbs; 69g, Fats; 11g Proteins; 11g, fiber; 3g

73. Barbecue Beef Stir-Fry

Preparation time: 5 minutes | **Cooking time:** 25 minutes | **Servings:** 4

Ingredients:

- Barbecue Sauce – ¼ cup
- Beef broth – three tbsp, low-sodium
- Beef sirloin steak – one lb., boneless, cut into strips
- Onion – one, sliced
- Carrot – one, thinly sliced
- Oil – one tablespoon
- Hot cooked long-grain white rice – two cups

Instructions:

1. Combine the broth and BBQ sauce into the bowl.
2. Rub one tbsp of meat and let stand for five minutes.
3. Add vegetable, meat, and oil into the skillet and cook over medium-high flame for four minutes.
4. Add remaining BBQ sauce mixture and combine well. Let simmer over medium-low flame for two minutes.
5. Serve and enjoy!

Nutrition: Calories; 310, Carbs; 34g, protein; 23g, fat; 9g

74. Stir-Fry Ground Chicken and Green Beans

Preparation time: 5 minutes | **Cooking time:** 5-10 minutes | **Serving:** 2

Ingredients:

- Green bean – 2 cups
- Oil – one tbsp
- Ginger – one slice
- Ground chicken – ½ lb.
- Soy sauce – 1 tbsp
- Rice wine – 1 tsp
- Sesame oil – 1 tsp
- Sugar – 1 tsp

Instructions:

1. Add green beans into the boiled water and cook until tender.

2. Drain it and put it into the bowl of ice water.
3. Add oil into the skillet and heat it. Then, add a ginger slice and fry for one to two minutes.
4. Add ground chicken and cook until no longer pink.
5. Add sugar, sesame oil, rice wine, and soy sauce and toss to combine.
6. Add drained green beans and cook them.
7. Serve and enjoy!

Nutrition: Calories; 162kcal, Carbohydrates; 10g, Fats; 18g Proteins; 22g, fiber; 2g

75. Pomegranate Salad

Preparation time: 5 minutes | **Cooking time:** 10 minutes | **Serving:** 4

Ingredients:
- Chives – one tsp, chopped
- Zucchini – 300g
- Baby spinach – 100g
- Red pepper – one, skinned
- Extra-virgin olive oil spray
- Dressing:
- Walnut oil – three tbsp
- Pomegranate juice – ¼ cup
- Dijon mustard – 2 tsp
- Salt – to taste

Instructions:
1. Add all ingredients into the bowl and beat until combined for dressing.
2. Slice zucchini into chunks. Let chop the chives.
3. Spray the zucchini and chives with olive oil.
4. Place a frypan over medium flame.
5. Add chives and zucchini and fry until golden brown.
6. Then, add baby spinach leaves and stir well.
7. Turn off the flame. Pour dressing over the salad.

Nutrition: Calories; 273, Carbs; 14.9g, Fats; 21.4g Proteins; 9.5g, fiber; 2g

SNACK

76. Papaya-Mango Smoothie

Preparation Time: 5 minutes | **Cooking Time:** 0 minutes | **Servings:** 2

Ingredients:
- 1 cup mango, diced
- 1 cup papaya chunks
- 1 cup almond or lactose-free milk
- 1 tablespoon honey or maple syrup

Instructions:
1. Blend all ingredients in a blender and then pulse until smooth.
2. Pour into a large glass.
3. Enjoy!

Nutrition: Calories: 554, Fat: 32g, Carbs: 14g, Sugar: 8g, Fiber: 2g, Protein: 50g, Sodium: 63mg

77. Cantaloupe Smoothie

Preparation Time: 5 minutes | **Cooking Time:** 0 minutes | **Servings:** 2

Ingredients:
- 1 cup cantaloupe, diced
- 1/2 cup vanilla yogurt or lactose-free yogurt
- 1/2 cup of orange juice
- 1 tablespoon honey or maple syrup
- 2 ice cubes

Instructions:
1. Merge all ingredients in a blender and then pulse until smooth.
2. Pour into a large glass.
3. Enjoy!

Nutrition: Calories: 179, Fat: 13g, Carbs: 6g, Sugar: 3g, Fiber: 1g, Protein: 10g, Sodium: 265 mg

78. Cantaloupe-Mix Smoothie

Preparation Time: 5-10 minutes | **Cooking Time:** 0 minutes | **Servings:** 2

Ingredients:

- 1 cup cantaloupe, diced
- 1/2 cup mango, diced
- 1/2 cup almond milk or lactose-free cow milk
- 1/2 cup of orange juice
- 2 tablespoons lemon
- 1 tablespoon honey or maple syrup
- 2 ice cubes

Instructions:

1. Merge all ingredients in a blender until smooth.
2. Pour into a large glass.
3. Enjoy!

Nutrition: Calories: 329, Fat: 17g, Carbs: 9g, Sugar: 3g, Fiber: 5g, Protein: 37g, Sodium: 430mg

79. Applesauce-Avocado Smoothie

Preparation Time: 5-10 minutes | **Cooking Time:** 0 minutes | **Servings:** 1

Ingredients:

- 1 cup unsweetened almond or lactose-free milk
- 1/2 avocado
- 1/2 cup applesauce
- 1/4 teaspoon ground cinnamon
- 1/2 cup ice
- 1/2 teaspoon stevia or 1 tablespoon honey, for sweetness (optional)

Instructions:

1. Blend all ingredients in a blender. Pulse the mix until smooth.
2. Pour into a large glass.
3. Enjoy!

Nutrition: Calories: 270, Fat: 11g, Carbs: 4g, Sugar: 1g, Fiber: 1g, Protein: 39g, Sodium: 664mg

80. Pina Colada Smoothie

Preparation Time: 5-10 minutes | **Cooking Time:** 0 minutes | **Servings:** 1

Ingredients:

- 1 cup papaya chunks
- 1/2 cup unsweetened almond milk or lactose-free milk
- 1 banana
- 1/2 teaspoon vanilla extract, to taste
- 1 tablespoon honey, maple syrup or 1 teaspoon stevia (optional)

Instructions:

1. Blend all ingredients in a blender and then pulse until smooth and creamy.
2. Pour into a large glass.
3. Enjoy!

Nutrition: Calories: 329, Fat: 17g, Carbs: 9g, Sugar: 3g, Fiber: 5g, Protein: 37g, Sodium: 430mg

81. Diced Fruits

Preparation Time: 10 minutes | **Cooking Time:** 40 minutes | **Servings:** 6

Ingredients:

- 4 peaches, skin removed and thinly sliced
- 1 pound apple, pitted and skin removed
- 1 teaspoon cinnamon powder
- 1 cup honey or maple syrup
- 1 teaspoon vanilla extract

Instructions:

1. In a large pot, cook the fruits in boiling water over medium heat until softened.
2. In a large bowl, mix well all ingredients (except the fruits).
3. Pour the syrup over fruits and let the compote be thickened.
4. Pour the compote into a jar. Serve hot or cold.
5. Enjoy!

Nutrition: Calories: 178, Fat: 4g, Carbs: 7g, Fiber: 2g, Protein: 27g

82. Applesauce

Preparation Time: 10 minutes | **Cooking Time:** 30 minutes | **Servings:** 4

Ingredients:

- 6 organic apples, peeled, cored and cubed
- 1/2 cup boiling water
- 1/2 teaspoon cinnamon powder
- 1/4 cup sugar or 4 tablespoons honey
- 2 tablespoons fresh lemon juice
- 1/4 teaspoon salt

Instructions:

1. In a large pot, cook apples with boiling water, lemon juice, cinnamon, sugar or honey, and salt over medium-low heat until softened.
2. Remove from the heat.
3. You can mash all ingredients by using a fork or blend with a blender or a food processor.
4. Pour the applesauce into a suitable container or jar.
5. Serve warm or cold.
6. Enjoy!

Nutrition: Calories: 51, Fat: 3g, Carbs: 4g, Fiber: 2g, Protein: 2g

83. Avocado Dip

Preparation Time: 10 minutes | **Cooking Time:** 0 minutes | **Servings:** 4

Ingredients:

- 6 avocados, peeled
- 1/2 tablespoon extra-virgin olive oil
- 1/4 cup chopped fresh cilantro
- 2 tablespoons fresh lime juice
- 1 teaspoon fresh lemon juice
- 1/2 teaspoon salt

Instructions:

1. In a large bowl, set avocados with a fork.
2. Add extra-virgin olive oil and the other ingredients.
3. Enjoy!

Nutrition: Calories: 75, Carbs: 0.1g, Protein: 13.4g, Fat: 1.7g, Sugar: 0g, Sodium: 253 mg

84. Homemade Hummus

Preparation Time: 10 minutes | **Cooking Time:** 60 minutes | **Servings:** 4

Ingredients:

- 1/4-pound dried chickpeas (soaked in water for a night)
- 11/2 tablespoon tahini
- 1 tablespoon lemon juice
- 2 tablespoons extra-virgin olive oil, divided
- 1/4 teaspoon cumin powder
- 1/2 teaspoon salt
- 1 tablespoon water
- 1 teaspoon baking soda (optional)
- 1 teaspoon paprika powder (optional)

Instructions:

1. First, you need to soak the chickpeas overnight in water and optionally add baking soda to the water.
2. Cook your chickpeas in a large pot with water, over medium heat for about 1 hour. Check if they are cooked well by crushing one of them with a fork in your hand.
3. When chickpeas are cooked, drain and put them in a blender.
4. Add 1 tablespoon of extra-virgin olive oil, lemon juice, tahini, cumin powder, and salt to the blender. Blend until your hummus gets a soft, creamy texture equally.
5. Drizzle with 1 tablespoon of extra-virgin olive oil or paprika powder (optional).
6. Serve immediately or fridge it.

Nutrition: Calories: 207, Fat: 16g, Carbs: 5g, Sugar: 2g, Fiber: 1g, Protein: 12g, Sodium: 366mg

85. Tofu

Preparation Time: 10 minutes | **Cooking Time:** 25 minutes | **Servings:** 4

Ingredients:

- 1 ½ cup firm tofu, pressed and drained

- 1 avocado, cubed
- 1 tablespoon extra-virgin olive oil
- Salt and pepper, to taste

Instructions:

1. Preheat your oven to 400°F.
2. Choose a baking sheet, cover it with parchment paper or spray extra-virgin olive oil. Cut tofu cubes of 1/2 inch and spray extra-virgin olive oil on them.
3. Let it bake for 15 minutes until golden brown and crispy. Flip tofu and cook for another 10 minutes. Remove from the oven. Let it rest for 10 minutes.
4. Cube the avocado on a plate. Add salt and pepper.
5. Mix the tofu with avocado in a bowl. Enjoy!

Nutrition: Calories: 645, Fat: 32g, Carbs: 65g, Fiber: 5g, Protein: 26g

86. Almond Butter Sandwich

Preparation Time: 10 minutes | **Cooking Time:** 5 minutes | **Servings:** 1

Ingredients:

- 2 slices white bread or white gluten-free bread
- 1 tablespoon organic smooth almond butter

Instructions:

1. Set 1 piece of bread with almond butter.
2. Toast and enjoy!

Nutrition: Calories: 178, Fat: 4g, Carbs: 7g, Fiber: 2g, Protein: 27g,

87. Gluten-Free Muffins

Preparation Time: 15 minutes | **Cooking Time:** 30 minutes | **Servings:** 10-15

Ingredients:

- 2 tablespoons extra-virgin olive oil
- 2 ½ cups almond flour, blanched
- 3 large organic free-range eggs
- 1/4 cup organic maple syrup
- 2 teaspoons vanilla extract
- 1/4 cup banana, mashed
- 1 teaspoon lemon juice
- 3/4 teaspoon baking soda
- 1/4 teaspoon cinnamon powder
- 1/2 teaspoon salt

Instructions:

1. Preheat your oven to 375°F.
2. In a bowl, set almond flour, cinnamon, baking soda, and salt. Mix well.
3. In another bowl, add extra-virgin olive oil, vanilla extract, eggs, ripe banana, maple syrup, and lemon juice.
4. Whisk well.
5. Mix both bowls and stir with a wooden spoon until the flour is mixed well with the other ingredients.
6. Prepare 10 muffin cups. Pour them to the top and then bake for 15 minutes.
7. To avoid browning quickly, loosely cover muffins with aluminum foil. Cook for another 15 minutes.
8. Put a toothpick in a muffin to check if it cooks well or not.
9. If cooked well, the toothpick should not stick to the muffin.
10. Remove from the oven. Let the muffins cool for 15 more minutes.
11. Enjoy!

Nutrition: Calories: 408, Fat: 26g, Carbs: 4g, Sugar: 1g, Fiber: 1g, Protein: 47g, Sodium: 426mg

DINNER

88. Italian Stuffed Zucchini Boats

Preparation Time: 10 minutes | **Cooking Time:** 25 minutes | **Servings:** 2

Ingredients:

- 6 large zucchinis
- 1/2 tablespoon olive oil
- Kosher salt
- Freshly ground black pepper

- 1/4 teaspoon garlic powder
- 1 small yellow onion, diced
- 2 garlic cloves, minced
- 1 pound ground turkey
- 1 (28 ounces) can crush tomatoes
- 4 ounces Mozzarella cheese, shredded
- 1 ounce Parmesan cheese, freshly grated
- Flat-leaf parsley for garnishing
- Cooking spray

Instructions:
1. Turn your oven on and allow to preheat up to 425°F and lightly grease a 9x13-inch baking dish with cooking spray.
2. Divide the zucchini in half lengthwise and then scoop out the seeds. Brush with olive oil and season with salt, pepper and garlic powder.
3. Roast in the prepared dish for 20 minutes, or until it begins to soften.
4. Meanwhile, sauté the onions and garlic in 1/2 tablespoon of olive oil over medium-high heat in a large skillet.
5. Cook for 3-4 minutes, then add the ground turkey and brown. Attach the tomatoes and bring them to a boil.
6. Reduce the heat to medium and then let simmer until the zucchini are done. Stir in 1/2 teaspoon salt and pepper to taste.
7. Set to bake for about 5 minutes or at least until the Mozzarella cheese you added has melted, about 3-5 minutes.
8. Serve hot, garnished with Parmesan cheese and parsley.

Nutrition: Calories: 2981, Fat: 7g, Carbs: 14g, Fiber: 2g, Protein: 25g

89. Chicken Cutlets

Preparation Time: 10 minutes | **Cooking Time:** 15 minutes | **Servings:** 4

Ingredients:
- 4 teaspoons red wine vinegar
- 2 teaspoons minced garlic cloves
- 2 teaspoons dried sage leaves
- 1 pound chicken breast cutlets
- Salt and pepper, to taste
- 1/4 cup refined white flour
- 2 teaspoons olive oil

Instructions:
1. Set a good amount of plastic wrap on the kitchen counter, sprinkle with half the combined sage, garlic and vinegar.
2. Put the chicken breast on the plastic wrap, sprinkle with the rest of the vinegar mixture. Season lightly with pepper and salt.
3. Secure the chicken with the second sheet of plastic wrap. Use a kitchen mallet to pound the breast until it is flattened. Let stand 5 minutes.
4. Set the chicken on both sides with flour. In a skillet, heat the oil over medium heat.
5. Add half of the chicken breast and cook for 1 ½ minute or until it is browned on the bottom.
6. Turn on the other side and let it cook for 3 minutes.
7. Remove the chicken breast and place it on an oven-proof serving plate so that you can keep warm.
8. Reduce the liquid by half. Pour the mixture over the chicken breast; serve immediately.

Nutrition: Calories: 549, Fat: 6g, Carbs: 7g, Fiber: 1g, Protein: 114g

90. Slow Cooker Salsa Turkey

Preparation Time: 8 minutes | **Cooking Time:** 7 hours | **Servings:** 4

Ingredients:
- 2 pounds turkey breasts, boneless and skinless
- 1 cup salsa
- 1 cup small tomatoes, diced, canned choose low sodium
- 2 tablespoons taco seasoning
- 1/2 cup celery, finely diced
- 1/2 cup carrots, shredded
- 3 tablespoons low-fat sour cream

Instructions:
1. Add the turkey to your slow cooker.

2. Season it with taco seasoning then top with salsa and vegetables.
3. Add in 1/2 cup of water. Set to cook on low for 7 hours (internal temperature should be 165°F when done).
4. Shred the turkey with 2 forks, add in sour cream and stir.
5. Enjoy.

Nutrition: Calories: 178, Fat: 4g, Carbs: 7g, Fiber: 2g, Protein: 27g

91. Sriracha Lime Chicken and Apple Salad

Preparation Time: 10 minutes | **Cooking Time:** 15 minutes | **Servings:** 4

Ingredients:

Sriracha Lime Chicken:
- 2 organic chicken breasts
- 3 tablespoons sriracha
- 1 lime, juiced
- 1/4 teaspoon fine sea salt
- 1/4 teaspoon freshly ground pepper

Fruit Salad:
- 4 apples, peeled, cored and diced
- 1 cup organic grape tomatoes
- 1/3 cup red onion, finely chopped

Lime Vinaigrette:
- 1/3 cup light olive oil
- 1/4 cup apple cider vinegar
- 2 limes, juiced
- A dash of fine sea salt

Instructions:
1. Use salt and pepper to season the chicken on both sides. Spread on the sriracha and lime and let sit for 20 minutes.
2. Cook the chicken per side over medium heat, or until done. Grill the apple with the chicken.
3. Meanwhile, whisk together the dressing and season to taste.
4. Arrange the salad, topping it with red onion and tomatoes.
5. Serve as a side to the chicken and apple.

Nutrition: Calories: 484, Fat: 28g, Carbs: 32g, Fiber: 8g, Protein: 30g

92. Pan-Seared Scallops with Lemon-Ginger Vinaigrette

Preparation Time: 10 minutes | **Cooking Time:** 10 minutes | **Servings:** 2

Ingredients:
- 1 pound sea scallops
- 1 tablespoon extra-virgin olive oil
- 1/4 teaspoon sea salt
- 2 tablespoons lemon-ginger vinaigrette
- A pinch of freshly ground black pepper

Instructions:
1. Heat the olive oil in a non-stick skillet or pan over medium-high heat until it starts shimmering.
2. Add the scallops to the skillet or pan after seasoning them with pepper and salt.
3. Cook for 3 minutes per side or until the fish is only opaque.
4. Serve with a dollop of vinaigrette on top.

Nutrition: Calories: 280, Fat: 16g, Carbs: 5g, Sugar: 1g, Fiber: 0g, Protein: 29g,

93. Roasted Salmon and Asparagus

Preparation Time: 5 minutes | **Cooking Time:** 15 minutes | **Servings:** 2

Ingredients:
- 1 tablespoon extra-virgin olive oil
- 1 pound salmon, cut into two fillets
- 1/2 lemon zest and slices
- 1/2-pound asparagus spears, trimmed
- 1 teaspoon sea salt, divided
- 1/8 teaspoon freshly cracked black pepper

Instructions:
1. Preheat the oven to 425°F.
2. Stir the asparagus with half of salt and olive oil.
3. At the base of a roasting tray, spread in a continuous sheet.

4. Season the salmon with salt and pepper. Place the asparagus on top of the skin-side down.
5. Lemon zest should be sprinkled over the asparagus, salmon, and lemon slices.
6. Set them over the top.
7. Roast for around 15 minutes until the flesh of the fish is opaque, in the preheated oven.

Nutrition: Calories: 308, Fat: 18g, Carbs: 5g, Sugar: 2g, Fiber: 2g, Protein: 36g, Sodium: 542mg

94. Orange and Maple-Glazed Salmon

Preparation Time: 15 minutes | **Cooking Time:** 15 minutes | **Servings:** 2

Ingredients:
- 1 orange zest
- 1 tablespoon low-sodium soy sauce
- 2 (4-6 ounces) salmon fillets, pin bones removed
- 1 orange juice
- 2 tablespoons pure maple syrup
- 1 teaspoon garlic powder

Instructions:
1. Preheat the oven to 400°F.
2. Set the orange juice and zest, soy sauce, maple syrup, and garlic powder in a little shallow bowl.
3. Place the salmon parts in the dish flesh-side down.
4. Allow resting 10 minutes for marinating.
5. Put the salmon on a rimmed baking dish, skin-side up, and bake for 15 minutes, or until the flesh is opaque.

Nutrition: Calories: 297, Fat: 11g, Carbs: 18g, Sugar: 15g, Fiber: 1g, Protein: 34g, Sodium: 528 mg

95. Cod with Ginger and Black Beans

Preparation Time: 10 minutes | **Cooking Time:** 15 minutes | **Servings:** 2

Ingredients:

- 2 (6 ounces) cod fillets
- 1/2 teaspoon sea salt, divided
- 3 minced garlic cloves
- 2 tablespoons chopped fresh cilantro leaves
- 1 tablespoon extra-virgin olive oil
- 1/2 tablespoon grated fresh ginger
- 2 tablespoons freshly ground black pepper
- 1/2 (14 ounces) can black beans, drained

Instructions:
2. Heat the olive oil in a big non-stick skillet or pan over medium-high heat until it starts shimmering.
3. Half of the salt, ginger, and pepper are used to season the fish. Cook for around 4 minutes per side in the hot oil until the fish is opaque.
4. Detach the cod from the pan and place it on a plate with aluminum foil tented over it.
5. Add the garlic to the skillet or pan and return it to the heat. Cook for 30 seconds while continuously stirring.
6. Mix the black beans and the remaining salt. Cook, stirring regularly, for 5 minutes.
7. Add the cilantro and serve the black beans on top of the cod.

Nutrition: Calories 419, Fat 2g, Carbs 33g, Sugar 1g, Fiber 8g, Protein 50g, Sodium 605mg

96. Halibut Curry

Preparation Time: 10 minutes | **Cooking Time:** 10 minutes | **Servings:** 2

Ingredients:
- 1 teaspoon ground turmeric
- 1 pound halibut, skin, and bones removed, cut into 1-inch pieces
- 1/2 (14 ounces) can coconut milk
- 1/8 teaspoon ground black pepper
- 1 tablespoon extra-virgin olive oil
- 1 teaspoon curry powder
- 2 cups no-salt-added chicken broth
- 1/4 teaspoon sea salt

Instructions:

1. Heat the olive oil in a non-stick skillet or pan over medium-high heat until it starts shimmering.
2. Add the curry powder and turmeric to a bowl. To bloom the spices, cook for 2 minutes, stirring continuously.
3. Stir in the halibut, coconut milk, chicken broth, pepper, and salt.
4. Lower the heat to medium-low and bring to a simmer.
5. Cook, stirring regularly, for 6-7 minutes, or until the fish is opaque.

Nutrition: Calories 428, Fat: 47g, Carbs: 5g, Sugar: 1g, Fiber: 1g, Protein: 27g, Sodium: 507mg

97. Chicken Cacciatore

Preparation Time: 10 minutes | **Cooking Time:** 20 minutes | **Servings:** 2

Ingredients:

- 1-pound skinless chicken, cut into bite-size pieces
- 1/4 cup black olives, chopped
- 1/2 teaspoon onion powder
- A pinch of freshly ground black pepper
- 1 tablespoon extra-virgin olive oil
- 1 (28 ounces) can crushed tomatoes, drained
- 1/2 teaspoon garlic powder
- 1/4 teaspoon sea salt

Instructions:

1. Heat the olive oil in a non-stick skillet or pan over medium-high heat until it starts shimmering.
2. Cook until the chicken is browned.
3. Add the tomatoes, garlic powder, olives, salt, onion powder, and pepper, then stir to combine. Cook, stirring regularly, for 10 minutes.

Nutrition: Calories: 305, Fat: 11g, Carbs: 34g, Sugar: 23g, Fiber: 13g, Protein: 19g, Sodium:1.171 mg

98. Chicken and Bell Pepper Sauté

Preparation Time: 5 minutes | **Cooking Time:** 15 minutes | **Servings:** 2

Ingredients:

- 1 chopped bell pepper
- 1-pound skinless chicken breasts, cut into bite-size pieces
- 1 ½ tablespoon extra-virgin olive oil
- 1/2 chopped onion
- 3 minced garlic cloves
- 1/8 teaspoon ground black pepper
- 1/4 teaspoon sea salt

Instructions:

1. Heat the olive oil in a non-stick skillet or pan over medium-high heat until it starts shimmering.
2. Add the onion, red bell pepper, and chicken. Cook, stirring regularly, for 10 minutes.
3. Stir in the salt, garlic, and pepper in a mixing bowl. Cook for 30 seconds while continuously stirring.

Nutrition: Calories: 179, Fat: 13g, Carbs: 6g, Sugar: 3g, Fiber: 1g, Protein: 10g

99. Chicken Salad Sandwiches

Preparation Time: 15 minutes | **Cooking Time:** 0 minutes | **Servings:** 2

Ingredients:

- 2 tablespoons anti-inflammatory mayonnaise
- 1 tablespoon chopped fresh tarragon leaves
- 1 cup chicken, chopped, cooked and skinless (from 1 rotisserie chicken)
- 1/2 minced red bell pepper
- 1 teaspoon Dijon mustard
- 4 slices whole-wheat bread
- 1/4 teaspoon sea salt

Instructions:

1. Combine the chicken, red bell pepper, mayonnaise, mustard, tarragon, and salt in a medium mixing bowl.

2. Spread on 2 pieces of bread and top it with the remaining bread.

Nutrition: Calories: 315, Fat: 9g, Carbs: 30g, Sugar: 6g, Fiber: 4g, Protein: 28g

100. Rosemary Chicken

Preparation Time: 15 minutes | **Cooking Time:** 20 minutes | **Servings:** 2

Ingredients:

- 1 tablespoon extra-virgin olive oil
- 1 pound chicken breast tenders
- 1 tablespoon chopped fresh rosemary leaves
- 1/8 teaspoon ground black pepper
- 1/4 teaspoon sea salt

Instructions:

1. Preheat the oven to 425°F.
2. Set the chicken tenders on a baking sheet with a rim.
3. Sprinkle with salt, rosemary, and pepper after brushing them with olive oil.
4. For 15-20 minutes, keep in the oven, just before the juices run clear.

Nutrition: Calories: 389, Fat: 20g, Carbs: 1g, Sugar: 0g, Fiber: 1g, Protein: 49g

101. Gingered Turkey Meatballs

Preparation Time: 10 minutes | **Cooking Time:** 10 minutes | **Servings:** 2

Ingredients:

- 1/2 cup shredded cabbage
- 1/2 tablespoon grated fresh ginger
- 1/2 teaspoon onion powder
- 1 pound ground turkey
- 2 tablespoons chopped fresh cilantro leaves
- 1/2 teaspoon garlic powder
- 1/4 teaspoon sea salt
- 1 tablespoon olive oil
- A pinch of freshly ground black pepper

Instructions:

1. Combine the cabbage, turkey, cilantro, ginger, onion powder, garlic powder, pepper, and salt in a big mixing bowl. Mix well. Make 10 (3/4 inch) meatballs out of the turkey mixture.
2. Heat the oil in a big non-stick skillet or pan over medium-high heat until it starts shimmering.
3. Cook for about 10 minutes, rotating the meatballs while they brown, and you are done.

Nutrition: Calories: 408, Fat: 26g, Carbs: 4g, Sugar: 1g, Fiber: 1g, Protein: 47g

102. Turkey and Kale Sauté

Preparation Time: 15 minutes | **Cooking Time:** 35 minutes | **Servings:** 2

Ingredients:

- 1 pound ground turkey breast
- 1/2 chopped onion
- 1/2 teaspoon sea salt
- 3 minced garlic cloves
- 1 tablespoon extra-virgin olive oil
- 1 cup stemmed and chopped kale
- 1 tablespoon fresh thyme leaves
- A pinch of freshly ground black pepper

Instructions:

1. Heat the olive oil in a big non-stick skillet or pan over medium-high heat until it starts shimmering.
2. Add the turkey, onion, kale, thyme, pepper, and salt. Cook, crumbling the turkey with a spoon until it browns, for about 5 minutes.
3. Garlic can be included now. Cook for 30 minutes while continuously stirring.

Nutrition: Calories: 413, Fat: 20g, Carbs: 7g, Sugar: 1g, Fiber: 1g, Protein: 50g, Sodium: 358mg

103. Turkey with Bell Peppers and Rosemary

Preparation Time: 15 minutes | **Cooking Time:** 10 minutes | **Servings:** 2

Ingredients:

- 1 chopped red bell peppers

- 1-pound boneless, skinless turkey breasts, cut into bite-size pieces
- 1/4 teaspoon sea salt
- 2 minced garlic cloves
- 2 tablespoons extra-virgin olive oil
- 1/2 chopped onion
- 1 tablespoon chopped fresh rosemary leaves
- A pinch of freshly ground black pepper

Instructions:
1. Heat the olive oil in a non-stick skillet or pan over medium-high heat until it starts shimmering.
2. Add the onion, red bell peppers, rosemary turkey, salt, and pepper. Cook until the turkey is cooked, and the veggies are soft.
3. Garlic can be included now. Cook for an additional 30 seconds.

Nutrition: Calories: 303, Fat: 14g, Carbs: 15g, Sugar: 10g, Fiber: 2g, Protein: 30g, Sodium: 387mg

104. Mustard and Rosemary Pork Tenderloin

Preparation Time: 15 minutes | **Cooking Time:** 15 minutes | **Servings:** 2

Ingredients:
- 2 tablespoons Dijon mustard
- 2 tablespoons fresh rosemary leaves
- 1/4 teaspoon sea salt
- 1/2 (1 ½ pound) pork tenderloin
- 1/4 cup fresh parsley leaves
- 3 garlic cloves
- 1 ½ tablespoon extra-virgin olive oil
- 1/8 teaspoon ground black pepper

Instructions:
1. Preheat the oven to 400°F.
2. Combine the mustard, parsley, garlic, olive oil, rosemary, pepper, and salt in a blender or food processor. Pulse 20 times in 1-second intervals before a paste emerges. Rub the tenderloin with the paste and place it on a rimmed baking sheet.

3. Bake the pork for around 15 minutes or until an instant-read meat thermometer, reads 165°F.
4. Allow resting for 5 minutes before slicing and serving.

Nutrition: Calories: 362, Fat: 18g, Carbs: 5g, Sugar: 1g, Fiber: 2g, Protein: 2g, Sodium: 515mg

105. Thin-Cut Pork Chops with Mustardy Kale

Preparation Time: 10 minutes | **Cooking Time:** 25 minutes | **Servings:** 2

Ingredients:
- 1 teaspoon sea salt, divided
- 2 tablespoons Dijon mustard, divided
- 1/2 finely chopped red onion
- 1 tablespoon apple cider vinegar
- 2 thin-cut pork chops
- 1/8 teaspoon ground black pepper, divided
- 1 ½ tablespoon extra-virgin olive oil
- 2 cups stemmed and chopped kale

Instructions:
1. Preheat the oven to 425°F.
2. Half of salt and pepper are used to season the pork chops. Place them on a rimmed baking sheet and spread 1 tablespoon of mustard over them. Bake for 15 minutes until an instant-read meat thermometer detects a temperature of 165°F.
3. When the pork cooks, heat the olive oil in a big non-stick skillet or pan over medium-high heat until it starts shimmering.
4. Add the red onion and kale. Cook, stirring regularly, for around 7 minutes, or until the veggies soften.
5. Whisk together the remaining tablespoon of mustard, the remaining half salt, the cider vinegar, and the remaining pepper in a wide mixing bowl. Toss with the kale. Cook for 2 minutes, stirring occasionally.

Nutrition: Calories: 504, Fat: 39g, Carbs: 10g, Sugar: 1g, Fiber: 2g, Protein: 28g, Sodium: 755mg

106. Beef Tenderloin with Savory Blueberry Sauce

Preparation Time: 10 minutes | **Cooking Time:** 15 minutes | **Servings:** 2

Ingredients:
- 1 teaspoon sea salt, divided
- 2 tablespoons extra-virgin olive oil
- 1/4 cup tawny port
- 1 ½ tablespoon very cold butter, cut into pieces
- 2 beef tenderloin fillets, about 3⁄4 inch thick
- 1/8 teaspoon ground black pepper, divided
- 1 finely minced shallot
- 1 cup fresh blueberries

Instructions:
1. Half salt and pepper are to be used to season the beef.
2. Heat the olive oil in a big skillet or pan over medium-high heat until it starts shimmering.
3. Add the seasoned steaks to the pan. Cook per side until an instant-read meat thermometer detects an internal temperature of 130°F. Set aside on a plate of aluminum foil tented over it.
4. Get the skillet or pan back up to heat. Add the port, shallot, blueberries, and the remaining salt and pepper to the pan. Scrape some browned pieces off the bottom of the skillet or pan with a wooden spoon. Set the heat to medium-low and bring to a simmer.
5. Cook, stirring from time to time, and gently crushing the blueberries for around 4 minutes or until the liquid has reduced by half.
6. Set in the butter 1 slice at a time. Toss the meat back into the skillet or pan. Mix it once with the sauce to coat it.
7. The rest of the sauce can be spooned over the meat before serving.

Nutrition: Calories: 554, Fat: 32g, Carbs: 14g, Sugar: 8g, Fiber: 2g, Protein: 50g, Sodium: 632mg

107. Ground Beef Chili with Tomatoes

Preparation Time: 10 minutes | **Cooking Time:** 15 minutes | **Servings:** 2

Ingredients:
- 1/2 chopped onion
- 1 (14 ounces) can kidney beans, drained
- 1/2-pound extra-lean ground beef
- 1 (28 ounces) can chopped tomatoes, undrained
- 1/2 tablespoon chili powder
- 1/4 teaspoon sea salt
- 1/2 teaspoon garlic powder

Instructions:
1. Cook the beef and onion in a big pot over medium-high heat for around 5 minutes.
2. Add the kidney beans, tomatoes, garlic powder, chili powder, salt, and stir to combine. Bring to boil, then reduce to low heat.
3. Cook for 10 minutes, stirring occasionally.

Nutrition: Calories: 890, Fat: 20g, Carbs: 63g, Sugar: 13g, Fiber: 17g, Protein: 116g, Sodium:562 mg

108. Fish Taco Salad with Strawberry Avocado Salsa

Preparation Time: 20 minutes | **Cooking Time:** 15 minutes | **Servings:** 2

Ingredients:
For the salsa:
- 2 hulled and diced strawberries
- 1/2 diced small shallot
- 2 tablespoons finely chopped fresh cilantro
- 2 tablespoons freshly squeezed lime juice
- 1/8 teaspoon cayenne pepper
- 1/2 diced avocado

- 2 tablespoons canned black beans, rinsed and drained
- 1 thinly sliced green onions
- 1/2 teaspoon finely chopped peeled ginger
- 1/4 teaspoon sea salt

For the fish salad:
- 1 teaspoon agave nectar
- 2 cups arugula
- 1 tablespoon extra-virgin olive or avocado oil
- 1/2 tablespoon freshly squeezed lime juice
- 1 pound light fish (halibut, cod, or red snapper), cut into 2 fillets
- 1/4 teaspoon ground black pepper
- 1/2 teaspoon sea salt

Instructions:
For the salsa:
1. Preheat the grill, whether it's gas or charcoal.
2. Add the avocado, beans, strawberries, shallot, cilantro, green onions, salt, ginger, lime juice, and cayenne pepper in a medium mixing cup.
3. Put aside after mixing until all the components are well combined.

For the fish salad:
1. Whisk the agave, oil, and lime juice in a small bowl. Set the arugula with the vinaigrette in a big mixing bowl.
2. Season the fish fillets with pepper and salt. Grill the fish for 7-9 minutes over direct high heat, flipping once during cooking.
3. The fish should be translucent and quickly flake.
4. Place 1 cup of arugula salad on each plate to eat.
5. Cover each salad with a fillet and a heaping spoonful of salsa.

Nutrition: Calories: 878, Fat: 26g, Carbs: 53g, Sugar: 15g, Fiber: 18g, Protein: 119g, Sodium: 582 mg

109. Beef and Bell Pepper Stir-Fry

Preparation Time: 5 minutes | **Cooking Time:** 10 minutes | **Servings:** 2

Ingredients:
- 3 scallions, white and green parts, chopped
- 1 tablespoon grated fresh ginger
- 2 minced garlic cloves
- 1/2-pound extra-lean ground beef
- 1 chopped red bell peppers
- 1/4 teaspoon sea salt

Instructions:
1. Cook the beef for around 5 minutes in a big non-stick skillet or pan until it browns.
2. Add the scallions, ginger, red bell peppers, and salt. Cook, stirring occasionally, for around 4 minutes or until the bell peppers are tender.
3. Garlic can be included now.
4. Cook for 30 seconds while continuously stirring. Switch off the flame, and you are done.

Nutrition: Calories: 599, Fat: 19g, Carbs: 9g, Sugar: 4g, Fiber: 2g, Protein: 97g, Sodium: 520mg

110. Veggie Pizza with Cauliflower-Yam Crust

Preparation Time: 5 minutes | **Cooking Time:** 1hour 10 minutes | **Servings:** 2

Ingredients:
- 1/2 medium peeled and chopped garnet yam
- 1 teaspoon sea salt, divided
- 1/2 tablespoon coconut oil, plus more for greasing pizza stone
- 1/4 cup sliced cremini mushrooms
- 1/4 medium head cauliflower, cut into small florets
- 1/2 tablespoon dried Italian herbs
- 1/2 cup flour brown rice
- 1/2 sliced small red onion
- 1/2 zucchini or yellow summer squash
- 2 tablespoons vegan pesto

- 1/2 cup spinach

Instructions:

1. Heat the oven to 400°F or preheat the pizza stone in case you have one.
2. Set a big pot with 1 inch of water, place a steamer basket.
3. Put the yam and cauliflower in the steamer basket and steam for 15 minutes, or until both are quickly pricked with a fork. If you overcook the vegetables, they can get too soggy.
4. Place the vegetables in a food blender or processor and pulse until smooth. Blend in the Italian herbs and half a teaspoon of salt until smooth.
5. Set the mixture in a big mixing bowl.
6. Gradually whisk in the flour until it is well mixed.
7. Use coconut oil to grease the pizza stone or a pizza plate.
8. In the middle of the pizza stone, pile the cauliflower mixture. Spread the pizza dough uniformly in a round or circular way (much like frosting) with a spatula until the crust is around 1/8 inches thick.
9. Bake for around 45 minutes. To get the top crispy, switch on the broiler and cook it for 2 minutes.
10. In a medium skillet or pan, melt the coconut oil over medium heat. Cook for 2 minutes after adding the onion. Add the squash, mushrooms, and the remaining ingredients to a large mixing bowl. Sauté for 3-4 minutes with a quarter teaspoon of salt.
11. Detach the spinach from the heat as soon as it starts to wilt.
12. Evenly, plate the pesto around the pizza crust.
13. Over the pesto, spread the sautéed vegetables. It's time to slice the pizza and eat it.

Nutrition: Calories: 329, Fat: 17g, Carbs: 9g, Sugar: 3g, Fiber: 5g, Protein: 37g, Sodium: 430mg

111. Toasted Pecan Quinoa Burgers

Preparation Time: 5 minutes | **Cooking Time:** 30 minutes | **Servings:** 2

Ingredients:

- 2 cups vegetable broth, divided
- 1 teaspoon sea salt
- 2 tablespoons sesame seeds
- 1/2 teaspoon dried oregano
- 1/4 cup canned black beans,
- 2 tablespoons pecans
- 1/2 cup quinoa, rinsed and drained
- 1/4 cup sunflower seeds
- 1/2 teaspoon ground cumin
- 1/2 shredded carrot
- Freshly ground black pepper
- 1/2 thinly sliced avocado
- 1/2 teaspoon coconut or sunflower oil

Instructions:

1. Preheat the oven to 375°F.
2. Roast the pecans for 5-7 minutes on a baking sheet.
3. In a big saucepan, bring 1 cup of broth, quinoa, and salt to a boil over medium-high heat. Set the heat to a minimum, cover, and cook for 20 minutes, stirring occasionally.
4. In a food processor, grind the pecans, cumin, sesame seeds, sunflower seeds, and oregano to a medium-coarse texture.
5. Combine a half cup of quinoa, carrots, nut mixture, and beans in a big mixing bowl. Slowly, pour the remaining cup of broth, constantly stirring, before the paste becomes tacky. Season with pepper and salt as per taste.
6. Set the mixture into 2 (1/2-inch thick) patties and cook, refrigerate them right away.
7. In a big skillet or pan over medium-high heat, melt the coconut oil. Cook for around 2 minutes on either side.
8. Carry on for the remaining patties in the same manner. Avocado slices can be placed on top of the burgers.

Nutrition: Calories: 432, Fat: 12g, Carbs: 12g, Sugar: 5g, Fiber: 3g, Protein: 57g, Sodium: 566mg

112. Sizzling Salmon and Quinoa

Preparation Time: 10 minutes | **Cooking Time:** 30 minutes | **Servings:** 2

Ingredients:

- 1/2 teaspoon extra-virgin olive oil
- 1/2 cup quinoa, rinsed and drained
- 1/4-pound sliced chanterelle mushrooms
- 1/2 cup frozen small peas
- 1 tablespoon chopped fresh basil
- 1 head garlic
- 1 ½ cup mushroom broth, divided
- 1 tablespoon coconut oil
- 1/2 cup shredded brussels sprouts
- 1 tablespoon nutritional yeast
- 1/2 tablespoon dried oregano
- Sea salt and freshly ground black pepper
- 1/4-pound salmon, skin, and bones removed, cut into 1-inch cubes

Instructions:

1. Preheat the oven to 350°F.
2. Detach the top of the garlic head to reveal the cloves. Cover the head in foil and drizzle with olive oil. Set in the oven for 50 minutes to roast.
3. Meanwhile, in a big saucepan, mix 1 cup of broth and the quinoa. Set to a boil over high heat, then reduce to low heat, cover, and simmer without stirring for 20 minutes. To make this dish, measure 1/4 cup of quinoa, reserving any leftovers for another use.
4. Heat the coconut oil in a big skillet or pan over medium heat. Sauté for 5 minutes, or before the mushrooms release liquid and become tender.
5. Cook for 3 minutes with the brussels sprouts, adding up to 1/4 cup of broth if required to keep the mushrooms and sprouts from sticking to the skillet or pan.
6. Sauté for 5 minutes, stirring regularly, with the peas, basil, nutritional yeast, and oregano.
7. Toss the salmon in the pan to mix. Squeeze the garlic cloves gently into it. Cook, secured, for 4-5 minutes, stirring periodically.
8. Stir in the remaining 1/4 cup of broth and 1/4 cup of quinoa in the skillet or pan until all is well mixed. Season with pepper and salt to taste.
9. Serve.

Nutrition: Calories: 599, Fat: 20g, Carbs: 10g, Sugar: 4g, Fiber: 6g, Protein: 88g, Sodium: 662mg

113. Lemon Chicken and Rice

Preparation time: 5 minutes | **Cooking time:** 20 minutes | **Servings:** 4

Ingredients:

- Butter – two tbsp
- Chicken breasts – 1 lb., cut into strips, boneless, skinless
- Onion – one, chopped
- Carrot – one, thinly sliced
- Garlic – two cloves, minced
- Cornstarch – one tbsp
- Chicken broth – 14 ounces
- Lemon juice – two tbsp
- Salt – ¼ tsp
- Frozen peas – one cup
- Uncooked instant rice – one and half cup

Instructions:

1. Add butter into the skillet and cook over medium-high flame.
2. Then, add garlic, carrot, chicken, onion and cook for five to seven minutes.
3. Combine the salt, lemon juice, broth, and cornstarch into the bowl, and then add to the skillet.
4. Let cook and stir for one to two minutes.
5. Add peas and rice and stir well.
6. When done, remove from the flame.
7. Let stand for five minutes.
8. Serve and enjoy!

Nutrition: Calories; 370, Carbs; 41g, protein; 29 g, fat; 9g

114. Peachy Pork with Rice

Preparation time: 5 minutes | **Cooking time:** 20 minutes | **Servings:** 4

Ingredients:

- Brown rice – one cup, cooked
- Pork tenderloin – 1lb, cut into 1-inch cubes
- Olive oil – two tbsp
- Taco seasoning – two tbsp, low-sodium
- Salsa – one cup
- Peach preserves – three tbsp

Instructions:

1. Add pork into the bowl and drizzle with oil. Sprinkle with taco seasoning and toss to combine.
2. Add pork into the skillet and cook for eight to ten minutes.
3. Add peach preserve and salsa and stir well.
4. Serve with cooked rice.

Nutrition: Calories; 387l, Carbs; 42g, protein; 25g, fat; 12g

115. Skillet Ham and Rice

Preparation time: 5 minutes | **Cooking time:** 20 minutes | **Servings:** 2

Ingredients:

- Olive oil – one tsp
- Onion – one, chopped
- Fresh mushrooms – one cup, sliced
- Ham – one cup, fully cooked, cubed
- Pepper – 1/8 tsp
- Chicken broth – half cup, low-sodium
- Water – ¼ cup
- Uncooked instant rice – ¼ cup
- Green onions – two, sliced
- Parmesan cheese – ¼ cup, shredded

Instructions:

1. Add oil into the skillet and cook over medium-high flame.
2. Add mushroom and onion and cook until tender.
3. Add water, pepper, broth, and ham and stir well.
4. Add rice and stir well. Lower the heat and simmer for five minutes.

5. Top with cheese and green onions.

Nutrition: Calories; 322, Carbs; 38g, protein; 24g, fat; 8g

116. Peanut Butter-Chocolate Chip Overnight Oats with Banana

Preparation time: 10 mins | **Cooking Time:** 8 hours 20 mins | **Servings:** 4

Ingredients:

- Divided unsweetened almond milk, 2 cups
- Divided natural peanut butter, 4 tablespoons
- Divided pure maple syrup, 8 teaspoons
- Divided rolled oats, 2 cups
- Divided salt, 4 pinches
- Divided mini chocolate chips, 4 tablespoons
- Halved & divided bananas, 2

Instructions:

1. Mix 1 tablespoon peanut butter, 2 teaspoons maple syrup & 1/2 cup milk in a bowl/ mason jar: whisk till blended.
2. Whisk in half cup oats, 1 tablespoon chocolate chips & a pinch of salt.
3. Use the different bowls for every serving; go over with the leftover ingredients. Cover-up & refrigerate it overnight.
4. Cut half the banana into every serving before serving.

Nutrition: Calories 409, Protein 10g, Carbs 59g, Fat 15g.

117. Baked Banana Cups

Preparation time: 15 minutes | **Cooking Time:** 50 minutes | **Servings:** 12

Ingredients:

- Rolled oats, 3 cups
- Low-fat milk, 11/2 cups
- Mashed ripe bananas, 2
- Packed brown sugar, 1/3 cup
- Lightly beaten eggs, 2
- Baking powder, 1 teaspoon
- Ground cinnamon, 1 teaspoon

- Vanilla extract, 1 teaspoon
- Salt, 1/2 teaspoon
- Toasted & chopped pecans, 1/2 cup

Instructions:

1. Oven Preheated to 375 degrees F. With cooking spray, coat the muffin tin.
2. Combine the milk, oats, brown sugar, bananas, baking powder, eggs, vanilla, salt & cinnamon in the bowl. Fold up the pecans.
3. Split the combination of around 1/3 cup each b/w the muffin cups. Bake till the toothpick injected in the middle gets out clean, around twenty-five minutes.
4. Let it cool in the skillet for ten minutes, then put it on the wire rack.

Nutrition: Calories 176, Protein 5g, Carbs 26g, Fat 6g.

118. Southwest Breakfast Quesadilla

Preparation time: 5 minutes | **Cooking Time:** 10 minutes | **Servings:** 1

Ingredients:

- Cooking spray (Nonstick)
- Thawed & frozen egg product, 1/4 cup
- Southwest chipotle seasoning mix (salt-free), 1/8-1/4 teaspoon
- Whole wheat flour tortilla, 1
- Chopped part-skim mozzarella cheese, 2 tablespoons
- Rinsed & drained canned black beans (no salt), 2 tablespoons
- Frozen fresh Pico de gallo, 2 tablespoons

Instructions:

1. With the non-stick cooking spray, spray a med non-stick pan. Preheat the pan on med heat. Put the egg on a hot pan, drizzle with seasoning mix.
2. Cook on med heat, without whisking, till egg starts to set around the edge & on the bottom.
3. Use the large spoon or spatula to lift & fold a somewhat cooked egg allowing the uncooked part to flow beneath.

4. Carry on the cooking on med heat for thirty to sixty seconds or till the egg is fully cooked.
5. Instantly put the cooked egg into the tortilla on one side.
6. Garnish with beans, cheese, & Pico de gallo 2 tablespoons. Fold the tortilla across filling to cover, press nicely.
7. With a paper towel, Clean the same pan. Spray the pan with cooking spray. Pan Preheated on med heat.
8. In the hot pan, cook the filled tortilla for around two minutes or till the tortilla color changes to brown & the filling is fully heated, flipping once.
9. Garnish with extra pico de gallo If desired.

Nutrition: Calories 175, Protein 19g, Carbs 24g, Fat 5g

119. Bean & Bacon Breakfast Tacos

Preparation time: 5 minutes | **Cooking Time:** 10 minutes | **Servings:** 1

Ingredients:

- Extra-virgin olive oil, 1 teaspoon
- Finely minced kale, 1 cup
- Rinsed canned cannellini beans (reduce-sodium), ½ cup
- Warmed corn tortillas, 2
- Shredded Cheddar cheese, 1 tablespoon
- Crumbled cooked bacon, 1 piece

Instructions:

1. In a med skillet, Heat the oil on med heat.
2. Put kale & beans, then cook, whisking, till hot, around two minutes.
3. Enjoy in corn tortillas garnished with bacon & cheese.

Nutrition: Calories 282, Protein 12g, Carbs 33g, Fat 12g

120. Garlic Mushroom Chicken

Preparation time: 15 minutes | **Cooking time:** 15 minutes | **Servings:** 4

Ingredients:

- 4 chicken breasts, boneless and skinless
- 3 garlic cloves, minced
- 1 onion, chopped
- 2 cups mushrooms, sliced
- 1 tbsp olive oil
- ½ cup chicken stock
- ¼ tsp pepper
- ½ tsp salt

Instructions:

1. Season chicken with pepper and salt.
2. Warm oil in a pan on medium heat, then put season chicken in the pan and cook for 5-6 minutes on each side.
3. Remove and place on a plate.
4. Add onion and mushrooms to the pan and sauté until tender, about 2-3 minutes. Add garlic and sauté for a minute.
5. Add stock and bring to boil. Stir well and cook for 1-2 minutes.
6. Pour over chicken and serve.

Nutrition: Calories: 331 Fat: 14.5g Protein: 43.9g Carbs: 4.6g Sodium 420 mg

121. Grilled Chicken

Preparation time: 15 minutes | **Cooking time:** 15 minutes | **Servings:** 4

Ingredients:

- 4 chicken breasts, skinless and boneless
- 1 ½ tsp dried oregano
- 1 tsp paprika
- 5 garlic cloves, minced
- ½ cup fresh parsley, minced
- ½ cup olive oil
- ½ cup fresh lemon juice
- Pepper
- Salt

Instructions:

1. Add lemon juice, oregano, paprika, garlic, parsley, and olive oil to a large zip-lock bag.

2. Season chicken with pepper and salt and add to bag.
3. Seal bag and shake well to coat chicken with marinade.
4. Let sit chicken in the marinade for 20 minutes.
5. Remove chicken from marinade and grill over medium-high heat for 5-6 minutes on each side.
6. Serve and enjoy.

Nutrition: Calories: 512 Fat: 36.5g Protein: 43.1g Carbs: 3g Sodium 110mg

122. Delicious Lemon Chicken Salad

Preparation time: 15 minutes | **Cooking time:** 5 minutes | **Servings:** 4

Ingredients:

- 1 lb. chicken breast, cooked and diced
- 1 tbsp fresh dill, chopped
- 2 tsp olive oil
- 1/4 cup low-fat yogurt
- 1 tsp lemon zest, grated
- 2 tbsp onion, minced
- ¼ tsp pepper
- ¼ tsp salt

Instructions:

1. Put all your fixing into the large mixing bowl and toss well.
2. Season with pepper and salt.
3. Cover and place in the refrigerator.
4. Serve chilled and enjoy.

Nutrition: Calories: 165 Fat: 5.4g Protein: 25.2g Carbs: 2.2g Sodium 153mg

123. Mustard Chicken Tenders

Preparation time: 15 minutes | **Cooking time:** 20 minutes | **Servings:** 4

Ingredients:

- 1 lb. chicken tenders
- 2 tbsp fresh tarragon, chopped
- 1/2 cup whole grain mustard
- 1/2 tsp paprika
- 1 garlic clove, minced

- 1/2 oz fresh lemon juice
- 1/2 tsp pepper
- 1/4 tsp kosher salt

Instructions:

1. Warm oven to 425 F. Add all ingredients except chicken to the large bowl and mix well.
2. Put the chicken in the bowl, then stir until well coated.
3. Place chicken on a baking dish and cover.
4. Bake within 15-20 minutes.
5. Serve and enjoy.

Nutrition: Calories: 242 Fat: 9.5g Protein: 33.2g Carbs: 3.1g Sodium 240 mg

124. Garlic Lime Marinated Pork Chops

Preparation Time: 15 minutes | **Cooking Time:** 5 minutes | **Serving:** 4

Ingredients:

- 4 (6 ounces each) lean boneless pork chops
- 4 cloves garlic, crushed
- 1 teaspoon cumin
- 1 teaspoon chili powder
- 1 teaspoon paprika
- Fresh black pepper to taste
- Juice of ½ lime (about 1 tablespoon)
- Zest of ½ lime

Instructions:

1. Season the pork with all the spices, lime juice, lime zest, and garlic in a bowl.
2. Marinate for 20 minutes.
3. Layer the broiler pan with tin foil.
4. Place the seasoned pork in the pan and broil for 5 minutes per side.

5. Serve warm.

Nutrition: Calories 402, Total Fat 9.8g, Saturated Fat 3.5g, Cholesterol 22 mg, Sodium 671 mg, Carbs 21.1g Fiber 3.1g Sugar 0.3g Protein 44 g

125. Crusted Pork Tenderloin

Preparation Time: 10 minutes | **Cooking Time:** 20 minutes | **Serving:** 2

Ingredients:

- 1-pound (16 ounces) pork tenderloin, trimmed of surface fat
- 1 tablespoon canola oil
- 1 tablespoon Cocoa powder, unsweetened
- 1 teaspoon instant coffee
- ½ teaspoon ground cinnamon
- ½ teaspoon chili powder
- Nonstick cooking spray

Instructions:

1. Set your oven to 400 degrees F.
2. Combine all the spices in a bowl.
3. Season the pork with this mixture along with oil.
4. Heat a greased cast iron pan and add seasoned pork.
5. Cook for 5 minutes per side.
6. Transfer the iron pan to the oven for 15 minutes.
7. Slice and serve.

Nutrition: Calories 511, Total Fat 24g Cholesterol 49 mg, Sodium 647 mg, Carbs 26.4 g Fiber 1.5 g S Protein 23.4 g

SAUCE

126. Green Goddess Sauce (FAST)

Preparation Time: 5 minutes | **Cooking Time:** 0 minutes | **Serving:** 8

Ingredients:

- 1 cup basil, chopped
- 1 cup flat leaf parsley, chopped

- ¼ cup green onion
- 1 clove of garlic, minced
- 1 tsp apple cider vinegar
- 2 tbsps. lemon juice, freshly squeezed
- ¼ cup olive oil
- 1 cup plain non-Fat Greek yogurt
- 1/8 tsp salt

- 1/8 tsp black pepper
- 1/8 tsp cayenne pepper

Instructions:
1. Place all ingredients in a food processor and blend until smooth.
2. Place in containers and store in the fridge until ready to use.

Nutrition: Calories 78, Fat 7g, Carbs 2g, Protein 3g, Fiber 0.4g, Sodium 13mg, Potassium 90mg

127. Garlicky Vegetable Soup (FAST)

Preparation Time: 5 Minutes | **Cooking Time:** 20 Minutes | **Servings:** 4

Ingredients:
- 5 medium heads garlic, peeled (each clove peeled)
- 6 cups Roasted Vegetable Stock
- 1 (6-ounce) can tomato paste
- 1 large yellow onion, peeled and diced
- 1/4 teaspoon lemon juice
- 2 tablespoons olive oil
- 2 tablespoons chopped basil

Instructions:
1. Place all ingredients except olive oil and basil into a 4–6-quart slow cooker. Stir.
2. Secure and cook on low for 8 hours or on high for 5 hours.
3. Add olive oil. Set an immersion blender or blend soup in batches in a standard blender until smooth.
4. Garnish with basil and serve.

Nutrition: Calories: 223 Carbs: 37g Fat: 8g Sugar: 16g Fiber: 9g Protein: 6g Sodium: 73mg

128. Peach Stew (FAST)

Preparation Time: 10 minutes | **Cooking Time:** 10 minutes | **Servings:** 6

Ingredients:
- 3 tbsp coconut sugar
- 5 cups peeled and cubed peaches
- 2 cup water

- 1 tsp grated ginger

Instructions:
1. In a pot, combine the peaches while using the sugar, ginger and water, toss, provide a boil over medium heat, cook for 10 mins, divide into bowls and serve cold.

Nutrition: Calories 142, Fat 1.5g, Carbs 7.8g, Protein 2.4g, Phosphorus 127mg, Potassium 199mg, Sodium 134g

129. Cream" of Cauliflower Soup (FAST)

Preparation Time: 5 Minutes | **Cooking Time:** 20 Minutes | **Servings:** 4

Ingredients:
- 1 large head cauliflower, chopped
- 3 large stalks celery, chopped
- 1 medium carrot, peeled and chopped
- 2 cloves garlic, peeled and minced
- 1 medium onion, peeled and chopped
- 2 teaspoons ground cumin
- 1/2 teaspoon ground black pepper
- 1 tablespoon chopped parsley
- 1/4 teaspoon dill

Instructions:
1. 1In a large soup pot, combine cauliflower, celery, carrot, garlic, onion, cumin, and black pepper.
2. Add water to just cover ingredients in pot. Bring to a boil over high heat.
3. Set heat to low.
4. Simmer until vegetables are tender. Stir in parsley and dill before serving.

Nutrition: Calories: 62 Carbs: 13g Fat: 1g Sugar:5g Fiber: 5g Protein: 4g Sodium: 94mg

130. Wonton Soup (FAST)

Preparation Time: 5 minutes | **Cooking Time:** 15 minutes | **Servings:** 8

Ingredients:
- 4 sliced scallions
- ¼ tsp. ground white pepper

- 2 cup sliced fresh mushrooms
- 4 minced garlic cloves
- 6 oz. dry whole-grain yolk-free egg noodles
- ½ lb. lean ground pork
- 1 tbsp minced fresh ginger
- 8 cup low-Sodium chicken broth

Instructions:
1. Place a stockpot over medium heat. Add the ground pork, ginger, and garlic and sauté for 5 mins.
2. Drain any excess Fat, then return to stovetop.
3. Add the broth and bring to a boil.
4. Once boiling, stir in the mushrooms, noodles, and white pepper.
5. Cover and simmer for 10 mins.
6. Remove pot from heat. Stir in the scallions and serve immediately.

Nutrition: Calories 143, Fat 4g, Carbs 14g, Protein 16g, Fiber 3g, Sodium 55mg, Potassium 125mg

131. Lentil And Lemon Soup

Preparation Time: 10 minutes | **Cooking Time:** 40 minutes | **Servings:** 4

Ingredients:
- 2 tsp olive oil
- 1 large onion finely chopped
- 5 oz red lentils
- 2 tsp tomato puree
- 1 garlic clove, peeled
- 1 pint vegetable stock
- 14 oz tin chopped tomatoes
- juice of 1/2 lemon

Instructions:
1. Heat the oil and cook onion and garlic for 10 mins.
2. Add the lentils and the stock and bring to the boil.
3. Add the tinned tomatoes and tomato puree and bring back to the boil (covered 15 mins).
4. Taste for seasoning and serve.

Nutrition: Calories 104, Fat 12g, Carbs 12g, Protein 11g

132. Halibut Soup (FAST)

Preparation Time: 5 Minutes | **Cooking Time:** 15 Minutes | **Servings:** 2

Ingredients:
- Table salt and black pepper to the taste
- 2 tbsp. ginger, chopped
- 1 mug water
- 1 yellow onion, sliced off
- 1-pound carrots, sliced
- 1 tablespoon coconut oil
- 1-pound halibut, slice into moderate chunks
- 12 mugs chicken stock

Instructions:
1. Warm up a pot with the oil over moderate heat, insert onion, shake and prepare for 6 minutes.
2. Insert ginger, carrots, water and stock, shake bring to a simmer, reduce tempera and prepare for 20 minutes.
3. Merge soup using an immersion blender, season with table salt and pepper and insert halibut pieces.
4. Shake gently and simmer soup for 5 minutes more.
5. Distribute into pots and serve.

Nutrition: Calories: 132 Carbs: 5g Fat: 6g Sod: 234mg

133. Egg Soup with Scallions and Bok Choy (FAST)

Preparation Time: 5 Minutes | **Cooking Time:** 20 Minutes | **Servings:** 3

Ingredients:
- 1 2-inch piece fresh ginger, peeled and slice into very thin matchstick-size strips
- 1-star anise
- 1-pound shiitake mushrooms, stemmed and sliced
- 1 tsp. five-spice grinding grains

- 1/4 mug fresh lemon juice
- 3 large eggs
- 6 scallions, thinly sliced
- 2 heads baby book choy, slice into 1/4-inch-thick slices
- 0.5-ounce sun-dried wakame
- 3 tbsp. unrefined coconut oil
- 2 shallots, chopped
- 1/4 tsp. black pepper
- 8 mugs Beef Bone Broth

Instructions:

1. In a very moderate pot Wrap up wakame with warm water.
2. Let indicate 10 minutes or till soft and pliable.
3. Drain well; rinse well and drain again. Slice strips of wakame into 1-inch items; put aside.
4. In a very large pot warmth coconut oil over moderate heat.
5. Insert shallots, ginger, and star anise.
6. Prepare and shake for regarding a pair of minutes or till shallots are translucent. I
7. nsert mushrooms; prepare and shake for two minutes.
8. Garnish 5-spice grinding grains and pepper over mushrooms; prepare and shake for one minute.
9. Insert reserved wakame, Beef Bone Broth, and lemon juice. Bring combine to simmering.
10. In an exceedingly little pot beat egg.
11. Drizzle overwhelmed eggs into simmering broth, swirling broth in an exceedingly figure-eight motion.
12. Remove soup from heat. Shake in scallions.
13. Distribute book choy among large, warmed pots.
14. Ladle soup into pots; serve instantly.

Nutrition: Calories: 123 Carbs: 5 g Fat: 11 g Fiber: 3 g Protein: 5 g Sodium: 16 mg

DIVERTICULITIS
CLEAR FLUID RECIPES

134. Strawberry overnight oats

Preparation Time: 5 minutes | **Cooking Time:** 0 minutes | **Total time:** 5 minutes | **Servings:** 1

Ingredients:
- ½ cup (50 grams) rolled or old-fashioned oats, use certified gluten-free oats if necessary
- 1 tablespoon chia
- ¾ cup (180 ml) non-dairy milk
- ½ teaspoon vanilla extract
- 1 tablespoon maple syrup (optional), use real maple syrup, not pancake syrup
- 1 tablespoon strawberry jam (optional - but recommended)
- Around ½ cup (60 grams) fresh strawberries, chopped

Instructions:
1. Add the oats and chia to a jar (or another covered container).
2. Stir in the milk, vanilla extract, and optional maple syrup.
3. Pour in the strawberry jam, followed by the cut strawberries.
4. Place the container in the fridge for at least 3 to 4 hours, but up to 72 hours is ok.
5. Eat the oats straight from the jar or transfer them to a bowl beforehand.

Nutrition: Calories: 388, Carbs 6g, Protein 14g, Fat 10g, Cholesterol 386 mg

135. Ginger peach smoothie

Preparation Time: 5 minutes | **Cooking Time:** 5 minutes | **Total time:** 10 minutes | **Servings:** 1

Ingredients:

- 2 ripe, juicy peaches, (you can use frozen peaches, but if you do, use a fresh banana and not a frozen one)
- 1 medium frozen banana (fresh or frozen)
- ¾ cup (180 ml) non-dairy milk
- 1 tablespoon maple syrup (optional - add to taste or not at all)
- 1 approx. 2½ inches long stick fresh ginger, roughly x ½inch wide
- Or ¼ to ½ teaspoon ground ginger

Instructions:
1. Remove the pits from the peaches and combine them with the remaining ingredients in a blender. I recommend using only half of the fresh ginger or 14 teaspoons of ground ginger to begin.
2. Blend until smooth, then taste it. If you want a stronger flavor, add a little more ginger.
3. Serve right away.

Nutrition: Calories: 337, Carbs 72g, Protein 9g, Fat 4g, Cholesterol 186 mg

136. Strawberry banana peanut butter smoothie

Preparation Time: 5 minutes | **Cooking Time:** 5 minutes | **Total time:** 10 minutes | **Servings:** 1

Ingredients:
- 2 cups (approx. 288 grams) strawberries, fresh or frozen
- 1 medium frozen banana, fresh and not frozen if using frozen strawberries
- 2 tablespoons peanut butter, or any other nut or butter
- 1 cup (240 ml) plant milk of choice

Optional
- 1 tablespoon maple syrup, or a medjool date
- 1 tablespoon flax
- 1 tablespoon chia

Instructions:
1. In a blender, combine all of the ingredients.
2. Blend until completely smooth.

3. Check the sweetness and, if required, add the optional maple syrup or date, then mix again to combine.

Nutrition: Calories 465, Carbs 60g, Protein 18g, Fat 21g, Cholesterol 276 mg

137. Granola

Preparation Time: 5 minutes|**Cooking Time:** 20 minutes|**Total time:** 25 minutes|**Servings:** 6

Ingredients:

- 2 cups (180 grams) rolled or old-fashioned oats, use certified gluten-free for gluten-free granola
- 1 cup (85 grams) raw almonds of choice, pecans, walnuts, etc. (or more pumpkin or sunflower for nut-free)
- ½ cup (80 grams) shelled pumpkin, sunflower or hemp, or a mix of all 3
- ½ cup (25 grams) puffed rice (optional) (adds fantastic texture - if you don't use it, make up the quantity with more oats.)
- 6 tablespoons creamy butter of choice
- ¾ cup (180 ml) brown rice syrup or maple syrup, brown rice syrup will give you bigger clusters
- ½ teaspoon fine sea salt, note that if you use iodized (table) salt instead, you will need to use less
- 1 teaspoon ground cinnamon
- 1 teaspoon vanilla extract
- 1 cup dried raisins, sultanas, cranberries, tart cherries or chocolate chips, or any other dried fruit (chopped if it's something like apricots or dates)

Instructions:

1. Preheat the oven to 350°f (175°c) and place a shelf on the bottom level.
2. Using parchment paper or a silicone baking mat, line a large baking pan.
3. Add the oats and optional puffed rice to a large mixing bowl. To mix, stir everything together.
4. In a medium mixing bowl, combine the butter, syrup, salt, cinnamon, and vanilla extract. To mix, whisk everything together.
5. Pour the wet mixture into the oat mixture and stir with a wooden spoon or spatula until everything is mixed, moist, and sticky.
6. Spread it evenly over the prepared tray, about 3/4 inch deep.
7. Bake for 10 minutes on the lowest oven shelf, then take from the oven and stir with a spatula to ensure equal cooking. After you've finished swirling it, firmly press it all over with a spatula or the bottom of a cup. This helps it cling together and forms wonderful large clumps when crumbled later.
8. Return to the oven and bake for another 10 to 15 minutes, or until the top is brown and the house smells toasty.
9. Remove from the oven and sprinkle with the dried fruit/chocolate chips, then leave to cool fully on the baking tray. As it cools, the granola will solidify.
10. Break up the granola into chunky pieces with your hands and place it in an airtight container. It will last 6 to 8 weeks.

Nutrition: Calories 250, Carbs 35gm Protein 8g, Fat 13g, Cholesterol 621 mg

138. Persimmon smoothie

Preparation Time: 5 minutes|**Cooking Time:** 5 minutes|**Total time:** 10 minutes|**Servings:** 1

Ingredients:

- 2 medium ripe persimmons
- 1 medium frozen banana
- 1 cup dairy-free milk
- About 10 cashews; if you don't have a high-powered blender, soak the cashew in hot water for 5 minutes before adding to the blender. See notes for cashew alternatives.
- ¼ teaspoon cinnamon, add a little more if you prefer a stronger cinnamon taste
- 1 tablespoon maple syrup

Instructions:

1. Remove and discard the persimmon leaves, then chop each fruit into a few pieces.

2. Blend them, together with the remaining ingredients except for the maple syrup, in a blender until smooth.

3. Use the blender to give it a brief taste and, if required, add the maple syrup.

4. After adding it, give it a brisk 5-second mix before serving.

Nutrition: Calories 298, Carbs 41g, Protein 11g, Fat 12g, Cholesterol 121 mg

139. Cranberry smoothie

Preparation Time: 5 minutes | **Cooking Time:** 0 minutes | **Total time:** 5 minutes | **Servings:** 1

Ingredients:

- 75g / ¾ cup frozen cranberries (or fresh cranberries but add a handful of ice too)
- 1 large apple cored and chopped into chunks
- 1 small handful / about 2 tablespoons raw pecans or walnuts (see notes for nut-free option)
- 1 tablespoon maple syrup
- 240mls / 1 cup non-dairy milk
- ¼ teaspoon ground cinnamon

Instructions:

1. Add all the ingredients to a blender.

2. Blend until smooth.

Nutrition: Calories 424, Carbs 61g, Protein 10g, Fat 19g, Cholesterol 251 mg

140. Kale apple smoothie

Preparation Time: 5 minutes | **Cooking Time:** 5 minutes | **Total time:** 10 minutes | **Servings:** 1

Ingredients:

- 2 large kale leaves, washed with stems removed. Use a couple of handfuls of baby kale instead for a milder kale flavor

- 1 large apple cored (no need to peel unless you want to).
- 1 tablespoon chia
- 2 teaspoons ground flax or whole flax
- 1 - 2 tablespoons maple syrup
- ½ medium lemon, juice only
- 180mls / ¾ cup plant-based milk, add up to a ¼ cup more too thin if you prefer it that way
- 5 ice cubes, optional but will make it colder and a bit thicker
- 1 tablespoon almond butter, optional - it's great with or without

Instructions:

1. Blend all of the ingredients in a blender until smooth. On my blended, I use the smoothie option.

2. Check the sweetness and, if required, add a bit more maple syrup.

3. Serve right away.

Nutrition: Calories 319, Carbs 63g, Protein 9g, Fat 7g, Cholesterol 266 mg

141. Glowing skin smoothie

Preparation Time: 5 minutes | **Cooking Time:** 5 minutes | **Total time:** 10 minutes | **Servings:** 2

Ingredients:

- ¼ cup cashew pieces or 1 very heaping ¼ cup of whole ones about 38g
- 1 cup | 240mls water or coconut water for an extra skin boost!
- 1 medium banana
- 1 very heaping cup frozen mango pieces around 140g, see recipe notes if you only have fresh mango
- 1 tablespoon chia, optional
- ⅛ teaspoon vanilla bean powder or ½ teaspoon vanilla extract
- ½ teaspoon ground cardamon
- ¼ teaspoon ground turmeric
- ⅛ teaspoon ground ginger or a small piece of fresh ginger

- 1 tablespoon of maple syrup or 1 large medjool date

Instructions:

1. If you don't have a high-powered blender, soak the cashew in boiling water for 15 minutes or cold water for 2 hours (this technique will maintain the nutrients), then drain.

2. Blend the cashew with the water in a blender until smooth. You've just created cashew milk!

3. Add the other ingredients and mix until smooth.

4. Serve with a decorative sprinkling of cardamon and turmeric if desired.

Nutrition: calories 342, Carbs 70g, Protein 8g, Fat 15g, Ch0oesterol 82 mg

142. Cranberry sauce

Preparation Time: 5 minutes | **Cooking Time:** 15 minutes | **Total time:** 20 minutes | **Servings:** 16

Ingredients:

- 24 oz / 680 g fresh or frozen cranberries
- ½ cup / 100 g sugar, granulated white or cane sugar is best
- ½ cup / 120 ml maple syrup (real, natural maple syrup, not pancake syrup)
- ⅓ cup / 80 ml vegan red wine or port, or orange juice for an alcohol-free alternative
- 1 large orange, zest and juice of
- 1 medium cinnamon stick
- 1 approx. 3-inch piece of fresh rosemary

Instructions:

To make on the stovetop

1. Wash the cranberries and remove any that are soft. 1 cup of them should be set aside, and the rest should be combined with everything else in a medium saucepan. Cook, frequently stirring, over medium heat until the sauce thickens and becomes jammy, and the cranberries break down. Usually, it takes approximately 15 minutes.

2. Remove the rosemary and cinnamon stick from the pan and set aside. Take a quick taste but be careful because it will be extremely hot. If you want to add more sugar, do so now because it will dissolve in the heat. But keep in mind that it's intended to taste tart. Its purpose is to cut through the richness of your holiday fare.

3. Stir in the cranberries that have been set aside. The residual heat will cook them sufficiently before the sauce cools, giving them a good texture.

4. Allow cooling completely before transferring to sterilized jars or freezer-safe containers.

To make in an instant pot

1. Wash the cranberries and remove any that are soft. Scoop out approximately 1 cup and set aside till the end. Place the remaining ingredients in the instant pot.

2. Stir in the sugar, maple syrup, red wine, orange juice, and zest. On top, place the cinnamon stick and rosemary.

3. Close the vent and replace the cover on the instant pot. Cook for 3 minutes on high pressure before allowing the pressure to release naturally.

4. Open the lid once the pin has dropped. Don't be alarmed if it appears frothy and unappealing.

5. Remove the cinnamon stick and rosemary, and then stir in the saved cranberries. The remaining heat is sufficient to cook them. Stir everything together thoroughly. It now appears to be in good condition. Take a short sip. Take cautious since it will be quite hot. If you find it too sour, add a bit of extra sugar now since it will dissolve in the heat. But keep in mind that a little acidity is excellent since it pairs well with your rich holiday meals.

6. Allow cooling completely before using. At this stage, the lid can be on or off, although it will cool faster with the cover off. Decant

into jars or freezer-safe containers once cold.

Nutrition: Calories 74, Carbs 18g, Protein 1g, Fat 1g, Cholesterol 80 mg

143. Chocolate tahini pumpkin smoothie

Preparation Time: 5 minutes | **Cooking Time:** 0 minutes | **Total time:** 5 minutes | **Servings:** 1

Ingredients:

- 1 frozen banana
- 1 tablespoon cocoa
- 8 tablespoons | ½ cup pumpkin puree canned or fresh
- 1 slightly heaping tablespoon tahini
- 2 tablespoons maple syrup
- 180mls | ¾ cup non-dairy milk

Instructions:

1. Add all ingredients to a blender.
2. Blend until completely smooth.
3. Serve immediately.

Nutrition: Calories 383, Carbs 73g, Fat 11g, Protein 7g, Cholesterol 32 mg

144. Caramel sauce

Preparation Time: 2 minutes | **Cooking Time:** 3 minutes | **Total time:** 5 minutes | **Servings:** 4

Ingredients:

- 100g | 1/2 cup coconut sugar (sometimes called coconut palm sugar (I have not tried this with any other sugar, so I can't guarantee it will work as well if you make a sub)
- 2 tablespoons water
- 2 tablespoons tahini (see recipe note)
- 2 tablespoons vegan butter or coconut oil (solid measurement)
- 1/8 - 1/4 teaspoon salt (add to taste)

Instructions:

1. In a saucepan, combine the coconut sugar and water.
2. Cook over medium heat until the sugar has fully dissolved, and the mixture is just beginning to bubble. Don't stir!!
3. Swirl the pan a little if necessary. It will take no more than two to three minutes.
4. If you leave it unattended for too long, it will quickly burn.
5. Take the pan off the heat and stir in the tahini, salt, and vegan butter or coconut oil. Stir vigorously until everything is fully incorporated. It's natural to see a few bright specks through it.
6. If you're having problems getting it to come together, place it back over low heat for 30 seconds or so.

Nutrition: Calories 195, Carbs 25g, Protein 1g, Fat 10g, Cholesterol 156 mg

145. Lemon cheesecake smoothie

Preparation Time: 5 minutes | **Cooking Time:** 5 minutes | **Total time:** 10 minutes | **Servings:** 2

Ingredients:

- 1 medium juicy lemon
- 1 cup (240 ml) light canned coconut milk
- ¼ heaping cup (50 grams) cooked chickpeas
- 1 to 2 medjool dates
- ¼ cup (25 grams) chopped pecan measured in pieces, not whole
- 1 cup (150 grams) frozen mango pieces
- ¼ teaspoon ground turmeric
- ¼ teaspoon salt
- ½ teaspoon apple cider vinegar
- 1 tablespoon maple syrup optional

Instructions:

1. To begin, zest the lemon. Blend the lemon zest, then remove the remaining peel and pith (the white stuff) from the lemon. I do this by cutting both sharp ends of the

lemon and then standing it up on the board.

2. Then, with a sharp knife, I sliced all the way around it, just deep enough to remove the pith while leaving the flesh intact.

3. After that, place the entire lemon in the blender and remove the pith and peel.

4. Except for the maple syrup, combine all of the remaining ingredients in a mixing bowl.

5. Blend until the mixture is totally smooth. It yields a thick smoothie. If you like it a little thinner, add a little extra coconut milk or a drop of water to thin it out.

6. If you want a little extra sweetness, add a little more maple syrup. It goes well with maple syrup. Blend for a second on low to disperse, then pour into a glass and serve.

Nutrition: Calories 549, Carbs 68g, Protein 6g, Fat 39g, Cholesterol 140 mg

146. Double chocolate scones

Preparation Time: 10 minutes | **Cooking Time:** 25 minutes | **Total time:** 35 minutes | **Servings:** 8

Ingredients:

- 125g | 1 cup all-purpose flour
- 97g | 3/4 cup wholewheat flour
- 25g | 1/4 cup cocoa powder
- 62g | 1/4 heaping cup natural cane sugar (you can sub this for any granulated sugar or coconut sugar)
- 1/2 teaspoon salt
- 1 tablespoon ground flax
- 1 tablespoon baking powder
- 1/4 packed cup coconut oil (it needs to be hard)
- 1 teaspoon vanilla extract
- 207mls | 3/4 cup + 2 tablespoons cup of non-dairy milk
- 130g | 3/4 cup dairy-free chocolate chips or chunks (I like to use semi-sweet, but you can use any kind you have to hand).
- A little sugar for sprinkling

For the drizzle (optional)

- 43g | 1/4 cup dairy-free chocolate
- 2 tablespoons non-dairy milk

Instructions:

1. Pre-heat the oven to 400°f.

2. Use parchment paper or a silicone baking mat to line a baking sheet.

3. In a large mixing basin, combine the flour and baking powder.

4. Mix in the coconut oil with your fingertips or a pastry cutter until the mixture resembles breadcrumbs.

5. Stir in all of the remaining dry ingredients, including the chocolate.

6. Add the vanilla extract to the milk and mix to blend, then add the liquid to the dry ingredients and swirl to combine.

7. It's now simpler to get your hands into the dough and shape it into a ball. Don't be too rough with it since the less you handle it, the better your scones will be.

8. Place on the prepared tray and press or roll into a 1-inch-thick round.

9. Divide the mixture into 8 equal wedges and divide them so that they all have some space between them.

10. Sprinkle with sugar and bake for 20 - 25 minutes, or until cooked through (if you're not sure, insert a toothpick or skewer and it should come out largely clean).

11. Allow cooling on a cooling rack.

12. optional chocolate drizzling

13. Place the chocolate and milk in a small dish and gently melt in a microwave or over a saucepan of boiling water.

14. Drizzle the melted chocolate mixture over the cooled scones using a spoon.

Nutrition: Calories 285, Carbs 41g, Protein 6g, Fat 12g, Cholesterol 90 mg

147. Apple Orange Juice

Preparation Time: 5 minutes | **Cooking Time:** 0 minutes | **Servings:** 2

Ingredients:

- 1 Gala apple, peeled, cored and sliced
- 2 oranges, peeled, halved and seeded
- 2 teaspoons honey (optional)
- 3/4 cup water

Instructions:

1. Squeeze each orange over a fine-mesh strainer.
2. Gently, press the pulp to extract as much liquid as possible.
3. Add in the apple, water, and orange juice in your blender and pulse.
4. Set a fine-mesh strainer in a bowl. Before transferring your juice into the strainer.
5. Once again, gently press the pulp to remove all possible liquid then discard it.
6. Stir in your honey then serve over ice.

Nutrition: Calories 180, Fat 1g, Carbs 43g, Fiber 1g, Protein 2g

148. Pineapple Mint Juice

Preparation Time: 5 minutes | **Cooking Time:** 0 minutes | **Servings:** 4

Ingredients:

- 3 cups pineapple, cored, sliced and chunks
- 10-12 mint leaves, or to taste
- 2 tablespoons sugar, or to taste (optional)
- 1 ½ cup water
- 1 cup ice cubes

Instructions:

1. Set all the ingredients into your blender, and pulse.
2. Set a fine-mesh strainer in a bowl. Before transferring your juice into the strainer.
3. Gently, press the pulp to extract all possible liquid then discard it.
4. Serve over ice.
5. Enjoy!

Nutrition: Calories: 78, Fat: 1g, Carbs: 22g, Fiber: 2g, protein: 1g

149. Celery Apple Juice

Preparation Time: 5 minutes | **Cooking Time:** 0 minutes | **Servings:** 2

Ingredients:

- 12 celery stalks, peeled and chopped
- 3 Apple, peeled, cored, seeded and sliced
- 1 inch ginger root, peeled and chopped
- 1/4 lemon juice
- 2 cups water

Instructions:

1. Set all the ingredients into your blender, and pulse.
2. Set a fine-mesh strainer in a bowl. Before transferring your juice into the strainer.
3. Gently, press the pulp to extract all possible liquid then discard it.
4. Serve over ice.
5. Enjoy!

Nutrition: Calories: 119, Fat: 1g, Carbs: 29g, Fiber: 7g, Protein: 2g

150. Homemade Banana Apple Juice

Preparation Time: 10 minutes | **Cooking Time:** 0 minutes | **Servings:** 2

Ingredients:

- 2 bananas, peeled and sliced
- 1/2 apple, peeled, cored and chopped
- 1 tablespoon honey
- 1 ½ cup water

Instructions:

1. Set all the ingredients into your blender, and pulse.
2. Set a fine-mesh strainer in a bowl. Before transferring your juice into the strainer.
3. Gently, press the pulp to extract all possible liquid then discard it.
4. Serve over ice.
5. Enjoy!

Nutrition: Calories: 132, Fat: 2g, Carbs: 27g, Fiber: 3g, Protein: 4g

151. Sweet Detox Juice

Preparation Time: 10 minutes | **Cooking Time:** 0 minutes | **Servings:** 2

Ingredients:

- 2 cups baby spinach, chopped
- 1 handful parsley, chopped
- 1 green apple, peeled, cored, seeded and sliced
- 1 large English cucumber, seeded and chopped
- 1 inch ginger, peeled
- 1 lemon, juiced

Instructions:

1. Set all the ingredients into your blender, and pulse.
2. Set a fine-mesh strainer in a bowl. Before transferring your juice into the strainer.
3. Gently, press the pulp to extract all possible liquid then discard it.
4. Serve over ice.
5. Enjoy!

Nutrition: Calories: 209, Fat: 2g, Carbs: 48g, Fiber: 17g, Protein: 12g

152. Pineapple Ginger Juice

Preparation Time: 35 minutes | **Cooking Time:** 0 minutes | **Servings:** 7

Ingredients:

- 10 cups pineapple, chopped
- 6 cups water
- 3 Fuji apples, chopped
- 4-inch ginger root, peeled and chopped
- 1/4 cup Lemon juice
- 1/4 cup sugar

Instructions :

1. Set all the ingredients into your blender, and pulse.
2. Set a fine-mesh strainer in a bowl. Before transferring your juice into the strainer.
3. Gently, press the pulp to extract all possible liquid then discard it.
4. Serve over ice.
5. Enjoy!

Nutrition: Calories: 71, Fat: 1g, Carbs: 20g, Fiber: 3g, Protein: 1g

153. Carrot Orange Juice

Preparation Time: 15 minutes | **Cooking Time:** 0 minutes | **Servings:** 2

Ingredients:

- 1 medium yellow tomato, cut into wedges
- 1 orange, peeled and quartered
- 1 apple, peeled, cored and chopped
- 4 jumbo carrots, peeled and chopped
- 2 cups water

Instructions:

1. Set all the ingredients into your blender, and pulse.
2. Set a fine-mesh strainer in a bowl. Before transferring your juice into the strainer.
3. Gently, press the pulp to extract all possible liquid then discard it.
4. Serve over ice.
5. Enjoy!

Nutrition: Calories: 111, Fat: 1g, Carbs: 24g, Fiber: 1g, Protein: 2g

154. Strawberry Apple Juice

Preparation Time: 5 minutes | **Cooking Time:** 0 minutes | **Servings:** 8-10

Ingredients:

- 2 cups strawberries (tops removed)
- 1 red apple, peeled, seeded, cored and chopped
- 1 tablespoon chia seeds
- 1 cup water

Instructions:

1. Set all the ingredients into your blender, and pulse.
2. Set a fine-mesh strainer in a bowl. Before transferring your juice into the strainer.
3. Gently, press the pulp to extract all possible liquid then discard it.
4. Add in your chia seeds then leave to sit for at least 5 minutes.
5. Serve over ice.
6. Enjoy!

Nutrition: Calories: 245, Fat: 5g, Carbs: 52g, Fiber: 7g, Protein: 4g

155. Autumn Energizer Juice

Preparation Time: 10 minutes | **Cooking Time:** 0 minutes | **Servings:** 2

Ingredients:

- 2 pears, peeled, seeded and chopped
- 2 Ambrosia apples, peeled, cored and chopped
- 2 Granny Smith apples, peeled, cored, chopped
- 2 mandarins, juiced
- 2 cups sweet potato, peeled and chopped
- 1 pint cape gooseberries
- 2 inches ginger root, peeled

Instructions:

1. Set all the ingredients into your blender, and pulse.
2. Set a fine-mesh strainer in a bowl. Before transferring your juice into the strainer.
3. Gently, press the pulp to extract all possible liquid then discard it.
4. Serve over ice.
5. Enjoy!

Nutrition: Calories: 170, Fat: 3g, Carbs: 33g, Fiber: 9g, Protein: 4g

156. Asian Inspired Wonton Broth

Preparation Time: 5 minutes | **Cooking Time:** 1 hour 30 minutes | **Servings:** 2

Ingredients:

- 1 chicken thigh, skin on
- 1 carrot, coarsely chopped
- 1 celery stalk, coarsely chopped
- 1 small onion, quartered
- 3 dime-sized ginger pieces
- 2 tablespoons kosher salt
- 1/4 teaspoon turmeric
- 1/8 teaspoon MSG (don't leave it out)
- 5 white peppercorns (can be substituted with black)
- 1 liter water

Instructions:

1. Transfer all the ingredients to your stockpot. Top with enough water to cover then allow to come to a boil on high heat slowly.
2. Switch to low heat and simmer for at least 1 hour and 30 minutes.
3. Set and pour the mixture through a fine-mesh strainer into a large bowl.
4. Taste and season with salt.
5. Serve hot.

Nutrition: Calories: 181, Fat: 7g, Carbs: 14g, Fiber: 1g, Protein: 14g

157. Mushroom, Cauliflower and Cabbage Broth

Preparation Time: 10 minutes | **Cooking Time:** 50 minutes | **Servings:** 2

Ingredients:

- 1 large yellow onion
- 1 cup celery stalks, chopped
- 2 carrots, diced or cubed
- 10 French beans
- 1/2 cabbage, diced
- 1-2 stalks celery leaves
- 1 ½ cup mushrooms, sliced
- 8 florets cauliflower
- 1 teaspoon garlic, chopped
- 1 teaspoon ginger, chopped
- 1 tablespoon oil
- 1 scallion stalk
- 1/2 teaspoon pepper, crushed

Instructions:

1. Transfer all the ingredients to your stockpot. Top with enough water to cover then allow to come to a boil on high heat slowly.
2. Switch to low heat and simmer for 50 minutes.
3. Set and pour the mixture through a fine-mesh strainer into a large bowl.
4. Mash the vegetables well to extract all their juices.
5. Taste and season with salt.

6. Enjoy.

Nutrition: Calories: 141, Fat: 5g, Carbs: 22g, Fiber: 7g, Protein: 5g

158. Indian Inspired Vegetable stock

Preparation Time: 10 minutes | **Cooking Time:** 11 minutes | **Servings:** 3

Ingredients:
- 3/4 cup onions, roughly chopped
- 3/4 cup carrot, roughly chopped
- 3/4 cup tomatoes, roughly chopped
- 3/4 cup potatoes, roughly chopped
- 1 teaspoon turmeric
- Salt to taste

Instructions:
1. Transfer all the ingredients to your stockpot. Top with enough water to cover then allow to come to a boil on high heat slowly.
2. Switch to low heat and simmer for 11 minutes.
3. Set and pour the mixture through a fine-mesh strainer into a large bowl.
4. Taste and season with salt.
5. Serve hot.
6. Enjoy!

Nutrition: Calories: 103, Fat: 0.2g, Carbs: 23.3g, Fiber: 3.1g, Protein: 2.2g

159. Beef Bone Broth

Preparation Time: 10 minutes | **Cooking Time:** 12 hours | **Servings:** 8

Ingredients:
- 2 pounds beef bones
- 1 onion, chopped in quarters
- 2 celery stalks, chopped in half
- 2 carrots, chopped in half
- 3 whole garlic cloves
- 2 bay leaves
- 1 tablespoon salt
- Filtered water (enough to cover bones)

Instructions:
1. Transfer the bones and vegetables to your stockpot. Top with enough water to cover then allow to come to a boil on high heat slowly.
2. Switch to low heat and simmer for at least 2 hours and up to 12 hours.
3. Set and pour the mixture through a fine-mesh strainer into a large bowl.
4. Taste and season with salt.
5. Serve hot.

Nutrition: Calories: 69, Fat: 4g, Carbs: 1g, Fiber: 0.1g, Protein: 6g

160. Ginger, Mushroom and Cauliflower Broth

Preparation Time: 10 minutes | **Cooking Time:** 50 minutes | **Servings:** 3

Ingredients:
- 1 large yellow onion
- 1 cup celery stalks, chopped
- 2 carrots, diced or cubed
- 10 French beans
- 1 ginger root, peeled, diced or grated
- 1-2 stalks celery leaves or coriander leaves
- 1 ½ cup mushrooms, sliced
- 8 florets cauliflower
- 1 teaspoon garlic, chopped
- 1 tablespoon oil
- 1 stalk spring onion greens or scallions
- 1/2 teaspoon crushed pepper or ground pepper

Instructions:
1. Transfer all the ingredients to your stockpot. Top with enough water to cover then allow to come to a boil on high heat slowly.
2. Switch to low heat and simmer for at least 50 minutes.
3. Set and pour the mixture through a fine-mesh strainer into a large bowl.
4. Taste and season with salt.
5. Serve hot. Enjoy!

Nutrition: Calories: 141, Fat: 5g, Carbs: 22g, Fiber: 7g, Protein: 5g

161. Fish Broth

Preparation Time: 15 minutes | **Cooking Time:** 45 minutes | **Servings:** 3

Ingredients:

- 1 large onion, chopped
- 1 large carrot chopped
- 1 fennel bulb and fronds, chopped (optional)
- 3 celery stalks, chopped
- Salt
- 2-5 pounds fish bones and heads
- 1 handful dried mushrooms (optional)
- 2-4 bay leaves
- 1 star anise pod (optional)
- 1-2 teaspoons thyme, dried or fresh
- 3-4 pieces dried kombu kelp (optional)

Instructions:

1. Transfer the bones and vegetables to your stockpot.
2. Top with enough water to cover then allow to come to a boil on high heat slowly.
3. Set to low heat and simmer for 45 minutes.
4. Set and pour the mixture through a fine-mesh strainer into a large bowl.
5. Taste and season with salt.
6. Serve hot.
7. Enjoy!

Nutrition: Calories: 29, Fat: 1g, Carbs: 2g, Fiber: 1g, Protein: 1g

162. Clear Pumpkin Broth

Preparation Time: 15 minutes | **Cooking Time:** 30 minutes | **Servings:** 6

Ingredients:

- 6 cups water
- 2 tablespoons ginger, minced
- 2 cups potatoes, peeled and diced
- 3 cups kabocha, peeled and diced
- 1 carrot, peeled and diced
- 1 onion, diced
- 1/2 cup scallions, chopped

Instructions:

1. Transfer the bones and vegetables to your stockpot.
2. Top with enough water to cover then allow to come to a boil on high heat slowly.
3. Switch to low heat and simmer for at least 30 minutes.
4. Set and pour the mixture through a fine-mesh strainer into a large bowl.
5. Taste and season with salt.
6. Serve hot.
7. Enjoy!

Nutrition: Calories: 216, Fat: 1g, Carbs: 37g, Fiber: 4g, Protein: 8g

163. Pork Stock

Preparation Time: 15 minutes | **Cooking Time:** 12 hours | **Servings:** 8

Ingredients:

- 2 Pounds pork bones, roasted
- 1 onion, chopped in quarters
- 2 celery stalks, chopped in half
- 2 carrots, chopped in half
- 3 whole garlic cloves
- 2 bay leaves
- 1 tablespoon salt
- Filtered water (enough to cover bones)

Instructions:

1. Transfer the bones and vegetables to your stockpot.
2. Top with enough water to cover then allow to come to a boil on high heat slowly.
3. Set to low heat and simmer for 12 hours.
4. Set and pour the mixture through a fine-mesh strainer into a large bowl.
5. Taste and season with salt.
6. Serve hot.
7. Enjoy!

Nutrition: Calories: 69, Fat: 4g, Carbs: 1g, Fiber: 0.1g, Protein: 6g

164. Slow Cooker Pork Bone Broth

Preparation Time: 15 minutes | **Cooking Time:** 24 hours | **Servings:** 12

Ingredients:

- 2 pounds pork bones, roasted
- 1/2 onion, chopped
- 2 medium carrots, chopped
- 1 stalk celery, chopped
- 2 whole garlic cloves
- 1 bay leaf
- 1 tablespoon sea salt
- 1 teaspoon peppercorns
- 1/4 cup apple cider vinegar
- Filtered water (enough to cover bones)

Instructions:

1. Transfer all the ingredients to your slow cooker.
2. Top with enough water to cover then allow to come to a boil on high heat slowly.
3. Switch to low heat and simmer for at least 24 hours.
4. Set and pour the mixture through a fine-mesh strainer into a large bowl.
5. Taste and season with salt.
6. Serve hot.
7. Enjoy!

Nutrition: Calories: 65, Fat: 2g, Carbs: 7g, Fiber: 4g, Protein: 6g

165. Brandy java ice

Preparation Time: 2 minutes | **Cooking time:** 2 minutes | **Total time:** 4 minutes | **Servings:** 2

Ingredients:

- Four scoops of vanilla ice cream large
- 2 oz brandy
- Two teaspoons of ground coffee, not instant granules

Instructions:

1. In a blender, combine all of the ingredients and blend until smooth.
2. Enjoy!

Nutrition: Calories 339, Carbs 21g, Protein 5g, Fat 15g, Cholesterol 10 mg

166. Apple raisin pancakes

Preparation time: 10 minutes | **Cooking time:** 30 minutes | **Total time:** 40 minutes | **Servings:** 4

Ingredients:

- Two eggs
- One cup unsweetened applesauce
- One teaspoon cinnamon
- Two teaspoons brown sugar
- One cup wheat flour
- ½ cup white flour
- Two teaspoons baking powder
- Two teaspoons vanilla
- ½ cup golden, seedless raisins
- Non-stick cooking spray

Instructions:

1. Whisk the eggs in a medium mixing basin until light and frothy.
2. Stir in the applesauce, cinnamon, sugar, flours, baking powder, vanilla, and raisins until smooth.
3. Over medium heat, heat a griddle or a pan. We are using nonstick frying spray, coat the pan.
4. Pour approximately 1/4 cup of batter each pancake onto a heated pan.
5. Cook until the pancakes' edges begin to boil.
6. Cook until golden on the other side.
7. If desired, top the pancakes with more applesauce.

Nutrition: Calories 55, Carbs 10g, Protein 13g, Fat 1g, Cholesterol 10 mg

167. Banana and blueberry fritters

Preparation time: 10 minutes | **Cooking time:** 5 minutes | **Total time:** 15 minutes | **Servings:** 6

Ingredients:

- Two ripe bananas
- 1/4 - 1/2 cup buckwheat flour (or plain flour)
- 1/4 cup blueberries
- Pinch of cinnamon (optional)

- One tablespoon coconut oil for frying

Instructions:
1. After mashing the bananas, add the flour and cinnamon.
2. Stir in the blueberries until they are evenly distributed.
3. Heat the coconut oil in a nonstick frying pan over high heat.
4. Reduce the heat to medium-low and pour one tablespoon of batter into the frying pan for each fritter.
5. Fry fritters until both sides are golden brown.
6. Remove the fritters from the pan and set them aside to cool slightly before serving.

Nutrition: Calories 62, Carbs 13g, protein 1g, Fat 2g, Cholesterol 18 mg

168. Banana and oat cookies

Preparation time: 10 minutes | **Cooking time:** 15 minutes | **Total time:** 25 minutes | **Servings:** 15

Ingredients:
- 2 ripe bananas
- 165g 1 3/4 cup oats

Instructions:
1. Preheat the oven to 180°c (350°f)/gas mark 4 and line a baking tray/sheet with parchment or baking paper.
2. Mash the bananas well in a large mixing basin until smooth. Mix in the oats until they are completely mixed.
3. To taste, add any other ingredients
4. Form tablespoon-sized cookies and put them on a baking sheet lined with parchment paper. (be careful to create cookie forms rather than balls, since they won't expand into shape like regular cookies)
5. Bake for about 15 minutes, or until golden brown and firm.
6. Allow time for the food to cool before eating.

Nutrition: Calories 55, Carbs 11g, Protein 1g, Fat 1g, Cholesterol 11mg

169. Sweet potato pancakes

Preparation time: 5 minutes | **Cooking time:** 12 minutes | **Total time:** 17 minutes | **Servings:** 13

Ingredients:
- 125 gram (1/2 cup) of sweet potato puree and mashed sweet potato
- Two eggs
- 3/4 tablespoon ground cinnamon (optional)
- 1/4 tablespoon ground ginger (optional)
- One tablespoon coconut oil (for frying)

Instructions:
1. Whisk the eggs and sweet potato together in a large mixing basin until thoroughly combined. Stir in the cinnamon and ginger (if using) until well combined.
2. Heat the oil in a frying pan over medium heat.
3. Spoon one spoonful of the mixture into the pan (little pancakes work best) and continue until the pan is completely filled.
4. Reduce the heat to medium/low and continue to cook for an additional 2 to 3 minutes.
5. Cook until done on the other side (approx 2-3 mins)
6. Repeat till you've used up all of the mixtures.

Nutrition: Calories 41, Carbs 2g, Protein 1g, Fat 1g, Cholesterol 25 mg

170. Lentil spinach pancakes

Preparation time: 5 minutes | **Cooking time:** 10 minutes | **Total time:** 15 minutes | **Servings:** 14

Ingredients:
- 180g (1 cup) red split lentils
- 1/3 cup water
- One garlic clove, minced
- One carrot, grated
- 1/4 tablespoon ground cumin
- 1/2 tablespoon smoked paprika

- Two handfuls of baby spinach (finely chopped into ribbons)
- Two tablespoon fresh lemon juice
- 1/4 tablespoon salt*
- One tablespoon oil (for frying)

Instructions:

1. Cover the lentils with water in a mixing dish. Allow soaking for at least one night.
2. Drain the lentils and combine them with the water in a blender or food processor. Blend until the batter is smooth. You may discover that you need to add additional water; if so, do so.)
3. Heat 1/2 tablespoon of the oil in a frying pan over medium-high heat. Reduce the heat to medium-low and sauté the carrot, garlic, smoked paprika, cumin, and spinach until softened (around 4-5 mins).
4. Combine the lentil batter, the sautéed veggies, and the lemon juice in a large mixing basin.
5. Over medium-high heat, heat a nonstick frying pan.
6. Add a sprinkle of oil when the pan is heated (or alternatively, use spray oil).
7. Place a spoonful of batter in the pan and spread it out with the back of your spoon (to make them thinner). To fill the pan, repeat the process.
8. Cook each side for at least 2 minutes (this will vary depending on the pan, heat and how thin your pancake is).
9. Look for bubbles to develop, and your pancakes should be able to be easily flipped.
10. Remove the pancakes from the pan and continue with the rest of the batter.
11. Serve

Nutrition: Calories 58, Carbs 9g, Protein 4g, Fat 1g, Cholestero 19 mg

171. Chickpea pancakes recipe

Preparation time: 10 minutes | **Cooking time:** 15 minutes | **Total time:** 25 minutes | **Servings:** 23

Ingredients:

- 1 cup (120g) chickpea flour
- 1 ½ cups 375ml water
- Two tablespoons of olive oil *see note 1
- 1 carrot, finely grated
- 1/4 red capsicum, finely chopped
- 1 spring onion, finely chopped
- 1/4 tablespoon turmeric
- 1/4 tablespoon cumin
- Two tablespoons of chopped coriander (cilantro)
- 1/4 tablespoon salt

Instructions:

1. Combine the chickpea flour and water in a mixing basin, constantly stirring to create a smooth, lump-free batter. Set aside.
2. Heat 1/2 tablespoon of the oil in a frying pan over medium-high heat. Combine the carrot, onion, turmeric, and cumin in a mixing bowl. Reduce the heat to medium-low and continue to simmer until the vegetables are softened (around 4-5 mins)
3. Combine the carrot mixture, chopped coriander, and salt in the chickpea batter (if using). Stir until everything is well mixed.
4. Over medium-high heat, heat a nonstick frying pan. When the pan is heated, pour in the olive oil (or alternatively, use spray oil). Place a tablespoon of batter in the pan and spread it out with the back of your spoon (to make them thinner). To fill the pan, repeat the process. (*please see note 3)
5. Cook each side for at least 2 minutes (this will vary depending on the pan, heat and how thin your pancake is). Look for bubbles to develop (as seen above), and your pancakes should be able to be easily flipped.
6. Remove the pancakes from the pan and repeat the process with the remaining batter.

Nutrition: Caloroies 32, Carbs 3g, Protein 1g, Fat 1g, Cholesterol 27 mg

172. Veggie chickpea sticks

Preparation time: 10 minutes | **Cooking time:** 15 minutes | **Total time:** 25 minutes | **Servings:** 6

Ingredients:

- 55 g (1/2 cup) grated carrots
- Two tablespoon chia
- 400 g can chickpeas (drained and washed)
- One tablespoon cream cheese
- 60 (1/2 cup) grated cheddar cheese
- One tablespoon olive oil
- One handful of spinach leaves (chopped)
- 60 g (1/2 cup) frozen peas
- 1/2 tablespoon smoked paprika
- 1/2 tablespoon mixed dried herbs

Instructions:

1. Preheat oven to 180°c/350°f/gas 4 and line two baking pans with reusable baking sheets.
2. Squeeze as much juice as possible from the carrots. Reserving the carrot juice, add water to produce a total of 80ml (1/3 cup) liquid.
3. Set aside the chia and carrot juice combination.
4. In a mixing bowl, combine all of the remaining ingredients and mix until smooth. Add the chia mixture and pulse until well combined.
5. Form a finger out of about a third of a spoonful of the mixture (alternatively, you could make cookie shape or nuggets). Repeat until the mixture is completed.
6. Bake for 15 minutes.

Nutrition: Calories 139, Carbs 5g, Protein 8g, Fat 6g, Cholesterol 31 mg

173. Apricot honey oatmeal

Preparation time: 5 minutes | **Cooking time:** 5 minutes | **Total time:** 10 minutes | **Servings:** 1

Ingredients:

- 1 cup water or milk or almond milk
- 1/4 cup dried apricots, chopped
- 1/2 cup rolled oats
- 1 tablespoon honey
- 1/4 teaspoon cinnamon

Instructions:

1. In a microwave-safe dish, combine the water or milk, apricots, honey, cinnamon, and oats.
2. Cook for about 2 minutes, stirring periodically until most of the liquid has been absorbed.

Nutrition: Calories 345, Carbs 1g, Protein 29g, Fat 9g, Cholesterol 105 mg

174. Asparagus and bean frittata

Preparation time: 20 minutes | **Cooking time:** 30 minutes | **Total time:** 50 minutes | **Servings:** 4

Ingredients:

- Two tablespoons olive oil
- One cup of chopped onion
- One minced garlic clove
- 14 oz drained and washed red, black, or white beans
- Four eggs 1 cup cooked and chopped asparagus
- A half teaspoon of salt
- 1/4 cup grated parmesan

Instructions:

1. Preheat the oven to 350°f.
2. One tablespoon olive oil, heated in a large oven-proof pan over medium-high heat cook until the onions, garlic, and red beans are tender (about 10 minutes). Place aside.
3. In a nice medium mixing bowl, combine eggs, salt, and asparagus; set aside.
4. Pour in the egg mixture and the remaining one tablespoon olive oil into the vegetable pan. Reduce the heat to medium-low and simmer for 10 to 15 minutes, or until the mixture is set and gently browned on the bottom.
5. Sprinkle the parmesan cheese on top of the mixture and broil for 3 to 5 minutes, or until the cheese is lightly browned and the eggs are cooked through.

Nutrition: Calories 446, Carbs 2g, Protein 43g, Fat 29g, Cholesterol 215 mg

175. Chocolate smoothie

Preparation time: 5 minutes | **Cooking time:** 0 minutes | **Total time:** 5 minutes | **Servings:** 2

Ingredients:

- Two scoops of chocolate-flavored whey protein
- Two cups of ice
- Two tablespoons southern comfort® liqueur (optional)
- ½ cup evaporated milk
- ¼ cup condensed milk
- ¼ teaspoon ground cinnamon
- Pinch of nutmeg

Instructions:

1. In a neat blender, combine all ingredients except the cinnamon and mix on high for 1–2 minutes, or until smooth.
2. To serve, top with whipped cream and sprinkle with cinnamon.

Nutrition: Calories 142, Carbs 17g, Protein 10g, Fat 4g, Cholesterol 120 mg

176. Orange and cinnamon biscotti

Preparation time: 10 minutes | **Cooking time:** 0 minutes | **Total time:** 10 minutes | **Servings:** 6

Ingredients:

- 1 cup sugar
- ½ cup unsalted butter, room temperature
- Two large eggs
- Two teaspoons grated orange peel
- One teaspoon vanilla extract
- Two cups all-purpose flour
- One teaspoon cream of tartar
- ½ teaspoon baking soda
- One teaspoon ground cinnamon
- ¼ teaspoon salt

Instructions:

1. Preheat the oven to 325 degrees fahrenheit.
2. Two baking sheets, sprayed with nonstick cooking spray

3. In a large mixing basin, combine the sugar and unsalted butter until thoroughly combined.
4. Add eggs one at a time, and mix thoroughly after each addition.
5. Mix in the orange peel and vanilla extract.
6. In a medium-sized mixing bowl, combine the flour, cream of tartar, baking soda, cinnamon, and salt.
7. Combine dry ingredients with butter mixture until everything is thoroughly mixed.
8. Cut the dough in half. Place one half on a prepared baking sheet. Form each half into a log shape 3 inches broad by three-quarters of an inch high using lightly floured hands. Bake for 35 minutes or until the dough logs are firm to the touch.
9. Take the dough logs out of the oven and put them aside to cool for 10 minutes.
10. Move logs to the work surface. Using a serrated knife, cut into 12-inch-thick slices on the diagonal. Place baking sheets cut side down on a baking sheet.
11. Bake for 12 minutes, or until the bottoms are brown.
12. Bake until the bottoms of the biscotti are brown, about twelve minutes more.
13. Place on a wire rack to cool before serving.

Nutrition: Calories 139, Carbs 33g, Protein 2g, Fat 6g, Cholesterol 27 mg

177. Banana bran muffins

Preparation time: 10 minutes | **Cooking time:** 30 minutes | **Total time:** 40 minutes

Servings: 12

Ingredients:

- 1 ½ cup all-bran cereal
- 2/3 cups milk
- Four eggs
- 1/4 cup canola oil
- 1 cup ripe banana, mashed (about two bananas)
- 1/2 cup brown sugar
- 1 cup whole wheat flour

- Two teaspoons baking powder
- 1/2 teaspoon salt

Instructions:
1. Preheat the oven to 400°f.
2. Set aside all-bran cereal and milk in a large mixing dish. Combine the eggs, oil, mashed banana, and brown sugar on a large mixing plate.
3. In a separate mixing bowl, whisk together the flour, baking powder, and salt. Stir in the dry ingredients until barely mixed with the banana mixture.
4. Bake 15 to 18 minutes, or until golden-brown and firm, in 12 greased or paper-lined muffin pans. Allow cooling completely before serving.

Nutrition: Calories 155, Carbs 4g, Protein 18g, Fat 4g, Cholesterol 172 mg

178. Banana breakfast smoothie

Preparation time: 10 minutes | **Cook time:** 5 minutes | **Total time:** 15 minutes | **Servings:** 1

Ingredients:
- One medium banana
- 1 cup milk, almond or regular
- 1/2 cup plain yogurt
- 1/4 cup 100% bran flakes
- One teaspoon vanilla extract
- Two teaspoons honey or agave syrup
- 1/2 cup ice
- One pinch cinnamon
- One pinch nutmeg

Instructions:
1. In a neat blender, combine all of the ingredients and mix on medium speed until smooth.
2. Garnish with cinnamon and/or nutmeg if desired.

Nutrition: Calories 58, Carbs 2g, Protein 3g, Fat 5g, Cholesterol 16 mg

179. Sweet & nutty bars

Preparation time: 15 minutes | **Cooking time:** 30 minutes | **Total time:** 45 minutes | **Servings:** 3

Ingredients:
- 2½ cups rolled oats, toasted
- ½ cup almonds
- ½ cup flax
- ½ cup peanut butter
- 1 cup dried cherries, blueberries or craisins®
- ½ cup honey

Instructions:
1. To toast the oats, place rolled oats on a baking sheet and bake for 10 minutes, or until golden brown.
2. Combine all of the ingredients in a large mixing bowl and stir until well mixed.
3. Press the protein mixture into a 9" × 9" pan that has been lightly oiled. Wrap in plastic wrap and place in the refrigerator for at least one hour or overnight.
4. Serve protein bars cut into appropriate squares.

Nutrition: Calories 283, Carbs 39g, Protein 7g, Fat 14g, Cholesterol 125 mg

180. Homemade herbed biscuits

Preparation time: 15 minutes | **Cooking time:** 0 minutes | **Total time:** 15 minutes | **Servings:** 4

Ingredients:
- 1¾ cups all-purpose flour
- One teaspoon cream of tartar
- ½ teaspoon baking soda
- ¼ cup mayonnaise
- ⅔ cup skim milk
- Three tablespoons chives or any other herb, fresh or dry to taste
- Nonstick cooking spray

Instructions:

1. Preheat the oven to 400 degrees (200 degrees celsius). Next, coat a cookie sheet with nonstick cooking spray.

2. In a large mixing basin, combine the flour, cream of tartar, and baking soda. Then, using a fork, stir in the mayonnaise until the mixture resembles coarse cornmeal.

3. Combine the milk and herbs in a separate bowl, then add to the flour mixture. Stir until everything is incorporated.

4. Place the heaping teaspoons of the mixture on the cookie sheet. 10 minutes in the oven

5. Place in the refrigerator until ready to use.

Nutrition: Calories 109, Carbs 15g, Protein 3g, Fat 4g, Cholesterol 152 mg

181. Spinach vegetable barley bean soup

Preparation Time: 20 minutes | **Cooking Time:** 60 minutes | **Total Time:** 80 minutes | **Servings:** 6

Ingredients:

- One tablespoon extra-virgin olive oil
- Two stalks of celery chopped
- One medium onion diced
- Two carrots chopped
- One medium leek white and pale green parts only washed thoroughly and thinly sliced
- One cup quick-cooking barley
- One tablespoon tomato paste
- 8 cups low sodium vegetable broth
- 15 oz cannellini beans or other beans rinsed and drained
- Two teaspoon sprigs of fresh thyme or one dried thyme
- One teaspoon stem fresh basil or one dried thyme
- Four handfuls of baby spinach

Instructions:

1. In a soup saucepan, heat the oil.

2. Cook until the celery, onion, carrots, and leeks are cooked, about 5 minutes, over medium heat.

3. Cook, constantly tossing, until the barley and tomato paste are covered and glossy, approximately 30 seconds.

4. Bring the broth, beans, thyme, and basil to a boil. Simmer for 1 hour on low heat.

5. Cook until the spinach is barely wilted (if you use Swiss chard or kale, it will take slightly longer to cook).

6. Take off the thyme branch and the wilted basil. Season with salt and taste.

Nutrition: Calories 277, Carns 47g, Protein 14g, Fat 5g, Cholesterol 221 mg

182. Blueberry Green Tea

Preparation Time: 5 minutes | **Cooking Time:** 5 minutes | **Servings:** 4

Ingredients:

- 1/2 cup fresh or frozen blueberries
- 1 quart water
- 2 bags green tea (caffeinated or decaffeinated)
- 1/3 cup honey, plus more if desired

Instructions:

1. In a saucepan over high heat, place the blueberries and water and bring to a boil.
2. Set the heat to low and stir for 5 minutes.
3. Detach from the heat and add the green tea bags.
4. Steep for 10 minutes.
5. Using a slotted spoon, set the tea bags and blueberries.
6. Attach the honey and stir until it dissolves.
7. Taste and add more honey, if desired. Serve hot.

Nutrition: Calories 95, Fat 0g, Carbs 26g, Fiber 1g, Protein 1g Sodium 7 mg

183. Homemade No Pulp Orange Juice

Preparation Time: 5 minutes | **Cooking Time:** 0 minutes | **Servings:** 1

Ingredients:

- 4 oranges

Instructions:

1. Lightly squeeze the oranges on a hard surface to soften the exterior. Slice each in half.
2. Squeeze each orange over a fine-mesh strainer.
3. Gently, press the pulp to extract all possible liquid.
4. Serve over ice.
5. Enjoy!

Nutrition: Calories: 50 Fat: 2 g Carbs: 11.5 g Protein: 0.8 g

184. Citrus Sports Drink

Preparation Time: 5 minutes | **Cooking Time:** 0 minutes | Servings: 8

Ingredients:

- 4 cups coconut water
- 4 large oranges juice (about 1 ½ cup), strained
- 2 tablespoons lemon juice, strained
- 2 tablespoons honey or maple syrup
- 1 teaspoon sea salt

Instructions:

1. Place the coconut water, orange juice, lemon juice, honey, and salt in a jug or pitcher.
2. Stir until the salt is dissolved.
3. Serve cold.

Nutrition: Calories: 59 Fat: 1 g Carbs: 14 g Fiber: 1 g Protein: 1 g Sodium: 304 mg

185. Pina Colada Infused Water

Preparation Time: 5 minutes + chilling time

Cooking Time: 0 minutes | **Servings:** 1

Ingredients:

- 1 cup peeled and thinly sliced pineapple
- 2 cups ice
- 6 cups Coconut Water

Instructions:

1. Pour out your pineapple into a large pitcher.
2. Top with ice.

3. Pour in water to the top and cover.
4. Refrigerate for 1 hour before serving.

Nutrition: Calories 1.3 Total Fat 0.0 g Carbohydrate 0.4 g Protein 0.0 g

186. Orange, Strawberry & Mint Infused Water

Preparation Time: 5 minutes + chilling time | **Cooking Time:** 0 minutes | **Servings:** 1

Ingredients:

- 2 oranges, cut into wedges
- ½ cup strawberries
- 4 leaves mint
- 6 cups water

Instructions:

1. Place all the ingredients into a pitcher.
2. Cover and allow to chill for a minimum of 2 hours or overnight.
3. Serve.

Nutrition: Calories 1.3 Total Fat 0.0 g Carbohydrate 0.4 g Protein 0.0 g

187. Watermelon Juice

Preparation Time: 5 minutes | **Cooking Time:** 0 minutes | **Serving:** 2

Ingredients

- 1 watermelon, peeled, deseeded, cubed
- 1 tablespoon date sugar
- ½ of key lime, juiced, zest
- 2 cups soft-jelly coconut water

Instructions:

1. Place watermelon pieces in a high-speed food processor or blender, add lime zest and juice, add date sugar and then pulse until smooth.
2. Take two tall glasses, fill them with watermelon mixture until two-third full, and then pour in coconut water.
3. Stir until mixed and then serve.
4. Storage instructions:
5. Divide drink between two jars or bottles, cover with a lid and then store the containers in the refrigerator for up to 3 days.

Nutrition: 55 Calories; 1.3 g Fats; 0.9 g Protein; 9.9 g Carbohydrates; 7 g Fiber.

188. Orange Juice

Preparation Time: 10 minutes | **Cooking Time:** 5 minutes | **Servings:** 1

Ingredients:

- 6 medium oranges; peeled, seeded, and pieced

Instructions:

1. In a juicer, add orange pieces and extract the juice according to manufacturer's Instructions.
2. Transfer into two glasses and serve immediately.

Nutrition: Calories 259 Fats 0.1 g Cholesterol 0 mg Carbs 64.9 g Fiber 13.3 g Protein 5.3 g

189. Key Lime Tea

Preparation Time: 5 minutes | **Cooking Time:** 5 minutes | **Servings:** 1

Ingredients:

- 1 sprig of dill weed
- 1/16 teaspoon cayenne pepper
- 1 tablespoon key lime juice
- 2 cups spring water

Instructions:

1. Take a medium saucepan, place it over medium-high heat, pour in water, and then bring it to a boil.
2. Boil for 5 minutes, and then strain the tea into a bowl.
3. Add lime juice stir until mixed and then stir in cayenne pepper.
4. Divide tea between two mugs and then serve

Nutrition: Calories 24, Fat 0g, Protein 0g, Carbs 0.5g, Fiber 0g

190. Strawberry Juice

Preparation Time: 10 minutes | **Cooking Time:** 5 minutes | **Servings:** 1

Ingredients:

- 2 cups fresh strawberries, hulled
- 1 teaspoon fresh key lime juice
- 2 cups chilled spring water

Instructions:

1. In a high-powered blender, put all Ingredients: and pulse well.
2. Through a strainer, strain the juice and transfer into 2 glasses.
3. Serve immediately.

Nutrition: Calories 46 Fats 0 g Cholesterol 0 mg Carbs 11.1 g Fiber 2.9 g Protein 1g

LUNCH

191. Healthier Apple Juice

Preparation Time: 5 minutes | **Cooking Time:** 0 minutes | **Servings:** 2

Ingredients:

- 8 medium apples, cored and quartered

Instructions:

1. Add the apples into a juicer and extract the juice according to the manufacturer's method.

2. Through a cheesecloth-lined sieve, strain the juice and transfer it into 2 glasses.
3. Serve immediately.

Nutrition: Calories: 164, Carbs: 123.6g, Protein: 2.4g, Fat: 1.6g, Sugar: 90g, Sodium: 123 mg, Fiber: 21.6g

192. Citrus Apple Juice

Preparation Time: 5 minutes | **Cooking Time:** 0 minutes | **Servings:** 2

Ingredients:

- 5 large apples, cored and chopped
- 1 small lemon
- 1 cup fresh orange juice

Instructions:
1. Attach all the ingredients in a blender and pulse until well combined.
2. Through a cheesecloth-lined sieve, strain the juice and transfer it into 2 glasses.
3. Serve immediately.

Nutrition: Calories: 148, Carbs: 90.6g, Protein: 2.4g, Fat: 1.3g, Sugar: 68.6g, Sodium: 6mg, Fiber: 14g

193. Richly Fruity Juice

Preparation Time: 15 minutes | **Cooking Time:** 10 minutes | **Servings:** 2

Ingredients:
- 5 large green apples, cored and sliced
- 2 cups seedless white grapes
- 2 teaspoon fresh lime juice

Instructions:
1. Set all ingredients into a juicer and extract the juice according to the manufacturer's method.
2. Through a cheesecloth-lined sieve, strain the juice and transfer it into 2 glasses.
3. Serve immediately.

Nutrition: Calories: 152, Carbs: 92.8g, Protein: 2.1g, Fat: 1.3g, Sugar: 73g, Sodium: 7 mg, Fiber: 14.3g

194. Delicious Grape Juice

Preparation Time: 15 minutes | **Cooking Time:** 0 minutes | **Servings:** 3

Ingredients:
- 2 cups white seedless grapes
- 1 ½ cup filtered water
- 6-8 ice cubes

Instructions:
1. Attach all the ingredients in a blender and pulse until well combined.
2. Through a cheesecloth-lined sieve, strain the juice and transfer it into 3 glasses.

3. Serve immediately.

Nutrition: Calories: 41, Carbs: 10.5g, Protein: 0.4g, Fat: 0.2g, Sugar: 10g, Sodium: 1 mg, Fiber: 10g

195. Lemony Grape Juice

Preparation Time: 15 minutes | **Cooking Time:** 0 minutes | **Servings:** 3

Ingredients:
- 4 cups seedless white grapes
- 2 tablespoons fresh lemon juice

Instructions:
1. Attach all the ingredients in a blender and pulse until well combined.
2. Through a cheesecloth-lined sieve, strain the juice and transfer it into 3 glasses.
3. Serve immediately.

Nutrition: Calories: 85, Carbs: 21.3g, Protein: 0.9g, Fat: 0.5g, Sugar: 20.1g, Sodium: 4 mg, Fiber: 1.1g

196. Holiday Special Juice

Preparation Time: 15 minutes | **Cooking Time:** 0 minutes | **Servings:** 4

Ingredients:
- 4 cups fresh cranberries
- 1 tablespoon fresh lemon juice
- 2 cups filtered water
- 1 teaspoon raw honey

Instructions:
1. Attach all the ingredients in a blender and pulse until well combined.
2. Through a cheesecloth-lined sieve, strain the juice and transfer it into 4 glasses.
3. Serve immediately.

Nutrition: Calories: 66, Carbs: 11.5g, Protein: 0g, Fat: 0g, Sugar: 5g, Sodium: 1 mg, Fiber: 4g

197. Vitamin C Rich Juice

Preparation Time: 15 minutes | **Cooking Time:** 0 minutes | **Servings:** 2

Ingredients:
- 8 oranges, peeled and sectioned

Instructions:

1. Add the orange sections into a juicer and extract the juice according to the manufacturer's method.
2. Through a cheesecloth-lined sieve, strain the juice and transfer it into 2 glasses.
3. Serve immediately.

Nutrition: Calories: 146, Carbs: 86.5g, Protein: 6.9g, Fat: 0.9g, Sugar: 68.8g, Sodium: 0 mg, Fiber: 17.7g

198. Incredible Fresh Juice

Preparation Time: 15 minutes | **Cooking Time:** 0 minutes | **Servings:** 4

Ingredients:

- 2 pounds carrots, trimmed and scrubbed
- 6 small oranges, peeled and sectioned

Instructions:

1. Add the carrots and orange sections into a juicer and extract the juice according to the manufacturer's method.
2. Through a cheesecloth-lined sieve, strain the juice and transfer it into 4 glasses.
3. Serve immediately.

Nutrition: Calories: 183, Carbs: 44.9g, Protein: 3.7g, Fat: 0.2g, Sugar: 29.1g, Sodium: 156 mg, Fiber: 10.2g

199. Favorite Summer Lemonade

Preparation Time: 15 minutes | **Cooking Time:** 0 minutes | **Servings:** 8

Ingredients:

- 8 cups filtered water
- 1/2 cup fresh lemon juice
- 1/4 teaspoon pure stevia extract
- Ice cubes, as required

Instructions:

- In a pitcher, place the water, lemon juice and stevia. Mix well.
- Through a cheesecloth-lined sieve, strain the lemonade in another pitcher.
- Refrigerate for 30-40 minutes.
- Set ice cubes in serving glasses and fill with lemonade.

- Serve chilled.

Nutrition: Calories: 4, Carbs: 0.3g, Protein: 0.1g, Fat: 0.1g, Sugar: 0.3g, Sodium: 3 mg, Fiber: 0.1g

200. Ultimate Fruity Punch

Preparation Time: 15 minutes | **Cooking Time:** 0 minutes | **Servings:** 12

Ingredients:

- 3 cups fresh pineapple juice
- 2 cups fresh orange juice
- 1 cup fresh ruby red grapefruit juice
- 1/4 cup fresh lime juice
- 2 cups seedless watermelon, cut into bite-sized chunks
- 2 cups fresh pineapple, cut into bite-sized chunks
- 2 oranges, peeled and cut into wedges
- 2 limes, quartered
- 1 lemon, sliced
- 2 (12 ounces) cans diet lemon-lime soda
- Crushed ice, as required

Instructions:

1. In a large pitcher, add all ingredients except for soda cans and ice. Stir to combine.
2. Set aside for 30 minutes.
3. Through a cheesecloth-lined sieve, strain the punch into another large pitcher.
4. Set the glasses with ice and top with punch about 3/4 of the mixture.
5. Add a splash of the soda and serve.

Nutrition: Calories: 95, Carbs: 23.4g, Protein: 1.3g, Fat: 0.3g, Sugar: 18.3g, Sodium: 152 mg, Fiber: 1.8g

201. Thirst Quencher Sports Drink

Preparation Time: 15 minutes | **Cooking Time:** 0 minutes | **Servings:** 8

Ingredients:

- 7 cups spring water
- 1 cup fresh apple juice
- 2-3 teaspoons fresh lime juice
- 2 tablespoons honey

- 1/4 teaspoon sea salt

Instructions:
1. In a large pitcher, add all ingredients and stir to combine.
2. Through a cheesecloth-lined sieve, strain the punch into another large pitcher.
3. Refrigerate to chill before serving.

Nutrition: Calories: 30, Carbs: 7.8g, Protein: 0.1g, Fat: 0g, Sugar: 7.3g, Sodium: 60 mg, Fiber: 0.1g

202. Refreshing Sports Drink

Preparation Time: 15 minutes | **Cooking Time:** 0 minutes | **Servings:** 9

Ingredients:
- 8 cups fresh cold water, divided
- 3/4 cup fresh orange juice
- 1/4 cup fresh lemon juice
- 1/4 cup fresh limes juice
- 3 tablespoons honey
- 1/2 teaspoon salt

Instructions:
1. In a large pitcher, add all ingredients and stir to combine.
2. Through a cheesecloth-lined sieve, strain the punch into another large pitcher.
3. Refrigerate to chill before serving.

Nutrition: Calories: 33, Carbs: 8.1g, Protein: 0.2g, Fat: 0.1g, Sugar: 7.6g, Sodium: 130 mg, Fiber: 0.1g

203. Perfect Sunny Day Tea

Preparation Time: 15 minutes | **Cooking Time:** 3 minutes | **Servings:** 6

Ingredients:
- 5 cups filtered water
- 5 green tea bags
- 1/4 cup fresh lemon juice, strained
- 1/4 cup fresh lime juice, strained
- 1/4 cup honey
- Ice cubes, as required

Instructions:
1. In a medium pan, add 2 cups of water and bring to a boil.
2. Set in the tea bags and turn off the heat.
3. Immediately, cover the pan and steep for 3-4 minutes.
4. With a large spoon, gently press the tea bags against the pan to extract the tea completely.
5. Detach the tea bags from the pan and discard them.
6. Set honey and stir until dissolved.
7. In a large pitcher, place the tea, lemon and lime juice and stir to combine.
8. Add the remaining cold water and stir to combine.
9. Refrigerate to chill before serving.
10. Attach ice cubes in serving glasses and fill with tea.
11. Serve chilled.

Nutrition: Calories: 46, Carbs: 12g, Protein: 0.1g, Fat: 0.1g, Sugar: 11.8g, Sodium: 3 mg, Fiber: 0.1g

204. Nutritious Green Tea

Preparation Time: 15 minutes | **Cooking Time:** 4 minutes | **Servings:** 4

Ingredients:
- 4 cups filtered water
- 4 orange peel strips
- 4 lemon peel strips
- 4 green tea bags
- 2 teaspoons honey

Instructions:
1. In a medium pan, add the water, orange, and lemon peel strips over medium-high heat and bring to a boil.
2. Set the heat to low and stir, uncovered, for about 10 minutes.
3. With a slotted spoon, remove the orange and lemon peel strips and discard them.
4. Attach in the tea bags and turn off the heat.
5. Immediately, cover the pan and steep for 3 minutes.

6. With a large spoon, gently press the tea bags against the pan to extract the tea completely.
7. Detach the tea bags from the pan and discard them.
8. Add honey and stir until dissolved.
9. Strain the tea in mugs and serve immediately.

Nutrition: Calories: 11, Carbs: 3g, Protein: 0g, Fat: 0g, Sugar: 2.9g, Sodium: 0 mg, Fiber: 0.1g

205. Simple Black Tea

Preparation Time: 10 minutes | **Cooking Time:** 3 minutes | **Servings:** 2

Ingredients:
- 2 cups filtered water
- 1/2 teaspoon black tea leaves
- 1 teaspoon honey

Instructions:
1. In a pan, add the water and bring to a boil.
2. Stir in the tea leaves and turn off the heat.
3. Immediately, cover the pan and steep for 3 minutes.
4. Add honey and stir until dissolved.
5. Strain the tea in mugs and serve immediately.

Nutrition: Calories: 11, Carbs: 2.9g, Protein: 0g, Fat: 0g, Sugar: 2.9g, Sodium: 123 mg, Fiber: 0g

206. Lemony Black Tea

Preparation Time: 10 minutes | **Cooking Time:** 3 minutes | **Servings:** 6

Ingredients:
- 1 tablespoon black tea leaves
- 1 lemon, sliced thinly
- 1 cinnamon stick
- 6 cups boiling water

Instructions:
1. In a large teapot, place the tea leaves, lemon slices and cinnamon stick.
2. Pour hot water over the ingredients and immediately cover the teapot.
3. Set aside for about 5 minutes to steep.

4. Strain the tea in mugs and serve immediately.

Nutrition: Calories: 1, Carbs: 0.2g, Protein: 0g, Fat: 0g, Sugar: 0.1g, Sodium: 0 mg, Fiber: 0.1g

207. Metabolism Booster Coffee

Preparation Time: 5 minutes | **Cooking Time:** 4 minutes | **Servings:** 1

Ingredients:
- 1/4 teaspoon coffee powder
- 1 ¼ cup filtered water
- 1 teaspoon fresh lemon juice
- 1 teaspoon honey

Instructions:
1. In a small pan, attach the water and coffee powder. Bring it to boil.
2. Cook for about 1 minute.
3. Detach from the heat and pour into a serving mug.
4. Add the honey and lemon juice then stir until dissolved
5. Serve hot.

Nutrition: Calories: 23, Carbs: 6g, Protein: 0.1g, Fat: 0g, Sugar: 5.9g, Sodium: 1 mg, Fiber: 0g

208. Best Homemade Broth

Preparation Time: 15 minutes | **Cooking Time:** 2 hours 5 minutes | **Servings:** 8

Ingredients:
- 1 (3 pounds) chicken, cut into pieces
- 5 medium carrots
- 4 celery stalks with leaves
- 6 fresh thyme sprigs
- 6 fresh parsley sprigs
- Salt to taste
- 9 cups cold water

Instructions:
1. In a large pan, attach all the ingredients over medium-high heat and bring to a boil.
2. Set the heat to medium-low and stir, covered for about 2 hours, skimming the foam from the surface occasionally.

3. Through a fine-mesh sieve, strain the broth into a large bowl.
4. Serve hot.

Nutrition: Calories: 275, Carbs: 4.3g, Protein: 49.7g, Fat: 5.2g, Sugar: 2g, Sodium: 160 mg, Fiber: 1.2g

209. Clean Testing Broth

Prep Time: 5 hours 50minutes | **Cooking Time:** 15 minutes | **Servings:** 10

Ingredients:
- 4 pounds chicken bones
- Salt to taste
- 10 cups filtered water
- 2 tablespoons apple cider vinegar
- 1 lemon, quartered
- 3 bay leaves
- 3 teaspoons ground turmeric
- 2 tablespoons peppercorns

Instructions:
1. Preheat the oven to 400°F.
2. Arrange the bones onto a large baking sheet and sprinkle with salt.
3. Roast for about 45 minutes.
4. Detach from the oven and transfer the bones into a large pan.
5. Add the remaining ingredients and stir to combine.
6. Put the pan over medium-high heat and bring to a boil.
7. Set the heat to low and stir, covered for about 4-5 hours, skimming the foam from the surface occasionally.
8. Through a fine-mesh sieve, strain the broth into a large bowl.
9. Serve hot.

Nutrition: Calories: 140, Carbs: 0.6g, Protein: 25g, Fat: 2.6g, Sugar: 0.1g, Sodium: 73 mg, Fiber: 0.1g

210. Healing Broth

Preparation Time: 10 hours 25 minutes | **Cooking Time:** 15 minutes | **Servings:** 12

Ingredients:
- 3 tablespoons extra-virgin olive oil
- 2 ½ pounds chicken bones
- 4 celery stalks, chopped roughly
- 3 large carrots, peeled and chopped roughly
- 1 bay leaf
- 1 tablespoon black peppercorns
- 2 whole cloves
- 1 tablespoon apple cider vinegar
- Warm water, as required

Instructions:
1. In a Dutch oven, heat the oil over medium-high heat and sear the bones for about 3-5 minutes or until browned.
2. With a slotted spoon, transfer the bones into a bowl.
3. In the same pan, add the celery stalks and carrots. Cook for about 15 minutes, stirring occasionally.
4. Add browned bones, bay leaf, black peppercorns, cloves and vinegar. Stir to combine.
5. Add enough warm water to cover the bones mixture completely and bring to a gentle boil.
6. Set the heat to low and stir, covered for about 8-10 hours, skimming the foam from the surface occasionally.
7. Through a fine-mesh sieve, strain the broth into a large bowl.
8. Serve hot.

Nutrition: Calories: 67, Carbs: 2g, Protein: 5.7g, Fat: 4.1g, Sugar: 1g, Sodium: 29 mg, Fiber: 0.5g

211. Veggie Lover's Broth

Preparation Time: 2 hours 5 minutes | **Cooking Time:** 15 minutes | **Servings:** 10

Ingredients:
- 4 carrots, peeled and chopped roughly
- 4 celery stalks, chopped roughly
- 3 parsnips, peeled and chopped roughly

- 2 large potatoes, peeled and chopped roughly
- 1 medium beet, trimmed and chopped roughly
- 1 large bunch fresh parsley
- 1 (1 inch) piece fresh ginger, sliced
- Filtered water, as required

Instructions:

1. In a pan, add all the ingredients over medium-high heat.
2. Add enough water to cover the veggie mixture and bring to a boil.
3. Set the heat to low and simmer, covered for about 2-3 hours.
4. Through a fine-mesh sieve, strain the broth into a large bowl.
5. Serve hot.

Nutrition: Calories: 82, Carbs: 19g, Protein: 1.9g, Fat: 0.2g, Sugar: 3.9g, Sodium: 37 mg, Fiber: 3.7g

212. Brain Healthy Broth

Preparation Time: 12 hours 5 minutes | **Cooking Time:** 10 minutes | **Servings:** 6

Ingredients:

- 12 cups filtered water
- 2 pounds non-oily fish heads and bones
- 1/4 cup apple cider vinegar
- Sea salt to taste

Instructions:

1. In a large pan, attach all the ingredients over medium-high heat.
2. Add enough water to cover the veggie mixture and bring to a boil.
3. Set the heat to low and simmer, covered for about 10-12 hours, skimming the foam from the surface occasionally.
4. Through a fine-mesh sieve, strain the broth into a large bowl.
5. Serve hot.

Nutrition: Calories: 75, Carbs: 0.1g, Protein: 13.4g, Fat: 1.7g, Sugar: 0g, Sodium: 253 mg, Fiber: 0g

213. Minerals Rich Broth

Preparation Time: 15 minutes | **Cooking Time:** 2 hours 25 minutes | **Servings:** 8

Ingredients:

- 5-7 pounds non-oily fish carcasses and heads
- 2 tablespoons olive oil
- 3 carrots, scrubbed and chopped roughly
- 2 celery stalks, chopped roughly

Instructions:

1. In a pan, heat the oil over medium-low heat and cook the carrots and celery for about 20 minutes, stirring occasionally.
2. Add the fish bones and enough water to cover by 1-inch and stir to combine.
3. Set the heat to medium-high and bring to a boil.
4. Set the heat to low, covered, for about 1-2 hours, skimming the foam from the surface occasionally.
5. Through a fine-mesh sieve, strain the broth into a large bowl.
6. Serve hot.

Nutrition: Calories: 113, Carbs: 2.5g, Protein: 13.7g, Fat: 5.2g, Sugar: 1.2g, Sodium: 234 mg, Fiber: 0.7g

214. Holiday Favorite Gelatin

Preparation Time: 15 minutes | **Cooking Time:** 2 hours 25 minutes | **Servings:** 6

Ingredients:

- 1 tablespoon grass-fed gelatin powder
- 1 ¾ cup fresh apple juice, warmed
- 1/4 cup boiling water
- 1-2 drops fresh lemon juice

Instructions:

1. In a medium bowl, pour in the tablespoon of gelatin powder.
2. Add just enough warm apple juice to cover the gelatin and stir well.
3. Set aside for about 2-3 minutes or until it forms a thick syrup.

4. Add 1/4 cup of the boiling water and stir until gelatin is dissolved completely.
5. Add the remaining juice and lemon juice then stir well.
6. Transfer the mixture into a parchment paper-lined baking dish and refrigerate for 2 hours or until the top is firm before serving.

Nutrition: Calories: 40, Carbs: 8.2g, Protein: 1.9g, Fat: 0.1g, Sugar: 7g, Sodium: 5 mg, Fiber: 0.2g

215. Green Chicken Soup

Preparation Time: 15 minutes | **Cooking Time:** 25 minutes | **Servings:** 12

Ingredients:
- Two quarts of chicken broth or stock
- 1 ½ pound boneless, skinless chicken breast
- Two celery stalks, chopped
- Two cups of green beans, cut into 1-inch pieces
- One and a half cups peas, fresh or frozen
- Two cups' asparagus, cut into 1-inch pieces, tops and middles (avoid tough ends)
- One cup of diced green onions
- 4-6 cloves garlic, minced
- Two cups of fresh spinach leaves, chopped and packed
- One bunch watercress, chopped with large stems removed
- 1/2 cup of fresh parsley leaves, chopped
- 1/3 cup of fresh basil leaves, chopped
- One teaspoon salt

Instructions:
1. In a large saucepan, boil the chicken broth over medium-high heat. Bring the chicken breasts to a simmer in the sauce. The cooking time is 15 minutes.
2. Combine the celery, green beans, peas, asparagus, onions, garlic, salt in a mixing bowl. Simmer for 5-10 minutes, or until the vegetables are soft, then remove from the heat.

3. Remove the chicken breasts and shred or cut them into bite-sized pieces with two forks. Back to the pot.
4. Combine the spinach, watercress, parsley, and basil in a mixing bowl. Season with salt to taste.

Nutrition: Calories: 105, Carbs: 7g, Protein: 15g, Fat: 2g, Cholesterol: 134 mg

216. Peach Milkshake

Preparation Time: 5 minutes | **Cooking Time:** 5 minutes | **Servings:** 4

Ingredients:
- 6 ripe peaches pitted, skins on
- 7 scoops of vanilla ice cream
- 3 tablespoons granulated sugar
- ½ teaspoon vanilla extract
- 1 pinch salt
- Optional: whipped cream and maraschino cherries

Instructions:
1. Remove the pits from the peaches and cut them in half.
2. Combine the peaches, ice cream, sugar, vanilla, and salt in a large blender.
3. Puree till smooth, covered.

Nutrition: Calories: 397, caarbs: 62g, Protein: 7 g, Fat: 9g, Cholesterol: 14 mg

217. Great Lemon Gelatin

Preparation Time: 10 minutes | **Cooking Time:** 0 minutes | **Servings:** 8

Ingredients:
- 3 tbsp. grass-fed gelatin powder
- 3 C. cold water, divided
- 1½ C. boiling water
- 1 C. plus 2 tbsp. fresh lemon juice
- 2 tsp. stevia extract

Instructions:
1. In a bowl, soak the gelatin in 1½ C. of cold water. Set aside for about 5 minutes.
2. Add boiling water and stir until gelatin is dissolved.

3. Add the remaining cold water, lemon juice and stevia extract and stir until dissolved completely.
4. Divide the mixture into 2 baking dishes and refrigerate until set before serving.

Nutrition: Calories: 24; Carbs: 0.7g; Protein: 4.4g; Fat: 0.3g; Sugar: 0.7g; Sodium: 11mg; Fiber: 0.1g

218. Jugo Verde (Green Juice)

Preparation Time: 10 minutes | **Cooking Time:** 0 minutes | **Servings:** 5

Ingredients:

- 2 cups orange juice
- 1 1/2 cups fresh pineapple chunks
- 1/2 nopal cactus paddle chopped (or substitute 1 celery stalk)
- 1 large cucumber with peel, cut into chunks
- 1/4 cup packed parsley or cilantro
1. **Instructions:**
2. In a blender, combine all of the ingredients. Add a bit of salt, close the lid tightly, and puree until smooth.
3. When the mixture is green and frothy, serve immediately or strain over a screen to remove the pulp.

Nutrition: Calories: 67, Carabs: 12g, Protein: 2 g, Fat: 2g, Cholesterol: 86 mg

219. Decaf Peppermint Tea

Preparation Time: 5 minutes | **Cooking Time:** 0 minutes | **Servings:** 1

Ingredients:

- 1 Teabag Peppermint Tea
- 8 oz water
- 2 tablespoon Artificial sweetener optional

Instructions:
1. Fill a coffee cup halfway with teabags.
2. Place a teapot on the burner with the water. Wait for the whistle to blow. Pour it over the teabag.
3. -OR- Place the microwavable coffee cup in the microwave and heat for 30 seconds.

Microwave for 2 minutes or until the desired temperature is reached.
4. Allow the tea to infuse for a few seconds in the water.
5. Stir in the artificial sweetener with a spoon until it dissolves. If the water is too hot for you, add an ice cube. Slurp, slurp, slurp!

Nutrition: Calories: 220, Carbs: 12g, Protein: 2g, Fat: 2g, Cholesterol: 86 mg

220. Grape Juice

Preparation Time: 10 minutes | **Cooking Time:** 5 minutes | **Servings:** 1

Ingredients:

- 2 cups seedless red grapes
- ½ lime
- 2 cups spring water

Instructions:
1. In a blender, put all Ingredients: and pulse well.
2. Through a strainer, strain the juice and transfer into 2 glasses.
3. Serve immediately.

Nutrition: Calories 63, Fats 0.1g Cholesterol 0 mg, Carbs 16.2g, Fiber 0.9g, Protein 0.6g

221. Mango Juice

Preparation Time: 10 minutes | **Cooking Time:** 5 minutes | **Servings:** 1

Ingredients:

- 4 cups mangoes; peeled, pitted, and chopped
- 2 cups spring water

Instructions:
1. In a blender, put all Ingredients: and pulse well.
2. Through a strainer, strain the juice and transfer into 4 glasses.
3. Serve immediately.

Nutrition: Calories 99, Fats 0.2g, Cholesterol 0 mg, Carbs 24.7g, Fiber 2.6g, Protein 1.4g

222. Apple & Kale Juice

Preparation Time: 10 minutes | **Cooking Time:** 5 minutes | **Servings:** 1

Ingredients:

- 2 large green apples, cored and sliced
- 4 cups fresh kale leaves
- ¼ cup fresh parsley leaves
- 1 tablespoon fresh ginger, peeled
- 1 key lime, peeled and seeded
- 1 cup chilled spring water

Instructions:

1. In a blender, put all Ingredients: and pulse well.
2. Through a strainer, strain the juice and transfer into 2 glasses.
3. Serve immediately.

Nutrition: Calories 196, Fats 0.1g, Cholesterol 0 mg, Carbs 47.9g, Fiber 8.2g, Protein 5.2g

223. Vanilla Apple Pie Protein Shake

Preparation Time: 5 minutes | **Cooking Time:** 0 minutes | **Servings:** 2

Ingredients:

- 1 cup low-fat milk
- 1 scoop (1/4 cup) vanilla protein powder
- 1 small apple, peeled, cored, and chopped.
- 1 teaspoon vanilla extract
- 2 teaspoons ground cinnamon
- ½ teaspoon ground nutmeg
- 5 ice cubes

Instructions:

1. In a blender, combine protein powder, apple, vanilla protein powder, cinnamon, nutmeg, ice cubes, and milk.
2. Blend until powder is well dissolved and no longer visible for at least 3-4 minutes.
3. Serve immediately or refrigerate for later usage.

Nutrition: Calories: 123, Protein: 14g, Total Carbs:14g, Dietary Fibers: 1g, Total Fat: 1g

SNACK

224. Roasted Carrot Sticks in a Honey Garlic Marinade

Preparation Time: 10 minutes | **Cooking Time:** 25-30 minutes | **Servings:** 4

Ingredients:

- 1 bunch carrots, halved lengthways
- 2 garlic cloves, minced
- 1 tablespoon honey
- 1 tablespoon lemon juice (alternatively apple cider vinegar)
- 40 g butter
- 3 tablespoons parsley, chopped

Instructions:

1. Place the halved carrots on baking paper.
2. For the marinade, first, melt the butter. Add the garlic, honey and lemon/vinegar, mix well.
3. Set over the carrots so that they are all covered with the marinade.
4. Bake in the oven at 180ºC for about 25-30 minutes. Turn regularly.
5. Garnish with parsley and serve with herb quark or yogurt.

Nutrition: Calories: 216, Fat: 1g, Carbs: 37g, Fiber: 4g, Protein: 8g

225. Apple and Pistachio Salad on Spinach

Preparation Time: 10 minutes | **Cooking Time:** 5 minutes | **Servings:** 4

Ingredients:

- 1 ½ tablespoon butter
- 1 pack baby spinach
- 1 apple, diced small
- 1 teaspoon ginger, grated

- 60 g pistachios
- 1 tablespoon mustard
- 40 g Ricotta cheese
- 1 tablespoon honey
- 1 tablespoon lemon juice
- Salt and pepper

Instructions:

1. Dissolve the butter in the pan, add the apple pieces, honey, ginger and mustard.
2. Fry over medium heat until the apples are lightly caramelized for (about 3-5 minutes).
2. Wash the spinach and divide between 2 bowls.
3. Place the apples on the salad, garnish with Ricotta and season with a little lemon juice, pistachios, salt and pepper as desired.

Nutrition: Calories: 37, Fat: 1g, Carbs: 3g, Fiber: 0g, Protein: 4g, Sodium: 58 mg

226. Tomato Cashew Pesto

Preparation Time: 10 minutes | **Cooking Time:** 0 minutes | **Servings:** 4

Ingredients:

- 95 g dried tomatoes
- 50 g cashew nuts
- 2 garlic cloves, minced
- 5 tablespoons extra-virgin olive oil
- 1 tablespoon oregano
- Parmesan cheese (optional)
- Salt and pepper

Instructions:

1. Puree the garlic, tomatoes, oregano, oil, and cashews with a hand blender until the mixture is even.
2. Mix with whole-wheat pasta and serve.
3. Flavor to taste with salt and pepper then garnish with Parmesan.

Nutrition: Calories: 29, Fat: 1g, Carbs: 2g, Fiber: 1g, Protein: 1g

227. Sweet Potato Aioli

Preparation Time: 10 minutes | **Cooking Time:** 35 minutes | **Servings:** 4

Ingredients:

- 1 sweet potato
- 3 tablespoons olive oil
- 1 tablespoon mayonnaise
- 2-3 garlic cloves
- 1 tablespoon parsley, chopped

Instructions:

1. Bake the sweet potato in the oven until it is soft (about 35 minutes at 200°C).
2. Set out of the oven, let cool down briefly, peel and mix with 1 tablespoon of mayonnaise, oil, garlic and parsley (use a hand blender).

Nutrition: Calories: 75, Carbs: 0.1g, Protein: 13.4g, Fat: 1.7g, Sugar: 0g, Sodium: 253 mg

228. Eggplant paste

Preparation Time: 10 minutes | **Cooking Time:** 25 minutes | **Servings:** 4

Ingredients:

- 1 eggplant
- 2 tablespoons tahini
- 2 garlic cloves
- 1 tablespoon lemon juice
- A pinch of turmeric
- 30 g black olives
- 1 tablespoon olive oil
- 1 tablespoon parsley, chopped
- Salt and pepper

Instructions:

1. Grill the eggplant in the oven at 190°C for at least 20 minutes (until it is soft!).
2. Let cool and remove the skin. Set the eggplant in a container and use a fork to mash the meat into a paste.
3. Add the tahini, garlic, turmeric, olives, olive oil and lemon juice; mix well. Season to taste with salt and pepper.
4. Garnish with parsley.

Nutrition: Calories: 75, Carbs: 0.1g, Protein: 13.4g, Fat: 1.7g, Sugar: 0g, Sodium: 253 mg

229. Catalan Style Spinach

Preparation Time: 10 minutes | **Cooking Time:** 5 minutes | **Servings:** 4

Ingredients:

- 200 g fresh spinach
- 2 garlic cloves
- 2 tablespoons cashew nuts
- 3 tablespoons raisins
- 2-3 tablespoons extra-virgin olive oil

Instructions:

1. Warm the oil and fry the garlic over medium heat.
2. After 1-2 minutes add the cashews and raisins. Fry for another minute.
3. Add the spinach (do not boil!), stir well.
4. Serve with Goat cheese and whole meal baguette.

Nutrition: Calories: 59, Fat: 1g, Carbs: 14g, Fiber: 1g, Protein: 1g, Sodium: 304 mg

230. Energy Balls

Preparation Time: 10 minutes | **Cooking Time:** 0 minutes | **Servings:** 4

Ingredients:

- 120 g oat bran
- 80 ml honey
- 120 g coconut flakes (health food store, drugstore)
- 60 g choice nuts, ground
- 60 g chia seeds, ground
- 40 g dark chocolate, finely chopped
- 1 teaspoon yeast flakes
- 1 teaspoon sea salt

Instructions:

1. Mix all ingredients well in a container. Let the chia seeds soak for a moment.
2. Set small balls and put them in the fridge for about 45 minutes.

Nutrition: Calories: 75, Carbs: 0.1g, Protein: 13.4g, Fat: 1.7g, Sugar: 0g, Sodium: 253 mg

231. Larabar snack bar

Preparation Time: 5 minutes | **Cooking Time:** 5 minutes | **Total time:** 10 minutes | **Servings:** 12

Ingredients:

- 2 cup raw almonds
- 3/4 cup pitted dates packed
- 1 cup dried unsweetened apples
- 1/4 cup raisins packed
- 1/2 teaspoon cinnamon
- 1/4 teaspoon sea salt

Instructions:

1. In a food processor, combine all of the ingredients and process until finely chopped and sticky.
2. Line an 8-inch baking dish with wax paper, leaving enough to hang over the sides to cover the mixture. Fill the dish halfway with the mixture and top with wax paper. Press or roll out the ingredients until it is smooth.
3. Remove the wax paper and bars from the pan and cut them into 12 equal bars. Wrap each piece in wax paper and store it in an airtight container.

Nutrition: Calories 153, Carbs 17g, Protein 17g, Fat 27g, Cholesterol 89 mg

232. Kulfi indian ice cream

Preparation Time: 10 minutes | **Cooking Time:** 160 minutes | **Total time:** 170 minutes | **Servings:** 16

Ingredients:

- 2 cups heavy cream
- 14 ounces can sweeten condensed milk
- 2 teaspoon ground cardamom
- 1 teaspoon vanilla extract
- ½ cup chopped pistachios
- 1 pinch saffron + 1 tbs warm water

Instructions:

1. In a small dish, combine 1 tablespoon hot tap water. Allow a pinch of saffron to soak to absorb its color and taste.

2. Meanwhile, prepare an electric mixer fitted with a whip attachment. Pour in the heavy cream, cardamom powder, and vanilla essence. Whip the mixture at high speed until firm peaks form.

3. Using a rubber spatula, scrape the bowl. Then add the saffron and water and mix well.

4. Fold in the sweetened condensed milk using a spatula. Fold in the chopped pistachios after the mixture is smooth and uniform.

5. Insert the kulfi in an airtight container and freeze it, or spoon it into tiny cups for popsicles and place a popsicle stick in the center of each one.

6. Freeze for a minimum of 3 hours.

Nutrition: Calories 200, Carbs 16g, Protein 14g, Fat 18g, Cholesterol 44 mg

233. Easy no-bake key lime pie recipe

Preparation Time: 20 minutes | **Cooking Time:** 240 minutes | **Total time:** 260 minutes | **Servings:** 8

Ingredients:
For the graham cracker crust
- 12 whole graham crackers crushed (about 1 ½ cups)
- Six tablespoons melted butter
- ¼ cup granulated sugar
- ¼ teaspoon salt
For the key lime pie filling
- Eight ounce cream cheese softened
- 14 ounce sweetened condensed milk
- ½ cup key lime juice
- 3-5 drops lime green food coloring if desired
- 8 ounce cool whip
- Lime zest for garnish

Instructions:
1. Prepare a 9-inch pie pan as well as a food processor. In a food processor, combine the graham crackers. Close the lid and pulse into a fine crumb. After that, stir in the melted butter, sugar, and salt. To mix, pulse the ingredients together.

2. Fill the pie pan halfway with the graham cracker crumble. Press it into an equal layer over the bottom and up the edges of the pan with your hands. Keep refrigerated until ready to use.

3. Wipe the food processor bowl clean. Then combine the cream cheese, sweetened condensed milk, and lime juice in a mixing bowl. Blend until smooth. (if wanted, add food coloring here.)

4. Take the food processor blade out of the machine. Scoop the cool whip into the lime mixture and stir well. Fold the cool whip into the mixture with a spatula until completely smooth.

5. Fill the pie crust with the filling. Then, store the mixture in the freezer for at least 4 hours, undisturbed.

6. If preferred, top with fresh lime zest when ready to serve. While still frozen, cut into pieces. Allow each piece to remain at room temperature for 10 minutes before serving somewhat softened.

Nutrition: Calories 451, Carbs 60g, Protein 63g, Fat 28g, Cholesterol 59 mg

234. Lemon cheesecake recipe (limoncello cake!)

Preparation Time: 20 minutes | **Cooking Time:** 60 minutes | **Total time:** 80 minutes | **Servings:** 16

Ingredients:
For the biscoff crust
- 8.8 oz biscoff cookies, 1 package
- 1/2 cup granulated sugar
- 1/2 teaspoon salt
- 1/2 cup unsalted butter, melted
For the limoncello cheesecake filling
- 24 oz cream cheese, softened
- 4 large eggs
- 3/4 cup granulated sugar
- 1 large lemon, zested and juiced (1/4 cup juice)

- 1/4 cup limoncello liqueur
- 1/2 teaspoon vanilla extract
- 1/2 teaspoon salt

For the sour cream topping
- 16 oz sour cream
- 1/4 cup granulated sugar
- 3 tablespoons limoncello liqueur

Instructions:

1. Preheat the oven to 350 degrees fahrenheit. Place one oven rack in the center and one at the bottom of the oven.
2. To catch any spillage, use a big rimmed baking sheet on the bottom rack. Preheat the oven to 350°f. Line the bottom of a 9 1/2-inch springform pan with parchment paper.
3. Then, securely tighten the ring around the bottom. (if desired, trim the paper edges.)
4. To make the crust: in a food processor, combine the biscoff cookies, sugar, and salt.
5. Pulse the cookies until they are finely ground. After that, add the melted butter and pulse to the mix.
6. Fill the prepared pan halfway with the crust mixture. With your hands, press the crumbs all over the bottom of the pan and approximately two-thirds of the way up the edges. 10 minutes in the oven
7. Meanwhile, prepare the limoncello cheesecake filling by placing the cream cheese in the bowl of an electric mixer. 2 minutes on high to soften and fluff the cream cheese.
8. Add the eggs one at a time, delaying adding another until the preceding egg is thoroughly mixed in. Using a spatula, scrape the bowl.
9. Then mix in the other ingredients until fully smooth—bake for 45 minutes after pouring the filling into the crust.
10. To make the sour cream topping, combine the sour cream, sugar, and limoncello in a medium mixing bowl and whisk until smooth.
11. Once the cheesecake has baked and is nearly set in the center, pour the sour cream filling over the top and return to the oven for 10-12 minutes.
12. 1 hour on the counter to cool the cheesecake. Then place in the refrigerator for at least 3 hours to cool.
13. Remove the ring from the springform pan and place the cheesecake on a cake plate. Cut into slices and serve chilled.

Nutrition: Calories 386, Cxarbs 35g, Protein 22g, Fat 17g, Cholestrol 108 mg

235. Dark Chocolate with Pomegranate Seeds

Preparation Time: 10 minutes | **Cooking Time:** 2-3 minutes | **Servings:** 3

Ingredients:
- 150 g dark chocolate (at least 70% cocoa)
- 120 g pomegranate seeds (from 1 pomegranate)
- 1 teaspoon sea salt

Instructions:

1. Scatter a layer of pomegranate seeds in a muffin tin (or muffin paper).
2. Melt the chocolate in the microwave.
3. Pour the chocolate into a bag, then cut a tiny hole so that it can be spread over the seeds. Add a layer of seeds and another of chocolate.
4. Sprinkle with a pinch of salt and chill in the refrigerator until the mixture is hard.
5. Enjoy cold.

Nutrition: Calories: 82, Carbs: 19g, Protein: 1.9g, Fat: 0.2g, Sugar: 3.9g, Sodium: 37 mg, Fiber: 3.7g

236. Covered Bananas

Preparation Time: 10 minutes | **Cooking Time:** 0 minutes | **Servings:** 3

Ingredients:
- 3 bananas
- 1 tablespoon oat bran
- 2 tablespoons cashew or almond butter
- 1 tablespoon honey
- 1 teaspoon chia seeds

- 1 teaspoon cinnamon

Instructions:
1. Mix the oat bran, seeds and cinnamon in a shallow bowl.
2. Mix the nut butter with honey.
3. Coat the bananas with nut butter and then add to the dry mixture so that they are coated on both sides.

Nutrition: Calories: 11, Carbs: 3g, Protein: 0g, Fat: 0g, Sugar: 2.9g, Sodium: 0 mg, Fiber: 0.1g

237. Hummus with Tahini and Turmeric

Preparation Time: 10 minutes | **Cooking Time:** 0 minutes | **Servings:** 4

Ingredients:
- 2 cans chickpeas, drained
- 50 ml lemon juice
- 60 ml tahini
- 1 garlic clove, minced
- 2 tablespoons extra-virgin olive oil
- 1/2 tablespoon turmeric powder
- 1/2 teaspoon sea salt

Instructions:
1. Mix the tahini and lemon juice with olive oil, garlic, turmeric and salt for about 30 seconds using a hand blender or kitchen utensil.
2. Add the chickpeas and puree, making sure that no chickpeas remain unmixed on the sides. Pound until a uniform mixture is obtained.
3. Garnish with paprika powder and enjoy with any snacks, such as vegetable sticks.

Nutrition: Calories: 33, Carbs: 8.g, Protein: 0.2g, Fat: 0.1g, Sugar: 7.6g, Sodium: 130 mg, Fiber: 0.1g

238. Pineapple orange creamsicle

Preparation Time: 10 minutes | **Cooking Time:** 12 minutes | **Total time:** 22 minutes | **Servings:** 10

Ingredients:
- Two cups of orange-pineapple juice

- One cup heavy cream
- ½ cup granulated sugar
- 2 teaspoons vanilla extract

Instructions:
1. In a microwave-safe bowl, combine 1/2 cup juice and 1/2 sugar. Warm the juice for 1-2 minutes or until the sugar melts. Then add the remaining juice and whisk to combine.
2. Pour the heavy cream, vanilla extract, and 1 1/4 cup of the sweetened juice into a separate dish (or measuring pitcher). Stir everything together thoroughly. Then divide the mixture evenly among ten regular popsicle molds.
3. For 1 hour, place the popsicles in the freezer. Then, drizzle the remaining juice over the tops of each popsicle and insert wooden popsicle sticks. Freeze for at least 3 hours more.

Nutrition: Calories 145, Carbs 15g, Protein 17g, Fat 8g, Cholesterol 76 mg

239. Easy peach cobbler recipe with bisquick

Preparation Time: 10 minutes | **Cooking Time:** 60 minutes | **Total time:** 70 minutes | **Servings:** 7

Ingredients:
- 48 oz fresh or frozen sliced peaches 6 ½ cups, with or without peels
- Two cups granulated sugar
- ½ teaspoon of pumpkin pie spice or apple pie spice blend
- Cups bisquick baking mix
- 1 cup of whole milk
- 1 cup of melted butter

Instructions:
1. Preheat the oven to 350 degrees fahrenheit. Prepare a 9-by-13-inch baking dish and a large mixing basin.
2. If you are using fresh peaches, cut them into wedges and remove the pits. Fill the baking dish halfway with fresh (or frozen)

peach slices. Then, over the peaches, add 1 cup sugar and the pumpkin pie spice. Toss the peach to coat it, then spread it out in an equal layer.

3. Combine the remaining 1 cup sugar, bisquick, and milk in a mixing basin. Whisk everything together well. Then add the melted butter and stir until combined.

4. Pour the batter over the peaches in an equal layer. Bake for 55- 60 minutes, depending on the size of the baking dish.

5. After 40 minutes, check on the cobbler. If the top begins to darken, loosely cover with foil and continue baking.

6. Allow at least 15 minutes for the cobbler to cool before serving. Serve in dishes with vanilla ice cream or whipped cream.

Notes: you don't like peaches? Replace the nectarines, plums, pitted cherries, or berries with an equal number of nectarines, plums, pitted cherries, or berries in this recipe.

How to keep leftovers: once the cobbler has completely cooled, cover it in plastic wrap or move it to a container with a lid. The fruit cobbler may be stored in the refrigerator for up to 4-5 days.

To put on ice: cook according to the recipe in a freezer-safe baking dish, cool, and cover the entire dish in plastic wrap. Wrap in tin foil and place in the freezer for up to 3 months. Unwrap and bake in a 350°f oven for 40-50 minutes, or until boiling.

Nutrition: Calories 420, Carbs 59g, Protein 11g, Fat 20g, Cholesterol 172 mg

240. Healthy 5-minute strawberry pineapple sherbet

Preparation Time: 5 minutes | **Cooking Time:** 5 minutes | **Total time:** 10 minutes | **Servings:** 16

Ingredients:

- One pound frozen strawberries
- One pound has frozen pineapple chunks
- 1/2 cups plain greek yogurt
- 1/2 cup honey or palm syrup
- Two teaspoon vanilla extract
- Pinch salt

Instructions:

1. In a large food mixer, combine all of the ingredients. Pulse the frozen fruit to break it up. Then purée until completely smooth.

2. Serve immediately as soft serve, or freeze in an airtight container. Thaw for 15 minutes before scooping and serving if frozen.

Notes: this sherbet has a distinct honey taste. If you dislike the flavor of honey, use palm syrup.

Nutrition: Calories 70, Carbs 16g, Protein 2g, Fat 1g, Cholesterol 1mg

241. Best coconut milk ice cream (dairy-free!)

Preparation Time: 3 minutes | **Cooking Time:** 30 minutes | **Total time:** 33 minutes | **Servings:** 16

Ingredients:

- 27 ounce canned full-fat unsweetened coconut milk 2 cans
- 13.6 ounce can coconut cream
- One cup granulated sugar
- Two teaspoons of vanilla extract or vanilla bean paste
- ¼ teaspoon salt

Instructions:

1. After making this ice cream numerous times, i learned that it does not always need to be heated/cooked before churning... This saves a huge amount of time. (this depends on the kind of coconut milk/cream and the kind of blender you use.) Put all ingredients in a blender and purée until smooth to see whether your ice cream has to be cooked. If the coconut ice cream mixture is smooth and free of clumps, you may churn it without heating.

2. Heat and stir: if there are any pieces of coconut cream in the recipe, they will freeze as hard waxy clumps in the ice cream. In this scenario, cook the mixture over medium heat until smooth, stirring often. Before churning, chill and cool to at least room temperature. * if you don't want to "test" the no-heat approach, simply

combine all ingredients in a saucepot and cook over medium heat until smooth, allowing the coconut clumps and sugar to dissolve. Then take a break.

3. Set out a 1.5-2 quart ice cream machine after the ice cream mixture has cooled. Turn on the machine and place the frozen bowl inside. Fill the machine halfway with the extremely smooth ice cream mixture. Cook for 20-25 minutes, or until the mixture is thick, hard, and smooth.

4. Serve right away, or transfer to an airtight container and freeze until ready to use.

Nutrition: Calories 224, Carbs 16g, Protein 2g, Fat 19g, Cholesterol 27 mg

242. Lemon crinkle cookies recipe

Preparation Time: 15 minutes | **Cooking Time:** 10 minutes | **Total time:** 25 minutes | **Servings:** 45

Ingredients:

- 1 cup unsalted butter, softened (2 sticks)

- ¾ cups granulated sugar

- 4 large eggs

- 2 tablespoons fresh lemon juice

- 2 tablespoon lemon zest

- 1 teaspoon vanilla extract

- 1 cup all-purpose flour (stir, spoon into the cup, and level)

- 2 teaspoon baking powder

- 1/2 teaspoon salt

- 1/4 teaspoon baking soda

- 2-5 drops yellow food coloring (optional)

- 2 cup powdered sugar

Instructions:

1. In the bowl of an electric stand mixer, combine the butter and granulated sugar. Cream the butter and sugar together on high for 3-5 minutes, or until light and creamy. Using a rubber spatula, scrape the bowl.

2. Mix in the eggs, lemon juice, lemon zest, and vanilla extract at low speed. Scrape the bowl once more. Mix in 1 cup of flour, baking powder, salt, baking soda, and food coloring on low. Once mixed, gently fold in the remaining 2 cups of flour until smooth. (be careful not to overwork the dough!)

3. Refrigerate the dough for at least 30 minutes, covered. (the longer the dough is chilled, the puffier the cookies.) Preheat the oven to 375 degrees fahrenheit. Set aside several baking sheets lined with parchment paper.

4. Set out a small dish of powdered sugar once the dough has cooled. To separate the dough into balls, use a 1 tablespoon cookie scoop. Roll each ball in powdered sugar, then place 2 inches apart on baking pans. (be careful to cover the cookies with powdered sugar generously.) You should not shrug them off.)

5. 9-10 minutes, or until the sides are golden brown and the middle appears slightly underbaked. Allow them to cool on the baking pans so that the centers continue to bake as they cool.

Note: storage suggestions: store the cookies in an airtight jar at room temperature. Consume within 7-10 days.

Citrus substitutions: in place of the lemon, you can use lime or orange juice and zest. You may also combine lemon and lime for a unique taste combination!

Nutrition: Calories 11, Carbs 16g, Protein 29g, Fat 18g, Cholesterol 63 mg

243. The best no-bake chocolate lasagna

Preparation Time: 20 minutes | **Cooking Time:** 120 minutes | **Total time:** 140 minutes | **Servings:** 12

Ingredients:

Oreo layer

- 40 oreo cookies
- 7 tablespoons melted butter
- Cream cheese layer –
- 8 oz cream cheese softened
- 3 tablespoons granulated sugar
- Two tablespoons of milk
- 16 oz of cool whip reserve half for later

Chocolate pudding layer
- 7.8 oz instant chocolate pudding mix two small boxes
- 2 ¾ cups of milk
- Two teaspoons instant coffee granules
- Whipped topping layer –
- Remaining cool whip
- 2 cup mini chocolate chips or ½ cup chocolate shavings

Instructions:
1. Set up a big food processor to make the oreo crust. In a mixing dish, combine the oreo cookies. Cover and pulse until tiny crumbs form. Then, pulse in the melted butter to coat. * if you don't have a food processor, you may smash the cookies with a rolling pin in a zip bag. Then, for the remaining processes, use a mixer.
2. Fill a 9 x 13 inch baking dish halfway with oreo crumbs. Chill after pressing into a uniform layer.
3. A layer of cream cheese: next, rinse off the food processor bowl. Combine the cream cheese, sugar, and milk in a mixing bowl. Blend until smooth. Then, using a knife, spoon half (8 oz) of the cool whip into the cream cheese. Fold the mixture with a spatula until it is smooth. Spread the mixture evenly over the crust in the baking dish. Chill.
4. Rinse the food processor bowl once more for the chocolate pudding layer. Combine the chocolate pudding powder, milk, and instant coffee in a mixing bowl. Puree till smooth, covered. In the baking dish, evenly distribute the ingredients.
5. Toppings: top the chocolate pudding with the remaining 8 oz of cool whip. Then, over the top, sprinkle with tiny chocolate chips or chocolate shavings.
6. Place in the refrigerator for at least 4 hours, covered. Freeze for 2-3 hours for optimum cutting results, then cut and serve. Allow 10-15 minutes for the frozen plated pieces to come to room temperature before serving.

Note: this is a fantastic make-ahead dessert that can be made 4-5 days ahead of time and stored in the freezer for up to 3 months.

Nutrition: Calories 533, Carbs 72g, Protein 16g, Fat 8g, Cholesterol 42 mg

244. Easiest healthy watermelon smoothie recipe

Preparation Time: 3 minutes | **Cooking Time:** 3 minutes | **Total time:** 6 minutes | **Servings:** 4

Ingredients:
- 4 cups fresh ripe watermelon cubes from a less melon
- 2 cup strawberry yogurt regular or a dairy-free variety
- 4 cups ice
- 1-2 tablespoons granulated sugar optional (only needed if the watermelon isn't very sweet.)

Instructions:
1. In a blender, combine the watermelon cubes and yogurt. Puree till smooth, covered. Taste to see if more sugar is required.
2. Pour in the ice cubes (and sugar if desired). After that, cover and purée until smooth.
3. Serve right away.

Note: garnish with cubes or slices of watermelon or cut strawberries.

Nutrition: Calories 120, Carbs 27g, Protein 27g, Fat 19g, Cholesterol 47 mg

245. Chicken Bone Broth

Preparation Time: 10 minutes | **Cooking Time:** 90 minutes | **Servings:** 8

Ingredients:

- 3-4 pounds bones (from 1 chicken)
- 4 cups water
- 2 large carrots, cut into chunks
- 2 large stalks celery
- 1 large onion
- 2 cups Fresh rosemary sprigs
- 3 fresh thyme sprigs
- 2 tablespoons apple cider vinegar
- 1 teaspoon kosher salt

Instructions:

1. Put all the ingredients in your pot and allow to sit for 30 minutes.
2. Pressure cook and adjust the time to 90 minutes.
3. Set the release naturally until the float valve drops and then unlock the lid.
4. Strain the broth and transfer it into a storage container. The broth can be refrigerated for 3-5 days or frozen for up to 6 months.

Nutrition: Calories: 140, Carbs: 0.6g, Protein: 25g, Fat: 2.6g, Sugar: 0.1g, Sodium: 73 mg, Fiber: 0.1g

246. Homemade Beef Stock

Preparation Time: 10 minutes | **Cooking Time:** 2-12 hours | **Servings:** 6

Ingredients:

- 2 pounds beef bones (preferably with marrow)
- 5 celery stalks, chopped
- 4 carrots, chopped
- 1 white or Spanish onion, chopped
- 2 garlic cloves, crushed
- 2 bay leaves
- 1 teaspoon dried thyme
- 1 teaspoon dried sage
- 1 teaspoon black peppercorns
- Salt

Instructions:

1. Preheat the oven to 425°F.
2. On a baking sheet, spread out the beef bones, celery, carrots, onion, garlic, and bay leaves. Sprinkle the thyme, sage, and peppercorns over the top.
3. Roast until the vegetables and bones have a rich brown color.
4. Transfer the roasted bones and vegetables to a large stockpot. Cover with water and slowly bring to a boil over high heat.
5. Set the heat to medium-low for at least 2 hours and up to 12 hours.
6. Pour the mixture through a fine-mesh strainer into a large bowl.
7. Taste and season with salt. Serve hot.

Nutrition: Calories: 37, Fat: 1g, Carbs: 3g, Fiber: 0g, Protein: 4g, Sodium: 58 mg

247. Three-Ingredient Sugar-Free Gelatin

Preparation Time: 5 minutes | **Cooking Time:** 0 minutes | **Servings:** 6-8 |

Ingredients:

- 1/4 cup room temperature water
- 1/4 cup hot water
- 1 tablespoon gelatin
- 1 cup orange juice, unsweetened

Instructions:

1. Combine your gelatin and room temperature water, stirring until fully dissolved.
2. Stir in hot water then leave to rest for about 2 minutes.
3. Add in the juice and stir until combined.

4. Transfer to serving size containers then place on a tray in the refrigerator to set for about 4 hours.
5. Enjoy!

Nutrition: Calories: 17, Fat: 0g, Carbs: 4g, Fiber: 0g, Protein: 0g

248. Cranberry-Kombucha Jell-O

Preparation Time: 5 minutes | **Cooking Time:** 0 minutes | **Servings:** 6

Ingredients:
- 1/4 cup room temperature water
- 1/4 cup hot water
- 1 tablespoon gelatin
- 1 cup cranberry kombucha, unsweetened

Instructions:
1. Combine your gelatin and room temperature water, stirring until fully dissolved.
2. Stir in hot water then leave to rest for about 2 minutes.
3. Add in the kombucha and stir until combined.
4. Transfer to serving size containers then place on a tray in the refrigerator to set for about 4 hours.
5. Enjoy!

Nutrition: Calories: 13, Fat: 0g, Carbs: 1g, Fiber: 0g, Protein: 0g

249. Strawberry Gummies

Preparation Time: 5 minutes | **Cooking Time:** 5 minutes | **Servings:** 20-40 mini gummies

Ingredients:
- 1 cup strawberries, hulled and chopped
- 3/4 cup water
- 2 tablespoons gelatin

Instructions:
1. Bring your water and berries to a boil on high heat. Detach from the heat as soon as the mixture begins to boil.
2. Transfer to the blender and pulse. Add in your gelatin then blend once more.

3. Pour the mixture into a silicone gummy mold.
4. Place on a tray in the refrigerator to set for about 4 hours.
5. Enjoy!

Nutrition: Calories: 3, Fat: 0g, Carbs: 0g, Fiber: 0g, Protein: 0g

250. Fruity Jell-O Stars

Preparation Time: 15 minutes | **Cooking Time:** 5 minutes | **Servings:** 4

Ingredients:
- 1 tablespoon gelatin, powdered
- 3/4 cup boiling water
- 3 ½ cups fruit
- 1 tablespoon honey
- 1 teaspoon lemon juice

Instructions:
1. Attach all your ingredients into a blender and pulse.
2. Add in the gelatin then blend once more.
3. Pour the mixture into a silicone gummy mold.
4. Place on a tray in the refrigerator to set for about 4 hours.
5. Enjoy!

Nutrition: Calories: 2, Fat: 14g, Carbs: 0g, Fiber: 1g, Protein: 0g

251. Sugar-Free Cinnamon Jelly

Preparation Time: 5 minutes | **Cooking Time:** 0 minutes | **Servings:** 2

Ingredients:
- 1 cup hot cinnamon tea
- 1 cup room temperature water
- 2 teaspoons gelatin
- 1/3 cup sweetener

Instructions:
1. Combine your gelatin and room temperature water, stirring until fully dissolved.
2. Stir in hot tea then leave to rest for about 2 minutes.

3. Add in the sweetener and stir until combined.
4. Transfer to serving size containers then place on a tray in the refrigerator to set for about 4 hours.
5. Enjoy!

Nutrition: Calories: 35, Fat: 0g, Carbs: 17g, Fiber: 0g, Protein: 0g

252. Homey Clear Chicken Broth

Preparation Time: 10 minutes | **Cooking Time:** 2-12 hours | **Servings:** 6

Ingredients:
- 2 pounds chicken neck
- 2 celery ribs with leaves, cut into chunks
- 2 medium carrots, cut into chunks
- 2 medium onions, quartered
- 2 bay leaves
- 2 quarts cold water
- Salt

Instructions:
1. Transfer the bones and vegetables to your stockpot. Top with enough water to cover then allow to come to a boil on high heat slowly.
2. Switch to low heat and simmer for at least 2 hours and up to 12 hours.
3. Set and pour the mixture through a fine-mesh strainer into a large bowl.
4. Taste and season with salt.
5. Serve hot.

Nutrition: Calories: 245, Fat: 14g, Carbs: 8g, Fiber: 2g, Protein: 21g

253. Oxtail Bone Broth

Preparation Time: 15 minutes | **Cooking Time:** 12 hours | **Servings:** 8 cups

Ingredients:
- 2 pounds Oxtail
- 1 Onion, chopped in quarters
- 2 celery stalks, chopped in half
- 2 carrots, chopped in half
- 3 whole garlic cloves
- 2 bay leaves

- 1 tablespoon salt
- Filtered water (enough to cover bones)

Instructions:
1. Transfer the bones and vegetables to your stockpot. Top with enough water to cover then allow to come to a boil on high heat slowly.
2. Switch to low heat and simmer for at least 2 hours and up to 12 hours.
3. Set and pour the mixture through a fine-mesh strainer into a large bowl.
4. Taste and season with salt.
5. Serve hot.

Nutrition: Calories: 576, Fat: 48g, Carbs: 48g, Fiber: 0g, Protein: 24g

254. Chicken Bone Broth with Ginger and Lemon

Preparation Time: 10 minutes | **Cooking Time:** 90 minutes | **Servings:** 8

Ingredients:
- 3-4 pounds bones (from 1 chicken)
- 8 cups water
- 2 large carrots, cut into chunks
- 2 large stalks celery
- 1 large onion
- 3 fresh rosemary sprigs
- 3 fresh thyme sprigs
- 2 tablespoons apple cider vinegar
- 1 teaspoon kosher salt
- 1 (1/2 inches) piece fresh ginger, sliced (peeling not necessary)
- 1 large lemon, cut into quarters

Instructions:
1. Put all the ingredients in your pot and allow to sit for 30 minutes.
2. Pressure cook and adjust the time to 90 minutes.
3. Set the broth using a fine-mesh strainer and transfer it into a storage container.
4. Can be refrigerated for 5 days or frozen for 6 months.

Nutrition: Calories: 44, Fat: 1g, Protein: 7g, Sodium: 312 mg, Fiber: 0g, Carbs: 0g, Sugar: 0g

255. Vegetable Stock

Preparation Time: 10 minutes | **Cooking Time:** 40 minutes | **Servings:** 8

Ingredients:

- 2 large carrots
- 1 large onion
- 2 large stalks celery
- 8 ounces white mushrooms
- 5 whole garlic cloves
- 2 cups parsley leaves
- 2 bay leaves
- 2 teaspoons whole black peppercorns
- 2 teaspoons kosher salt
- 10 cups water

Instructions:

1. Place all the ingredients in your pot. Secure the lid.
2. Pressure cook and adjust the time to 40 minutes.
3. Set the broth using a fine-mesh strainer and transfer it into a storage container.

Nutrition: Calories: 9, Fat: 0g, Protein: 0g, Sodium: 585 mg, Fiber: 0g, Carbs: 2g, Sugar: 1g

256. Chicken Vegetable Soup

Preparation Time: 23 minutes | **Cooking Time:** 15 minutes | **Servings:** 8

Ingredients:

- 2 tablespoons avocado oil
- 1 small yellow onion, peeled and chopped
- 2 large carrots, peeled and chopped
- 2 large stalks celery, ends removed and sliced
- 3 garlic cloves, minced
- 1 teaspoon dried thyme
- 1 teaspoon salt
- 8 cups chicken stock
- 3 boneless, skinless, frozen chicken breasts

Instructions:

1. Heat the oil for 1 minute. Add the onion, carrots, and celery and sauté for 8 minutes.
2. Add the garlic, thyme, and salt then sauté for another 30 seconds.

3. Press the Cancel button.
4. Add the stock and frozen chicken breasts to the pot. Secure the lid.
5. Pressure cook and adjust the time to 6 minutes.
6. Allow cooling into bowls to serve.

Nutrition: Calories: 209, Fat: 7g, Protein: 21g, Sodium: 687 mg, Fiber: 1g, Carbs: 12g, Sugar:5g

257. Carrot Ginger Soup

Preparation Time: 20 minutes | **Cooking Time:** 21 minutes | **Servings:** 4

Ingredients:

- 1 tablespoon avocado oil
- 1 large yellow onion, peeled and chopped
- 1-pound carrots, peeled and chopped
- 1 tablespoon fresh ginger, peeled and minced
- 1 ½ teaspoon salt
- 3 cups vegetable broth

Instructions:

1. Add the oil to the inner pot, allowing it to heat for 1 minute.
2. Attach the onion, carrots, ginger, and salt then sauté for 5 minutes. Press the Cancel button.
3. Add the broth and secure the lid.
4. Adjust the time to 15 minutes.
5. Allow the soup to cool a few minutes and then transfer it to a large blender.
6. Merge on high until smooth and then serve.

Nutrition: Calories: 99, Fat: 4g, Protein: 1g, Sodium: 1,348 mg, Fiber: 4g, Carbs: 16g, Sugar:7g

258. Turkey Sweet Potato Hash

Preparation Time: 10 minutes | **Cooking Time:** 12 minutes | **Servings:** 4

Ingredients:

- 1 ½ tablespoon avocado oil
- 1 medium yellow onion, peeled and diced
- 2 garlic cloves, minced

- 1 medium sweet potato, cut into cubes (peeling not necessary)
- 1/2-pound lean ground turkey
- 1/2 teaspoon salt
- 1 teaspoon Italian seasoning blend

Instructions:
1. Attach the oil and allow it to heat for 1 minute. Add the onion and cook until softened, about 5 minutes. Attach the garlic and cook for an additional 30 seconds.
2. Add the sweet potato, turkey, salt, and Italian seasoning and cook for another 5 minutes.

Nutrition: Calories: 172, Fat: 9g, Protein: 12g, Sodium: 348 mg, Fiber: 1g, Carbs: 10g, Sugar:3g

259. Chicken Tenders with Honey Mustard Sauce

Preparation Time: 5 minutes | **Cooking Time:** 10 minutes | **Servings:** 4

Ingredients:
- 1 pound chicken tenders
- 1 tablespoon fresh thyme leaves
- 1/2 teaspoon salt
- 1/4 teaspoon black pepper
- 1 tablespoon avocado oil
- 1 cup chicken stock
- 1/4 cup Dijon mustard
- 1/4 cup raw honey

Instructions:
1. Dry the chicken tenders with a towel and then season them with thyme, salt, and pepper.
2. Attach the oil and let it heat for 2 minutes.
3. Add the chicken tenders and seer them until brown on both sides, about 1 minute per side. Press the Cancel button.
4. Remove the chicken tenders and set them aside. Add the stock to the pot. Use a spoon to scrape up any small bits from the bottom of the pot.

5. Set the steam rack in the inner pot and place the chicken tenders directly on the rack.
6. While the chicken is cooking, prepare the sauce.
7. In a bowl, combine the Dijon mustard and honey then stir to combine.
8. Serve the chicken tenders with the honey mustard sauce.

Nutrition: Calories: 223, Fat: 5g, Protein: 22g, Sodium: 778 mg, Fiber: 0g, Carbs: 19g

260. Chicken Breasts with Cabbage and Mushrooms

Preparation Time: 10 minutes | **Cooking Time:** 18 minutes | **Servings:** 4

Ingredients:
- 2 tablespoons avocado oil
- 1-pound sliced Baby Bella mushrooms
- 1 ½ teaspoon salt, divided
- 2 garlic cloves, minced
- 8 cups chopped green cabbage
- 1 ½ teaspoon dried thyme
- 1/2 cup chicken stock
- 1 ½ pound boneless, skinless chicken breasts

Instructions:
1. Add the oil. Allow it to heat for 1 minute. Attach the mushrooms and 1/4 teaspoon of salt. Sauté until they have cooked down and released their liquid, about 10 minutes.
2. Add the garlic and sauté for another 30 seconds. Press the Cancel button.
3. Attach the cabbage, 1/4 teaspoon of salt, thyme, and the stock to the inner pot. Stir to combine.
4. Dry the chicken breasts and sprinkle both sides with the remaining salt. Place on top of the cabbage mixture.
5. Transfer to plates and spoon the juices on top.

Nutrition: Calories: 337, Fat: 10g, Protein: 44g, Sodium: 1,023 mg, Fiber: 4g, Carbs: 14g, Sugar:2g

261. Duck with Bok Choy

Preparation Time: 15 minutes | **Cooking Time:** 12 minutes | **Servings:** 6

Ingredients:

- 2 tablespoons coconut oil
- 1 onion, sliced thinly
- 2 teaspoons fresh ginger, grated finely
- 2 minced garlic cloves
- 1 tablespoon fresh orange zest, grated finely
- 1/4 cup chicken broth
- 2/3 cup fresh orange juice
- 1 roasted duck, meat picked
- 3 pounds bok choy leaves
- 1 orange, peeled, seeded and segmented

Instructions:

1. In a sizable skillet, melt the coconut oil on medium heat. Attach the onion, sauté for around 3 minutes. Add ginger and garlic then sauté for about 1-2 minutes.
2. Stir in the orange zest, broth and orange juice.
3. Add the duck meat and cook for around 3 minutes.
4. Transfer the meat pieces to a plate. Add the bok choy and cook for about 3-4 minutes.
5. Divide the bok choy mixture into serving plates and top with duck meat.
6. Serve with the garnishing of orange segments.

Nutrition: Calories: 290, Fat: 4g, Fiber: 6g, Carbs: 8g, Protein: 14g

262. Beef with Mushroom and Broccoli

Preparation Time: 60 minutes | **Cooking Time:** 12 minutes | **Servings:** 4

Ingredients:

For Beef Marinade:

- 1 garlic clove, minced
- 1-piece fresh ginger, minced
- Salt and freshly ground black pepper
- 3 tablespoons white wine vinegar
- 3/4 cup beef broth
- 1 pound flank steak, trimmed and sliced into thin strips

For Vegetables:

- 2 tablespoons coconut oil
- 2 garlic cloves
- 3 cups broccoli rabe
- 4 ounces shiitake mushrooms
- 8 ounces cremini mushrooms

Instructions:

For the marinade:

1. In a substantial bowl, mix all ingredients except the beef. Add it and coat with the marinade generously. Refrigerate to soak for around 1/4 hour.
2. In a substantial skillet, warm oil on medium-high heat.
3. Detach the beef from the bowl, reserving the marinade.

For the Vegetables:

1. Attach the beef and garlic and cook for about 3-4 minutes or till browned.
2. In the same skillet, add the reserved marinade, broccoli and mushrooms. Cook for approximately 3-4 minutes.
3. Set in the beef and cook for about 3-4 minutes.

Nutrition: Calories: 200, Carbs: 31g, Cholesterol: 93 mg, Fat: 4g, Protein: 10g, Fiber: 2 g

263. Beef with Zucchini Noodles

Preparation Time: 15 minutes | **Cooking Time:** 9 minutes | **Servings:** 4

Ingredients:

- 1 teaspoon fresh ginger, grated
- 2 medium garlic cloves, minced
- 1/4 cup coconut aminos
- 2 tablespoons fresh lime juice
- 1 ½ pound NY strip steak, trimmed and sliced thinly

- 2 medium zucchinis, spiralized with blade C
- Salt to taste
- 3 tablespoons essential olive oil
- 2 medium scallions, sliced
- 1 teaspoon red pepper flakes, crushed
- 2 tablespoons fresh cilantro, chopped

Instructions:

1. In a big bowl, merge ginger, garlic, coconut aminos and lime juice. Add the beef and coat with the marinade generously. Refrigerate to soak for approximately 10 minutes.
2. Set zucchini noodles over a large paper towel and sprinkle with salt.
3. Keep aside for around 10 minutes.
4. In a big skillet, heat oil on medium-high heat. Attach the scallions and red pepper flakes then sauté for about 1 minute.
5. Attach the beef with the marinade and stir fry for around 3-4 minutes or till browned.
6. Stir in the fresh cilantro, then add the zucchini and cook for approximately 3-4 minutes.
7. Serve hot.

Nutrition: Calories: 1366, Carbs: 166g, Cholesterol: 6 mg, Fat: 67g, Protein: 59g, Fiber.41g

264. Spiced Ground Beef

Preparation Time: 10 minutes | **Cooking Time:** 22 minutes | **Servings:** 5

Ingredients:

- 2 tablespoons coconut oil
- 2 whole cloves
- 2 whole cardamoms
- 1 (2 inches) piece cinnamon stick
- 2 bay leaves
- 1 teaspoon cumin seeds
- 2 onions, chopped
- Salt to taste
- 1/2 tablespoon garlic paste
- 1/2 tablespoon fresh ginger paste
- 1-pound lean ground beef

- 1 ½ teaspoon fennel seeds powder
- 1 teaspoon ground cumin
- 1 ½ teaspoon red chili powder
- 1/8 teaspoon ground turmeric
- Freshly ground black pepper, to taste
- 1 cup coconut milk
- 1/4 cup water
- 1/4 cup fresh cilantro, chopped

Instructions:

1. In a sizable pan, warm oil on medium heat. Mix cloves, cardamoms, cinnamon stick, bay leaves and cumin seeds; cook for about 20 seconds.
2. Attach the onion and 2 pinches of salt then sauté for about 3-4 minutes.
3. Add the garlic-ginger paste and stir fry for about 2 minutes.
4. Attach the beef and cook for about 4-5 minutes, entering pieces using the spoon. Stir in spices and cook.
5. Set in the coconut milk and water; cook for about 7-8 minutes. Flavor with salt and take away from the heat.
6. Serve hot using the garnishing of cilantro.

Nutrition: Calories: 216, Protein: 8.83g, Fat: 11.48g, Carbs: 21.86g

265. Ground Beef with Veggies

Preparation Time: 60 minutes | **Cooking Time:** 22 minutes | **Servings:** 4

Ingredients:

- 1-2 tablespoons coconut oil
- 1 red onion,
- 2 red jalapeño peppers
- 2 minced garlic cloves
- 1-pound lean ground beef
- 1 small head broccoli, chopped
- 1/2 head cauliflower
- 3 carrots, peeled and sliced
- 3 celery ribs
- Chopped fresh thyme, to taste
- Dried sage, to taste
- Ground turmeric, to taste
- Salt and freshly ground black pepper

Instructions:
1. In a large skillet, dissolve the coconut oil on medium heat.
2. Stir in the onion, jalapeño peppers and garlic. Sauté for about 5 minutes.
3. Attach the beef and cook for around 4-5 minutes, entering pieces using the spoon.
4. Add the remaining ingredients and cook, stirring occasionally for about 8-10 minutes.
5. Serve hot.

Nutrition: Calories: 141, Cholesterol: 50 mg, Carbs: 6g, Fat: 1g, Sugar: 3g, Fiber: 2g

266. Ground Beef with Greens and Tomatoes

Preparation Time: 15 minutes | **Cooking Time:** 15 minutes | **Servings:** 4

Ingredients:
- 1 tablespoon organic olive oil
- 1/2 white onion, chopped
- 2 garlic cloves, finely chopped
- 1 jalapeño pepper, finely chopped
- 1-pound lean ground beef
- 1 teaspoon ground coriander
- 1 teaspoon ground cumin
- 1/2 teaspoon ground turmeric
- 1/2 teaspoon ground ginger
- 1/2 teaspoon ground cinnamon
- 1/2 teaspoon ground fennel seeds
- Salt and freshly ground black pepper
- 8 fresh cherry tomatoes, quartered
- 8 collard green leaves, stemmed and chopped
- 1 teaspoon fresh lemon juice

Instructions:
1. In a big skillet, warm oil on medium heat.
2. Add the onion and sauté for approximately 4 minutes.
3. Stir in the garlic and jalapeño pepper. Sauté for approximately 1 minute.

4. Attach the beef and spices; cook for approximately 6 minutes breaking into pieces while using a spoon.
5. Set in tomatoes and greens. Cook, stirring gently for about 4 minutes.
6. Whisk in lemon juice and take away from the heat.

Nutrition: Calories: 444, Fat: 15g, Carbs: 20g, Fiber: 2g, Protein: 37g,

267. Ginger Root Tea

Preparation time: 5 minutes | **Cooking time:** 20 minutes | **Serving:** 2

Ingredients:
1. Fresh ginger root – two tbsp
2. Water – four cups
3. Fresh lime juice – one tbsp, optional
4. Honey – one to two tbsp
5. Instructions:
6. Peel the ginger and cut it into pieces.
7. Add sliced ginger and water into the pot and boil it for ten minutes.
8. Let boil for twenty minutes.
9. When done, remove from the flame.
10. Pass tea through a strainer and then add lime juice and honey.
11. Serve and enjoy!

Nutrition: Calories; 42, Carbs; 11g, Protein; 0g, Fat; 0g

268. Pork Bone Broth

Preparation Time: 5 minutes | **Cooking Time:** 8 hours | **Servings:** 4

Ingredients:
- Cooked pork bones – two pounds
- Olive oil – two tbsp
- Yellow onions – two, quartered
- Celery ribs – two, cut into 4-inch segments
- Garlic – four cloves, peeled
- Peppercorns – twenty
- Apple cider vinegar – two tbsp
- Sea salt – half tsp

Instructions:

1. Firstly, add olive oil into the stockpot and place it over medium flame.
2. Then, add garlic, celery, and onions and cook for five minutes until softened.
3. Add bones, bay leaves, apple cider vinegar, five quarts of cold water, and peppercorns, and boil it. Remove brown foam through a strainer.
4. Cook over medium-low flame for six to eight hours. Add sea salt when half-hour left.
5. When done, pass broth through a mesh strainer.
6. Place broth into the bowls and serve!

Nutrition: Calories; 31, Carbs; 2.9g, Protein; 4.7g, Fat; 0.2g,

269. Banana Tea

Preparation time: 2 minutes | **Cooking time:** 8 minutes | **Serving:** 1

Ingredients:

- Banana – one, peeled, ends trimmed off
- Water – 1 ¼ cup
- Cinnamon – one stick, optional
- Vanilla extract – ¼ tsp

Instructions:

1. Add banana, water, and cinnamon stick into the pot and boil it.
2. Cover with a lid and simmer on low for eight to ten minutes.
3. When done, remove from the flame.
4. Pass the mixture through a strainer. Add vanilla extract and sweetener if desired.
5. Serve and enjoy!

Nutrition: Calories; 1, Carbs; 0g, Protein; 0g, Fat; 0g,

270. Lemon Jello

Preparation time: 10 minutes | **Cooking time:** 7 minutes | **Chill time:** 4 hours | **Servings:** 12-15

Ingredients:

- Lemon juice – half cup, squeezed
- Sparkling water – 1 ½ cups

- Gelatin – two tbsp, grass-fed
- Honey – two tbsp

Instructions:

1. Firstly, rinse and slice the lemon in half. Then, place a strainer over the mixing bowl. Squeeze the lemon until you get a half cup of lemon juice.
2. Add water and lemon juice into the saucepan. Add gelatin into the lemon juice. Stir well. Let stand for two to three minutes.
3. Cook it over medium-low flame for five to seven minutes.
4. When done, remove from the flame. Then, add honey and stir well.
5. Place mixture into the Jello mold.
6. Place it into the refrigerator for three to four hours.
7. Serve and enjoy!

Nutrition: Calories; 18, Carbs; 4g, Fat; 9g, Protein; 1g

271. Vegetable Consommé

Preparation Time: 5 minutes | **Cooking Time:** 55 minutes | **Servings:** 3

Ingredients:

- 2 egg whites
- 14 oz. vegetable stock

Instructions:

1. Whisk the egg whites 'til they begin to foam slightly.
2. Blend the egg whites with the vegetable stock until it is almost smooth. In a deep pan over low heat, add the stock.
3. Bring to a simmer, constantly stirring, until the egg whites shape a crust on the surface.
4. Scoop the egg white crust into a sieve lined with muslin or a clean tea towel (not washed with soap or detergent). Slowly pour the stock into the egg whites and sieve until enough of the liquid has passed through (don't force it).
5. Return the liquid to the pan and heat it until it is warm (do not boil).

Nutrition: Calories: 20, Protein: 4g, Total Carbs:1g, Dietary Fibers: 0g, Total Fat: 0g

272. Chicken Consommé

Preparation Time: 5 minutes | **Cooking Time:** 55 minutes | **Servings:** 4

Ingredients:
- 2 egg whites
- 16 oz. homemade chicken stock

Instructions:
1. Whisk the egg whites until they begin to foam slightly.
2. In a separate bowl, whisk together the egg whites and chicken stock until smooth.
3. In a deep pan over low heat, add the chicken stock.
4. Bring to a simmer, constantly stirring, until the egg whites shape a crust on top.
5. Scoop the egg white crust into a sieve lined with muslin or a clean tea towel (not washed with soap or detergent).
6. Slowly pour the stock into the egg whites and sieve until enough of the liquid has passed through (don't force it).
7. Return the liquid to the pan and heat it until it is warm (do not boil).

Nutrition: Calories: 51, Protein: 5g, Total Carbs:4g, Dietary Fibers: 0g, Total Fat: 1g

273. Peppermint Tea

Preparation Time: 5 minutes | **Cooking Time:** 0 minutes | **Servings:** 4

Ingredients:
- Peppermint Leaf (1/2 Cup, dried)
- Water (4 cups, hot)

Instructions:
1. Set Water on to boil.
2. Once boiling, add in peppermint leaves and remove them from heat.
3. Cover and let rest for at least 5 minutes.
4. Strain, serve, and enjoy.

Nutrition: Calories: 34.2, Protein: 0.1g, Total Carbs: 0g, Dietary Fibers: 0g, Total Fat: 0.0g

274. Pecan Tea

Preparation Time: 5 minutes | **Cooking Time:** 0 minutes | **Servings:** 2

Ingredients:
- Pecan (5 tablespoons, grounded)
- Water (1 cup)
- Cinnamon (1 tsp.)

Instructions:
1. Heat a cup of water in a saucepan and then stir in the remaining ingredients.
2. Serve hot.

Nutrition: Calories: 40, Protein: 1.51 g, Total Carbs: 1.4 g, Dietary Fibers: 0g, Total Fat: 3.58g

275. Ginger Tea

Preparation Time: 10 minutes | **Cooking Time:** 0 minutes | **Servings:** 2

Ingredients:
- Gingerroot (3 tablespoons, grated)
- Boiling Water (3 cups)

Instructions:
1. Combine all ingredients and allow to rest.
2. Covered for at least 10 minutes.
3. Serve hot.

Nutrition: Calories: 26.8, Protein: 0.1 g, Total Carbs: 6.8g, Dietary Fibers: 0g, Total Fat: 0g

276. Orange Vanilla Tea

Preparation Time: 5 minutes | **Cooking Time:** 0 minutes | **Servings:** 2

Ingredients:
- Vanilla Extract (1/4 tsp.)
- 2 medium peeled and sliced oranges
- Water (1/4 cup)

Instructions:
1. Combine all ingredients in a saucepan and boil it.
2. Remove from heat and let it rest for at least 5 minutes.
3. Strain and serve hot.

Nutrition: Calories: 60, Protein: 1g, Total Carbs: 14g, Dietary Fibers: 3g, Total Fat: 0g

277. Peanut Tea

Preparation Time: 5 minutes | **Cooking Time:** 0 minutes | **Servings:** 2

Ingredients:

- Peanuts (5 tsp., grounded)
- Cinnamon (1 tsp.)
- Water (1 cup)

Instructions:

1. Heat a cup of water in a saucepan and then stir in the remaining ingredients.
2. Serve hot.

Nutrition: Calories: 40, Protein: 1.51 g, Total Carbs: 1.4g, Dietary Fibers: 2g, Total Fat: 3.58g

278. Chamomile Tea

Preparation Time: 5 minutes | **Cooking Time:** 0 minutes | **Servings:** 2

Ingredients:

- 2 cups Water
- 3 teaspoons Dried Chamomile

Instructions:

1. Take a saucepan and start heating water on high heat.
2. Once the water starts boiling, switch off the heat and add the dried Chamomile.
3. Keep it covered for a minute. Strain the chamomile tea into the teacups, swirl, and serve it.

Nutrition: Calories: 1, Protein: 0.0 g, Total Carbs: 0.4g, Dietary Fibers: 0.7g, Total Fat: 0 g

SAUCE

279. Baked Eggplants in Tomato Sauce

Preparation time: 10 minutes | **Cooking time:** 40 minutes | **Servings:** 4

Ingredients:

- 4 eggplants
- 4 tomatoes, quartered
- 3 cups tomato puree
- 1 onion, finely chopped
- 4 cloves garlic, minced
- 1 teaspoon oregano
- Salt
- Black pepper
- Olive oil

Instructions:

1. Slice eggplants in half and sprinkle with salt. Let the eggplants rest at room temperature for 20-30 minutes, until they have sweat some water out. Pat dry with paper towel, detach all excess water and salt.
2. Preheat oven to 400F, brush a casserole dish with olive oil.
3. Mix tomato with salt, and black pepper to taste. Add oregano, garlic, and onion, and pour into casserole dish.
4. Place eggplants in casserole dish, face down, and bake in oven for 20 minutes.
5. Remove from oven, turn eggplant over, cover with aluminum foil, and bake for another 20 minutes or until the eggplants are fork tender.

Nutrition: Calories: 308, Carbs: 58g, Fat: 9g, Sugar: 30g, Protein: 10g, Sodium: 362mg

280. Spaghetti with Tomato Sauce (FAST)

Preparation Time: 5 Minutes | **Cooking Time:** 15 Minutes | **Servings:** 2

Ingredients:

- 4 ounces' spaghetti
- 2 green onions, greens, and whites separated
- 1/8 teaspoon coconut sugar
- 3 ounces' tomato sauce
- 1 tablespoon olive oil
- 1/3 teaspoon salt

- 1/4 teaspoon ground black pepper

Instructions:

1. Prepare the spaghetti, and for this, cook it according to the Instructions on the packet and then set aside.
2. Then take a skillet pan, place it over medium heat, add oil and when hot, attach white parts of green onions and cook.
3. Add tomato sauce, season with salt and black pepper and bring it to a boil.
4. Switch heat to medium-low level, simmer sauce for 1 minute, then add the cooked spaghetti and toss until mixed.
5. Divide spaghetti between two plates, and then serve.

Nutrition: Calories: 265, Carbs: 8g, Fat: 2g, Protein: 7g

281. Summer Rolls with Peanut Sauce (FAST)

Preparation time: 15 minutes | **Cooking time:** 0 minutes | **Servings:** 4-6

Ingredients:

- 6 to 8 Vietnamese/Thai round rice paper wraps
- 1 (13-ounce) package organic, extra-firm smoked or plain tofu, drained, cut into long, thin slices
- 1 cucumber, cored, cut into matchsticks (about 1 cup)
- 1 cup carrot, cut into matchsticks
- 1 cup mung bean or soybean sprouts
- 4 to 6 cups of spinach
- 12 to 16 basil leaves
- 3 to 4 mint sprigs
- Sweet Peanut Dressing

Instructions:

1. Place the rice paper wrap under running water or in a large bowl of water for a moment, then set it on a plate or cutting board to absorb the water for 30 seconds.
2. The wrap should be transparent and pliable.
3. Place your desired amount of filling on each wrap, being careful not to overfill because they will be hard to close.
4. Tightly fold the bottom of the wraps over the ingredients, and then fold in each side.
5. Continue rolling each wrap onto itself to form the rolls. Enjoy your rolls dipped in sweet peanut dressing.

Nutrition: Calories: 216, Fat: 6g Carbs: 32g, Protein: 13g

DIVERTICULITIS
HIGH FIBER RECIPES

282. Cherry Spinach Smoothie

Preparation time: 5 minutes | **Serving:** 1

Ingredients:

- Kefir – one cup, low-fat
- Frozen cherries – one cup
- Baby spinach leaves – half cup
- Avocado – ¼ cup, mashed
- Salted almond butter – one tbsp
- Ginger – ½-inch piece, peeled
- Chia seeds – one tsp

Instructions:

1. Add all ingredients into the blender and blend on high, about two to three minutes.
2. Pour smoothie into the glass.
3. Garnish with chia seeds.

Nutrition: Calories; 410, Carbs; 46.6g, Fats; 20.1g Proteins; 17.4g, fiber; 10.1g

283. Banana cacao smoothie

Preparation time: 5 minutes | **Serving:** 2

Ingredients:

- Frozen banana – two, sliced
- Cacao Bliss – ¼ cup
- Almond butter – ¼ cup
- Hemp hearts – 2 tbsp
- Non-dairy milk – 2 cups
- Ice – ½ cup

Instructions:

1. Add all ingredients into the blender and blend on high, about two to three minutes.
2. Pour smoothie into the glass.

Nutrition: Calories; 515, Carbs; 48g, Fats; 31g Proteins; 22g, fiber; 11g

284. Spinach and Egg Scramble with Raspberries

Preparation time: 10 minutes | **Serving:** 1

Ingredients:

- Canola oil – 1 tsp
- Baby spinach – 1 ½ cups
- Eggs – 2, beaten
- Kosher salt – one pinch
- ground pepper – one pinch
- Whole-grain bread – one slice, toasted
- Fresh raspberries – half cup

Instructions:

1. Add oil into the skillet and heat it over medium-high flame.
2. Add spinach and cook for one to two minutes until wilted.
3. Transfer the spinach to the medium plate.
4. Clean the pan and place it over medium flame. Then, add eggs and cook for one to two minutes.
5. Add pepper, salt, and spinach and stir well.
6. Top with raspberries.
7. Serve with toasted bread.

Nutrition: Calories; 296, Carbs; 20.9g, Fats; 15.7g Proteins; 17.8g, fiber; 7g

285. Blackberry Smoothie

Preparation time: 5 minutes | **Serving:** 1

Ingredients:

- Fresh blackberries – one cup
- Banana – half
- Plain whole-milk Greek yogurt – half cup
- Honey – one tbsp
- Fresh lemon juice – 1 ½ tsp
- Fresh ginger – 1 tsp, chopped

Instructions:

1. Add all ingredients into the blender and blend on high, about two to three minutes.
2. Pour smoothie into the glass.

Nutrition: Calories; 316, Carbs; 53g, Fats; 7g Proteins; 15g, fiber; 10g

286. Veggie Frittata

Preparation time: 5 minutes | **Cooking time:** 10 minutes | **Serving:** 1

Ingredients:

- Canola oil – one tbsp
- Scallions – two green and white parts separated, thinly sliced
- Mixed veggies – one cup carrots, broccoli, and cauliflower, chopped
- Salt – 1/8 tsp
- Eggs – 2, beaten
- Cheddar cheese – 2 tbsp, shredded
- Orange – 1, cut into wedges

Instructions:

1. Pour eggs over the vegetables and sprinkle with cheese.
2. Add oil into a skillet and place it over medium-high flame.
3. Add salt, veggies, and whites scallions and cook for three to five minutes until browned. Add green scallions and stir well.
4. Cover with a foil and remove from the flame.
5. Let sit for four to five minutes.
6. Serve with orange wedges.

Nutrition: Calories; 491, Carbs; 37g, Fats; 29g Proteins; 22g, fiber; 7g

287. Chocolate Banana Protein Smoothie

Preparation time: 5 minutes | **Serving:** 1

Ingredients:

- Banana – one, frozen
- Red lentils – half cup, cooked
- Milk – half cup, non-fat
- Unsweetened cocoa powder – 2 tsp
- Pure maple syrup – one tsp

Instructions:

1. Mix the syrup, cocoa, milk, lentils, and banana into the blender and blend until smooth.
2. Serve!

Nutrition: Calories; 310, Carbs; 63.8g, Fats; 1.8g Proteins; 15.3g, fiber; 8.5g

288. Cocoa Almond French toast

Preparation time: 10 minutes | **Serving:** 2

Ingredients:

- Unsweetened almond milk – ½ cup
- Egg – 1
- Ground cinnamon – ½ tsp
- Ground nutmeg – ½ tsp
- Almond – ¼ cup, chopped
- Non-stick cooking spray
- Whole wheat bread – four slices
- Chocolate syrup – 2 tbsp, sugar-free
- Raspberries – ¼ cup

Instructions:

1. Add nutmeg, cinnamon, eggs, and almond milk into the dish and keep ½ tbsp of chopped almonds to garnish.
2. Place remaining chopped almonds in another bowl.
3. Let coat the griddle with a cooking spray.
4. Heat the griddle over medium flame.
5. Meanwhile, immerse each bread slice into the egg mixture.
6. Then, dip soaked bread in the almonds and coat on both sides.
7. Place coated bread slices onto the griddle and cook for four to six minutes until golden brown.
8. Cut bread in half, lengthwise. Place onto the two serving plates.
9. Drizzle with chocolate syrup.
10. Top with raspberries and chopped almonds.

Nutrition: Calories; 250, Carbs; 28.6g, Fats; 11.7g Proteins; 15g, fiber; 7.9g

289. Muesli with Raspberries

Preparation time: 5 minutes | **Serving:** 1

Ingredients:

- Muesli – 1/3 cup
- Raspberries – one cup
- Milk – ¾ cup, low-fat

Instructions:

1. Place muesli into the bowl. Top with raspberries.
2. Serve with warm or cold water.

Nutrition: Calories; 288, Carbs; 51.8g, Fats; 6.6g Proteins; 13g, fiber; 13.3g

290. Mocha Overnight Oats

Preparation time: 10 minutes | **Chill time:** 8 hours | **Serving:** 1

Ingredients:

- Rolled oats – half cup
- Milk – half cup, low fat
- Cooled coffee – ¼ cup
- Pure maple syrup – one tbsp
- Chia seeds – 1 ½ tsp
- Cocoa powder – 1 ½ tsp
- Walnuts – 1 tbsp, toasted, chopped
- Cacao nibs – one tsp

Instructions:

1. Mix the cocoa powder, chia seeds, maple syrup, coffee, milk, and oats into the bowl.
2. Cover with a lid and put it into the fridge overnight or for eight hours.
3. Top with cacao nibs and walnuts.

Nutrition: Calories; 379, Carbs; 53g, Fats; 15.1g Proteins; 12.6g, fiber; 9.1g

291. Baked Banana-Nut Oatmeal Cups

Preparation time: 10 minutes | **Baking time:** 25 minutes | **Serving:** 12

Ingredients:

- Rolled oats – three cups
- Low-fat milk – 1 ½ cups
- Bananas – two, mashed
- Brown sugar – 1/3 cup
- Eggs – two, beaten
- Baking powder – one tsp
- Ground cinnamon – one tsp
- Vanilla extract – one tsp
- Salt – half tsp
- Pecans – half cup, chopped, toasted

Instructions:

1. Preheat the oven to 375 degrees Fahrenheit.
2. Let coat the muffin tin with cooking spray.

3. Mix the salt, vanilla, cinnamon, baking powder, eggs, brown sugar, bananas, milk, and oats into the bowl.
4. Fold in the pecans. Place mixture into the muffin cups and bake for twenty-five minutes.
5. Let cool it for ten minutes.
6. Serve and enjoy!

Nutrition: Calories; 176,   Carbs; 26.4g, Protein; 5.2g, Fat; 6.2g, Fiber; 3.1g

292. Pineapple Green Smoothie

Preparation time: 5 minutes | **Serving:** 1

Ingredients:

- Unsweetened almond milk – half cup
- Plain Greek yogurt – 1/3 cup, non-fat
- Baby spinach – one cup
- Frozen banana slices – one cup
- Frozen pineapple chunks – half cup
- Chia seeds – one tbsp
- Pure maple syrup or honey – one to two tsp

Instructions:

1. Add yogurt and almond milk into the blender and blend until smooth.
2. Then, add spinach, pineapple, bananas, honey or maple syrup, and chia into the blender and blend until smooth.
3. Serve and enjoy!

Nutrition: Calories; 297,   Carbs; 54.3g, protein; 12.8g, fat; 5.7g, fiber; 9.8g

293. Pumpkin Bread

Preparation time: 10 minutes | **Cooking time:** 1 hour 15 minutes | **Serving:** 12

Ingredients:

- Water – five tbsp
- Flaxseed meal – two tbsp
- Unsweetened almond milk – ¾ cup
- Sugar – ¾ cup
- Canola oil – 1/3 cup
- Vanilla extract – one tsp
- Unseasoned pumpkin puree – 1 ½ cups

- White whole-wheat flour – two cups
- Baking powder – two tsp
- Pumpkin pie spice or cinnamon – one tsp
- Salt – half tsp
- Bittersweet chocolate chips – half cup

Instructions:
1. Preheat the oven to 350 degrees Fahrenheit.
2. Let coat the loaf pan with cooking spray.
3. Mix the flaxseed meal and water into the bowl. Let sit for few minutes.
4. Whisk the flaxseed mixture, vanilla, oil, sugar, and almond milk into the bowl. Then, add pumpkin puree and stir well.
5. Whisk the salt, pumpkin pie spice, flour, and baking powder into the bowl. Add wet ingredients and stir well.
6. Add chocolate chips and stir well.
7. Transfer the batter to the pan. Bake for one hour and fifteen minutes.
8. Let cool it for one hour.
9. Serve and enjoy!

Nutrition: Calories; 191, Carbs; 30.5g, protein; 3.3g, fat; 7g, fiber; 3.3g

294. Banana-Bran Muffins

Preparation time: 10 minutes | **Cooking time:** 25 minutes | **Serving:** 12

Ingredients:
- Eggs – two
- Brown sugar – 2/3 cup
- Ripe bananas – one cup, mashed
- Buttermilk – one cup
- Unprocessed wheat bran – one cup
- Canola oil – ¼ cup
- Vanilla extract – one tsp
- Whole-wheat flour – one cup
- All-purpose flour – ¾ cup
- Baking powder – 1 ½ tsp
- Baking soda – half tsp
- Ground cinnamon – half tsp
- Salt – ¼ tsp
- Chocolate chips – half cup
- Walnuts – 1/3 cup, chopped

Instructions:
1. Preheat the oven to 400 degrees Fahrenheit.
2. Let coat twelve muffin cups with cooking spray.
3. Whisk the brown sugar and eggs into the bowl until smooth.
4. Add vanilla, oil, wheat bran, buttermilk, and bananas and whisk it well.
5. Whisk the salt, cinnamon, baking soda, baking powder, flour, all-purpose flour, and whole-wheat flour into the bowl.
6. Make a well in the middle of the dry ingredients and then add wet ingredients and stir well.
7. Add chocolate chips and stir well. Place batter into the muffin cups and sprinkle with walnuts. Bake it for fifteen to twenty-five minutes until golden brown.
8. Let cool it for five minutes.
9. Serve and enjoy!

Nutrition: Calories; 200, Carbs; 34.1g, protein; 4.8g, fat; 7g, fiber; 3.9g

295. Banana Bread

Preparation time: 15 minutes | **Cooking time:** 1 hour | **Serving:** 10

Ingredients:
- White whole-wheat flour – 1 ¾ cups
- Baking powder – 1 ½ tsp
- Ground cinnamon – one tsp
- Salt – half tsp
- Baking soda – ¼ tsp
- Sugar – ¾ cup
- Unsalted butter or coconut oil – ¼ cup, softened
- Eggs – two
- Ripe bananas – 1 ½ cups, mashed
- Buttermilk – ¼ cup
- Vanilla extract – one tsp
- Walnuts or chocolate chips – half cup, chopped

Instructions:
1. Preheat the oven to 350 degrees Fahrenheit.

2. Let coat the loaf pan with cooking spray.
3. Whisk the baking soda, salt, cinnamon, flour, and baking powder into the bowl.
4. Add butter and sugar into the bowl and beat it well using an electric mixer over medium-high heat.
5. Add eggs and beat it well. Add flour mixture and beat on low speed and then fold in chocolate chips or walnuts.
6. Place batter into the pan. Bake for forty-five to fifty-five minutes.
7. Serve and enjoy!

Nutrition: Calories 221, Carbs39.4g, Protein; 4.7g, fat; 5.9g, fiber; 3.1g

296. Chocolate-Raspberry Oatmeal

Preparation time: 10 minutes | **Serving:** 4

Ingredients:
- Regular rolled oats – 1 ½ cups
- Unsweetened cocoa powder – two tbsp
- Salt – ¼ tsp
- Unsweetened almond milk – three cups
- Fresh red raspberries – one cup
- Chocolate syrup – four tsp

Instructions:
1. Add salt, cocoa powder, and oats into the saucepan. Add almond milk and stir well. Let boil it over medium flame. Lower the heat and simmer for five to seven minutes.
2. Remove from the flame. Let stand for two minutes.
3. Place oatmeal mixture into the serving bowls.
4. Top with ¼ cup of raspberries.
5. Drizzle with one tsp chocolate syrup.

Nutrition: Calories; 157, Carbs; 26.2g, Protein; 5.4g, Fat; 4.7g, Fiber; 6.6g

297. Chai Chia Pudding

Preparation time: 10 minutes | **Chill time:** 8 hours | **Serving:** 1

Ingredients:
- Unsweetened almond milk – half cup
- Chia seeds – two tbsp

- Pure maple syrup – two tsp
- Vanilla extract – ¼ tsp
- Ground cinnamon – ¼ tsp
- Pinch of ground cardamom
- Pinch of ground cloves
- Banana – half cup, sliced
- Unsalted pistachios – one tbsp, chopped, roasted

Instructions:
1. Add cloves, cardamom, cinnamon, vanilla, maple syrup, chia, and almond milk into the bowl and stir well.
2. Cover with a lid and place it into the refrigerator for eight hours.
3. When ready to serve, combine it well. Place half of the pudding into the glass and top with half of pistachios and bananas.
4. Then, add the remaining pudding and top with remaining pistachios and bananas.
5. Serve and enjoy!

Nutrition: Calories; 264, Carbs; 38.2g, protein; 6.3g, fat; 11.2g, fiber; 10.8g

298. Apple Cinnamon Oatmeal

Preparation time: 5 minutes | **Cooking time:** 40 minutes | **Serving:** 4

Ingredients:
- Crisp apples – four
- Steel-cut oats – one cup
- Water – four cups
- Brown sugar – three tbsp
- Ground cinnamon – half tsp
- Salt – ¼ tsp
- Nonfat plain Greek yogurt – half cup

Instructions:
1. Firstly, cut two apples with a box grater.
2. Add oats into the saucepan and cook over medium-high flame until toasted, for two minutes.
3. Then, add shredded apples and water and boil it.
4. Then, lower the heat and cook for ten minutes.

5. During this, chop two apples.
6. When oats have cooked, add salt, cinnamon, two tbsp brown sugar, chopped apples and stir well for fifteen to twenty minutes.
7. Place between four bowls.
8. Top with ¾ tsp brown sugar and two tbsp yogurt.

Nutrition: Calories; 282,   Carbs; 59.1g, protein; 8g, fat; 2.7g, fiber; 6.3g

299. Apple Butter Bran Muffins

Preparation time: 5 minutes | **Cooking time:** 40 minutes | **Serving:** 12

Ingredients:

- Raisins – half cup
- Whole-wheat flour – ¾ cup
- All-purpose flour – ¾ cup
- Baking powder – 2 ½ tsp
- Salt – ¼ tsp
- Ground cinnamon – half tsp
- Unprocessed wheat bran – ¾ cup
- Egg – one, beaten
- Low-fat milk – half cup
- Spiced apple butter – half cup
- Brown sugar – half cup
- Canola oil – ¼ cup
- Molasses – three tbsp
- Apple – one cup, diced, peeled

Instructions:

1. Preheat the oven to 375 degrees Fahrenheit.
2. Let coat twelve muffin cups with cooking spray.
3. Add raisins into the bowl and cover with hot water and keep it aside.
4. Whisk the cinnamon, salt, baking powder, flour, all-purpose flour, and whole-wheat flour into the bowl. Then, add bran and stir well.
5. Whisk the molasses, oil, brown sugar, apple butter, egg, and milk into the bowl. Make a well in the dry ingredients and place in the wet ingredients. Then, drain

the raisins and add them to the bowl with diced apple. Stir well.
6. Place batter into the pan. Bake for eighteen to twenty-two minutes.
7. Let cool the pan for five minutes.
8. Serve and enjoy!

Nutrition: Calories; 204,   Carbs; 37.6g, protein; 3.9g, fat; 5.7g, fiber; 3.7g

300. Pineapple Raspberry Parfaits

Preparation time: 5 minutes | **Serving:** 4

Ingredients:

- Nonfat peach yogurt – two cups
- Raspberries – half pint
- Pineapple chunks – 1 ½ cups

Instructions:

1. Place pineapple, raspberries, and yogurt into the four glasses.
2. Serve and enjoy!

Nutrition: Calories; 155,   Carbs; 33g, protein; 5.7g, fat; 0.5g, fiber; 2.9g

301. Berry Chia Pudding

Preparation time: 5 minutes | **Chill time:** 8 hours | **Serving:** 2

Ingredients:

- Blackberries, raspberries or diced mango – 1 ¾ cups
- Unsweetened almond milk – one cup
- Chia seeds – ¼ cup
- Pure maple syrup – one tbsp
- Vanilla extract – ¾ tsp
- Whole-milk plain Greek yogurt – half cup
- Granola – ¼ cup

Instructions:

1. Add milk and 1 ¼ cups fruit into the blender and blend until smooth.
2. Transfer it to the medium bowl. Add vanilla, syrup, and chia and combine well. Place it into the refrigerator for eight hours.
3. Place pudding into the two bowls. Layering each serving with two tbsp granola, ¼ cup yogurt, and remaining ¼ cup of fruit.
4. Serve!

Nutrition: Calories; 343, Carbs; 39.4g, protein; 13.8g, fat; 15.4g, fiber; 14.9g

302. Spinach avocado smoothie

Preparation time: 5 minutes | **Serving:** 1

Ingredients:

- Nonfat plain yogurt – one cup
- Fresh spinach – one cup
- Banana – one, frozen
- Avocado – ¼
- Water – two tbsp
- Honey – one tsp

Instructions:

1. Mix the honey, water, avocado, banana, spinach, and yogurt into the blender and blend until smooth.
2. Serve and enjoy!

Nutrition: Calories; 375, Carbs; 57.8g, protein; 17.7g, fat; 8.2g, fiber; 7.8g

303. Strawberry pineapple smoothie

Preparation time: 5 minutes | **Serving:** 1

Ingredients:

- Frozen strawberries – one cup
- Fresh pineapple – one cup, chopped
- Unsweetened almond milk – ¾ cup, chilled
- Almond butter – one tbsp

Instructions:

1. Mix the almond butter, almond milk, pineapple, and strawberries into the blender and process until smooth.
2. Add almond milk more if required.
3. Serve and enjoy!

Nutrition: Calories; 255, Carbs; 39g, protein; 5.6g, fat; 11.1g, fiber; 7.8g

304. Peach Blueberry Parfaits

Preparation time: 10 minutes | **Serving:** 2

Ingredients:

- Vanilla, Peach or blueberry fat-free yogurt – six ounce

- Sweetener multigrain clusters cereal – one cup
- Peach – one, pitted and sliced
- Fresh blueberries – half cup
- Ground cinnamon – ¼ tsp

Instructions:

1. Add half of the yogurt into the two glasses.
2. Top with half of the cereal. Top with half of cinnamon, blueberries, and peaches.
3. Place remaining blueberries, peaches, cereal, and yogurt.
4. Serve and enjoy!

Nutrition: Calories; 166, Carbs; 34g, protein; 11g, fat; 1g, fiber; 7g

305. Raspberry Yogurt Cereal Bowl

Preparation time: 5 minutes | **Serving:** 1

Ingredients:

- Nonfat plain yogurt – one cup
- Wheat cereal – half cup, shredded
- Fresh raspberries – ¼ cup
- Mini chocolate chips – two tsp
- Pumpkin seeds – one tsp
- Ground cinnamon – ¼ tsp

Instructions:

1. Add yogurt into the bowl.
2. Top with cinnamon, pumpkin seeds, chocolate chips, raspberries, and shredded wheat.
3. Serve and enjoy!

Nutrition: Calories; 290, Carbs; 47.8g, protein; 18.4g, fat; 4.6g, fiber; 6g

306. Avocado toast

Preparation time: 10 minutes | **Serving:** 1

Ingredients:

- Mixed salad greens – one cup
- Red-wine vinegar – one tsp
- Extra-virgin olive oil – one tsp
- Pinch of salt
- Pinch of pepper
- Sprouted whole-wheat bread – two slices, toasted

- Plain hummus – ¼ cup
- Alfalfa sprouts – ¼ cup
- Avocado – ¼, sliced
- Unsalted sunflower seeds – two tsp

Instructions:
1. Firstly, toss greens with pepper, salt, oil, and vinegar into the bowl.
2. Spread each slice of toast with two tbsp hummus and top with greens, sprouts, avocado, and spinach.
3. Sprinkle with sunflower seeds.
4. Serve and enjoy!

Nutrition: Calories; 429, carbohydrates; 46.4g, protein; 16.2g, fat; 21.9g, fiber; 15.1g

307. Loaded Pita Pockets

Preparation time: 5 minutes | **Serving:** 1

Ingredients:
- Whole wheat pita – one, halved
- Low-fat cottage cheese – half cup
- Walnut halves – four, chopped
- Banana – one, sliced

Instructions:
1. Fill each pita with banana, walnuts, and cottage cheese.

Nutrition: Calories; 307, Carbs; 46g, protein; 21g, fat; 8.5g, fiber; 11g

308. Homestyle Pancake Mix

Preparation Time: 10 minutes | **Cooking Time:** 30 minutes | **Servings:** 16

Ingredients:
- 6 cups whole-wheat pastry flour
- 1 ½ cups (210 g) cornmeal
- 1/2 cup (100 g) sugar
- 11/2 cups (102 g) non-fat dry milk
- 2 tablespoons (28 g) baking powder

Instructions:
1. Merge all ingredients and store them in a tightly covered jar. To cook, attach 1 cup of water to 1 cup of the mix; use less water if you want a thicker pancake. Stir only until lumps disappear.

2. Coat a non-stick skillet or griddle with non-stick vegetable oil spray and preheat until drops of cold-water bounce and sputter.
3. Drop the batter to the desired size and cook until bubbles form and edges begin to dry.
4. Turn only once.

Nutrition: Calories: 75, Carbs: 0.1g, Protein: 13.4g, Fat: 1.7g, Sugar: 0g, Sodium: 253 mg

309. Multigrain Pancakes

Preparation Time: 10 minutes | **Cooking Time:** 30 minutes | **Servings:** 6

Ingredients:
- 1 ½ cup whole-wheat pastry flour
- 1/4 cup (35 g) cornmeal
- 1/4 cup (20 g) rolled oats
- 2 tablespoons oat bran
- 2 tablespoons wheat germ
- 2 tablespoons (18 g) toasted wheat cereal, such as Wheaten
- 1 teaspoon baking soda
- 1/2 teaspoon baking powder
- 1 teaspoon vanilla extract
- 11/2 cups (355 ml) skim milk
- 2 egg whites

Instructions:
1. Mix all dry ingredients. Add milk to make the batter. The thicker batter makes thicker pancakes. Set aside to rest for half an hour. Beat the egg whites until stiff peaks form.
2. Gently, fold into the batter after it has rested. Spoon onto the moderate griddle and cook until bubbles break. Turn and cook until done.
3. Bake more slowly than with regular pancakes because of the heavy batter.

Nutrition: Calories: 303, Fat: 14g, Carbs: 15g, Sugar: 10g, Fiber: 2g, Protein: 30g, Sodium: 387mg

310. Cinnamon–Oat Bran Pancakes

Preparation Time: 10 minutes | **Cooking Time:** 30 minutes | **Servings:** 6

Ingredients:

- 3/4 cup (75 g) oat bran
- 3/4 cup whole-wheat pastry flour
- 1 tablespoon sugar
- 1/2 teaspoon baking powder
- 1/2 teaspoon cinnamon
- 1/4 teaspoon baking soda
- 1 ¼ cup (295 ml) buttermilk
- 1 tablespoon (15 ml) canola oil
- 1/2 cup (55 g) finely chopped pecans

Instructions:

1. In a medium mixing bowl, combine all dry ingredients. Set aside.
2. In another mixing bowl, combine the buttermilk and oil. Add to dry ingredients, stirring until just combined. Stir in the pecans.
3. Cook on the hot griddle. Set 1/4 cup of the batter for each pancake.

Nutrition: Calories: 297, Fat: 11g, Carbs: 18g, Sugar: 15g, Fiber: 1g, Protein: 34g, Sodium: 528mg

311. Whole-Wheat Buttermilk Pancakes

Preparation Time: 10 minutes | **Cooking Time:** 30 minutes | **Servings:** 6

Ingredients:

- 1 cup whole-wheat flour
- 1/2 teaspoon baking soda
- 1/4 teaspoon cinnamon
- 1 ¼ cup (295 ml) buttermilk
- 2 eggs
- 3 tablespoons (45 ml) canola oil

Instructions:

1. Blend all dry ingredients.
2. Merge the wet ingredients except for oil. Mix both mixtures. It will be slightly lumpy.

3. Heat oil in a cast-iron skillet.
2. Pour 1/4 of the batter into the pan.
3. When the pancake bubbles, turn and cook for 1-2 minutes more.

Nutrition: Calories: 207, Fat: 16g, Carbs: 5g, Sugar: 2g, Fiber: 1g, Protein: 12g, Sodium: 366mg

312. Cornmeal Pancakes

Preparation Time: 10 minutes | **Cooking Time:** 30 minutes | **Servings:** 6

Ingredients:

- 1 cup (235 ml) boiling water
- 3/4 cup (105 g) cornmeal
- 1 ¼ cup (295 ml) buttermilk
- 2 eggs
- 1 cup whole-wheat pastry flour
- 1 tablespoon baking powder
- 1/4 teaspoon baking soda
- 1/4 cup (60 ml) canola oil

Instructions:

1. Pour water over the cornmeal, stir until thick. Add the buttermilk; beat in the eggs.
2. Mix flour, baking powder, and baking soda.
2. Add to the cornmeal mixture.
3. Stir in canola oil.
4. Bake on a hot griddle.

Nutrition: Calories: 280, Fat: 16g, Carbs: 5g, Sugar: 1g, Fiber: 0g, Protein: 29g, Sodium: 508mg

313. Oven-Baked Pancake

Preparation Time: 10 minutes | **Cooking Time:** 30 minutes | **Servings:** 6

Ingredients:

- 3 eggs
- 1/2 cup whole-wheat pastry flour
- 1/2 cup (120 ml) skim milk
- 1/4 cup (55 g) unsalted butter, divided
- 2 tablespoons (26 g) sugar
- 2 tablespoons (18 g) slivered almonds, toasted
- 2 tablespoons (30 ml) lemon juice

Instructions:

1. Set the eggs with an electric mixer at medium speed until well blended. Gradually add flour, beating until smooth. Add milk and 2 tablespoons (28 g) melted butter; beat until the batter is smooth.
2. Pour the batter into a 10-inch (25 cm) skillet coated with non-stick vegetable oil spray. Bake at 400°F for 15 minutes until the pancake is puffed and golden brown.
3. Sprinkle with sugar and toasted almonds. Combine the remaining butter and lemon juice, heat until butter melts. Serve over the hot pancake.

Nutrition: Calories: 429, Fat: 47g, Carbs: 5g, Sugar: 1g, Fiber: 1g, Protein: 27g

314. Baked Pancake

Preparation Time: 10 minutes | **Cooking Time:** 30 minutes | **Servings:** 4

Ingredients:

- 1 ½ cup whole-wheat pastry flour
- 1 ½ cup (355 ml) skim milk
- 4 eggs, slightly beaten
- 1/4 cup (55 g) unsalted butter
- 1 cup (170 g) sliced strawberries

Instructions:

1. Gradually, add flour and milk to the eggs. Melt the butter in 9 x 13-inch (23 x 33 cm) pan.
2. Pour the batter over melted butter. Bake at 400°F for about 30 minutes.
3. Serve with fresh sliced strawberries.

Nutrition: Calories: 270, Fat: 11g, Carbs: 4g, Sugar: 1g, Fiber: 1g, Protein: 39g, Sodium: 664mg

315. Wheat Waffles

Preparation Time: 10 minutes | **Cooking Time:** 30 minutes | **Servings:** 8

Ingredients:

- 2 cups whole-wheat pastry flour
- 4 teaspoons (18 g) baking powder
- 2 tablespoons (40 g) honey

- 1 ¾ cup (410 ml) skim milk
- 4 tablespoons (60 ml) canola oil
- 2 eggs

Instructions:

1. Mix all dry ingredients.
2. Stir in the remaining ingredients.
3. For lighter waffles, separate the eggs. Beat the egg whites and carefully fold in.
2. Set into a waffle iron coated with non-stick vegetable oil spray.

Nutrition: Calories: 389, Fat: 20g, Carbs: 1g, Sugar: 0g, Fiber: 1g, Protein: 49g, Sodium: 381mg

316. Oatmeal Waffles

Preparation Time: 10 minutes | **Cooking Time:** 30 minutes | **Servings:** 5

Ingredients:

- 1 ½ cup whole-wheat pastry flour
- 1 cup (80 g) quick-cooking oats
- 1 tablespoon baking powder
- 1 teaspoon cinnamon
- 2 tablespoons (30 g) brown sugar
- 3 tablespoons (42 g) unsalted butter
- 1 ½ cup (355 ml) skim milk
- 2 eggs, slightly beaten

Instructions:

1. In a bowl, merge all dry ingredients and set aside.
2. Melt the butter, add milk and eggs. Mix well and then add to the flour mixture.
3. Stir until well blended.
2. Set into a waffle iron coated with non-stick vegetable oil spray.

Nutrition: Calories: 224, Fat: 14g, Carbs: 15g, Sugar: 10g, Fiber: 5g, Protein: 12g

317. Bran Applesauce Muffins

Preparation Time: 10 minutes | **Cooking Time:** 30 minutes | **Servings:** 12

Ingredients:

- 3/4 cup (30 g) bran flakes cereal, crushed
- 1/2 cup (100 g) sugar

- 1 teaspoon baking soda
- 1 teaspoon cinnamon
- 1/2 teaspoon nutmeg
- 1 cup (245 g) applesauce
- 1/2 cup (120 ml) canola oil
- 1 teaspoon vanilla extract
- 2 eggs
- 1/2 cup (75 g) raisins
- 1 tablespoon sugar
- 1/2 teaspoon cinnamon

Instructions:
1. Heat the oven to 400°F (200°C, gas mark 6). Set 12 muffin cups with baking paper or sprinkle with non-stick vegetable oil spray.
2. In a bowl, combine all ingredients except the sugar and cinnamon; mix well.
3. Set the batter into the prepared muffin cups, filling 2/3 full.
4. In a bowl, combine the sugar and cinnamon, sprinkle over the top of each muffin.
5. Bake at 400°F for 20 minutes or until a toothpick inserted in the center comes out clean.
6. Immediately remove from pan. Serve warm.

Nutrition: Calories: 270, Fat: 11g, Carbs: 4g, Sugar: 1g, Fiber: 1g, Protein: 39g, Sodium: 664mg

318. Oat Bran Muffins

Preparation Time: 10 minutes | **Cooking Time:** 15-17 minutes | **Servings:** 12

Ingredients:
- 2 ¼ cup (225 g) oat bran
- 1 tablespoon baking powder
- 1/4 cup (35 g) raisins
- 1/4 cup (28 g) chopped pecans
- 2 eggs
- 2 tablespoons (28 ml) olive oil
- 1/4 cup (85 g) honey
- 1 ¼ cup (295 ml) water

Instructions:
1. Preheat the oven to 425°F (220°C, gas mark 7).
2. Put all dry ingredients, raisins, and pecans in a mixing bowl.
3. Beat the eggs, olive oil, honey, and water lightly.
2. Attach this mixture to the dry ingredients and stir until moistened.
3. Line muffin pans with paper liners or spray with non-stick vegetable oil spray and fill about half full.
4. Bake for 15-17 minutes.

Nutrition: Calories: 270, Fat: 11g, Carbs: 4g, Sugar: 1g, Fiber: 1g, Protein: 39g, Sodium: 664mg

319. Orange Bran Muffins

Preparation Time: 10 minutes | **Cooking Time:** 25 minutes | **Servings:** 12

Ingredients:
- 2 ½ cups (300 g) whole-wheat pastry flour
- 1 tablespoon baking soda
- 3 cups (177 g) raisin bran cereal
- 1/2 cup (100 g) sugar
- 1 teaspoon cinnamon
- 1 ½ tablespoon orange peel
- 2 cups (460 g) plain fat-free yogurt
- 2 eggs, beaten
- 1/2 cup (120 ml) cooking oil

Instructions:
1. In a bowl, merge flour and baking soda.
2. Add the cereal, sugar, cinnamon, and orange peel, mixing well.
2. Briefly, but thoroughly mix in the yogurt, beaten eggs, and cooking oil.
3. Set into muffin tins lined with paper liners or sprayed with non-stick vegetable oil spray.
4. Bake for 20 minutes in a 375°F (190°C, gas mark 5) oven.

Nutrition: Calories: 270, Fat: 11g, Carbs: 4g, Sugar: 1g, Fiber: 1g, Protein: 39g

320. Pasta Fritters

Preparation Time: 10 minutes | **Cooking Time:** 30 minutes | **Servings:** 6

Ingredients:

- 2 cups (280 g) leftover spaghetti
- 1/4 cup (25 g) chopped scallions
- 1/2 cup (56 g) shredded zucchini
- 78 ml canola oil
- 1 egg
- 1 cup whole-wheat pastry flour
- 1teaspoon black pepper
- 1 cup (235 ml) water

Instructions:

1. About 35 minutes before serving, coarsely chop the cooked spaghetti, onions, and shred zucchini; set aside. In a 12-inch (30 cm) skillet, over high heat, heat canola oil until very hot.
2. Meanwhile, prepare the batter.
3. In a bowl, with a wire whisker or fork, mix the egg, flour, pepper, and water.
4. Stir in the spaghetti mixture.
5. Drop it into hot oil in the skillet by 1/4 cup into 4 mounds about 2 inches (5 cm) apart.
6. With a spatula, flatten each to make 3-inch (7.5 cm) pancake.
7. Set the fritters until golden brown on both sides; drain them on paper towels.
8. Keep warm. Repeat with the remaining mixture, adding more oil to the skillet if needed.

Nutrition: Calories: 178, Fat: 4g, Carbs: 7g, Fiber: 2g, Protein: 27g

321. Cinnamon Honey Scones

Preparation Time: 10 minutes | **Cooking Time:** 20 minutes | **Servings:** 5

Ingredients:

- 1 ¾ cup (220 g) whole-wheat pastry flour
- 1 ½ teaspoon baking powder
- 1/4 teaspoon cinnamon
- 6 tablespoons (85 g) unsalted butter, softened
- 1 tablespoon (20 g) honey

- 1/2 cup (120 ml) skim milk
- 1 egg

Instructions:

1. Preheat the oven to 450°F (230°C, gas mark 8). Line a baking sheet with aluminum foil.
2. In a bowl, merge the flour, baking powder, and cinnamon with a wooden spoon.
3. Work the butter into the mixture by hand until it is yellow.
4. Add honey and milk, then the egg. Stir with a wooden spoon until thoroughly mixed.
5. Scoop a spoonful of dough and drop it onto the baking sheet.
6. Leave 1 inch (2.5 cm) between each. Bake for 15 minutes or until golden brown.
7. Cool for 5 minutes.

Nutrition: Calories: 179, Fat: 13g, Carbs: 6g, Sugar: 3g, Fiber: 1g, Protein: 10g, Sodium: 265mg

322. Oatmeal Raisin Scones

Preparation Time: 10 minutes | **Cooking Time:** 20-25 minutes | **Servings:** 5

Ingredients:

- 2 cups whole-wheat pastry flour
- 3 tablespoons (45 g) brown sugar
- 1 teaspoon baking powder
- 1/2 teaspoon baking soda
- 1/2 cup unsalted butter, chilled
- 1 ½ cup (120 g) rolled oats
- 1/2 cup (75 g) raisins
- 1 cup (235 ml) buttermilk
- 2 tablespoons cinnamon
- 2 tablespoons (26 g) sugar

Instructions:

1. Heat the oven to 375°F (190°C, gas mark 5). Merge flour, brown sugar, baking powder, and baking soda.
2. Divide in the butter until the mixture resembles coarse crumbs.
2. Stir in oats and raisins.
3. Add the buttermilk and mix with a fork until the dough forms a ball.

4. Set out on a lightly floured board and knead for 6-8 minutes.
5. Pat the dough into 1/2-inch (1 cm) thickness.
6. Divide 8-10 rounds or wedges and place them on an ungreased baking sheet.
7. Sprinkle with sugar and cinnamon.
8. Bake for 20-25 minutes.

Nutrition: Calories: 329, Fat: 17g, Carbs: 9g, Sugar: 3g, Fiber: 5g, Protein: 37g, Sodium: 430mg

323. Whole Grain Scones

Preparation Time: 10 minutes | **Cooking Time:** 30 minutes | **Servings:** 5

Ingredients:

- 1 egg
- 1/2 cup (100 g) sugar
- 5 tablespoons (75 ml) canola oil
- teaspoon lemon peel
- 1/2 cup (40 g) rolled oats
- 1/4 cup (25 g) wheat bran
- 1 ½ cup whole-wheat pastry flour
- 2 tablespoons poppy seeds
- 1 tablespoon baking powder
- 1/2 teaspoon cinnamon
- 1/2 cup (120 ml) skim milk

Lemon Topping:

- 3 tablespoons (45 ml) lemon juice
- 1/4 cup (25 g) confectioners' sugar

Instructions:

1. Preheat the oven to 375°F (190°C, gas mark 5).
2. Set the egg, sugar, and oil together in a bowl.
3. Mix the lemon peel and all the dry ingredients in a separate bowl.
4. Stir with a wooden spoon until all of them are evenly dispersed throughout.
2. Slowly, add the dry ingredients into the egg, sugar, and oil.
3. Mix to create a thick dough.
4. Add the milk and mix well.

5. Coat a baking sheet with non-stick vegetable oil spray
6. Bake until the crust is barely golden brown, and the dough is dry.
7. Detach from the oven and let cool for 10 minutes.
8. With a fork, mix the lemon topping ingredients until the sugar is completely melded in.
9. Drizzle 1 tablespoon over each scone.

Nutrition: Calories: 280, Fat: 16g, Carbs: 5g, Sugar: 1g, Fiber: 0g, Protein: 29g, Sodium: 508mg

324. Granola

Preparation Time: 10 minutes | **Cooking Time:** 30 minutes | **Servings:** 30

Ingredients:

- 6 cups (480 g) rolled oats
- 6 cups rolled wheat
- 2 cups (290 g) sunflower seeds
- 4 ounces (113 g) sesame seeds
- 2 cups (190 g) peanuts
- 3 cups (255 g) coconut
- 1 cup (112 g) wheat germ
- 1 ½ cup (355 ml) canola oil
- 1 cup (340 g) honey
- 1/2 cup (170 g) molasses
- 1 tablespoon (15 ml) vanilla extract
- 1 cup (145 g) raisins

Instructions:

1. Merge all dry ingredients in a large bowl.
2. Put aside.
2. Heat the oil, honey, molasses, and vanilla together and mix with the dry ingredients.
3. Spread the mixture on baking sheets.
4. Bake at 350°F until light brown. Stir frequently to brown evenly. Detach from the oven and add the raisins or any other dried fruit.

Nutrition: Calories: 270, Fat: 11g, Carbs: 4g, Sugar: 1g, Fiber: 1g

325. Toasty Nut Granola

Preparation Time: 10 minutes | **Cooking Time:** 35 minutes | **Servings:** 30

Ingredients:

- 6 cups (480 g) rolled oats
- 1 cup (110 g) chopped pecans
- 3/4 cup (84 g) wheat germ
- 1/2 cup (115 g) firmly packed brown sugar
- 1/2 cup (40 g) shredded coconut
- 1/2 cup (72 g) sesame seeds
- 1/2 cup (120 ml) canola oil
- 1/2 cup (170 g) honey
- 1 ½ teaspoon vanilla extract

Instructions:

1. Toast the oats in a 9 x 13-inch (23 x 33 cm) pan at 350°F (180°C, gas mark 4) for 10 minutes.
2. Merge the remaining ingredients in a large bowl and add the toasted oats.
3. Bake on 2 baking sheets at 350°F (180°C, gas mark 4) for 20-25 minutes.
4. Stir when cool and store in the refrigerator.

Nutrition: Calories: 270, Fat: 11g, Carbs: 4g, Sugar: 1g, Fiber: 1g, Protein: 39g, Sodium: 664mg

326. Breakfast Bars

Preparation Time: 10 minutes | **Cooking Time:** 30 minutes | **Servings:** 30

Ingredients:

- 1 cup (80 g) quick-cooking oats
- 1/2 cup whole-wheat flour
- 1/2 cup (58 g) crunchy wheat-barley cereal, such as Grape-Nuts
- 1/2 teaspoon cinnamon
- 1 egg
- 1/4 cup (60 g) applesauce
- 1/4 cup (85 g) honey
- 3 tablespoons (45 g) brown sugar
- 2 tablespoons (28 ml) canola oil
- 1/4 cup (36 g) sunflower seeds, unsalted

- 1/4 cup (30 g) chopped walnuts
- 7 ounces (198 g) dried fruit

Instructions:

1. Preheat the oven to 325°F (170°C, gas mark 3). Set a 9-inch (23 cm) square baking pan with aluminum foil.
2. Spray the foil with non-stick vegetable oil.
2. In a bowl, stir together the oats, flour, cereal, and cinnamon.
3. Add the egg, applesauce, honey, brown sugar, and oil. Merge well.
4. Stir in the sunflower seeds, walnuts, and dried fruit. Spread the mixture evenly in the prepared pan.
5. Bake for 30 minutes or until firm and lightly browned around the edges. Let cool. Use the foil to lift from the pan.
6. Cut into bars and store in the refrigerator.

Nutrition: Calories: 280, Fat: 16g, Carbs: 5g, Sugar: 1g, Fiber: 0g, Protein: 29g

327. Whole-Wheat Coffee Cake

Preparation Time: 10 minutes | **Cooking Time:** 30-45 minutes | **Servings:** 12

Ingredients:

For the cake:

- 1 ¾ cup (210 g) whole-wheat pastry flour
- 1 teaspoon baking powder
- 1 teaspoon baking soda
- 1/2 cup (112 g) unsalted butter, softened
- 1 cup (133 g) sugar
- 2 eggs
- 1 teaspoon vanilla extract
- 1 cup (230 g) sour cream

For the Bran Nut Filling:

- 1 cup (75 g) packed brown sugar
- 1/2 cup bran flakes (20 g) cereal
- 1/2 cup (60 g) chopped walnuts
- 1 teaspoon cinnamon

Instructions:

For the cake:

1. Merge flour, baking powder, and baking soda; set aside.

2. In a large bowl, beat the butter, sugar, eggs, and vanilla until light and fluffy. At low speed stir in the sour cream alternately with the flour mixture until blended.

For the Bran Nut Filling:

3. Combine all filling ingredients in a small bowl. To assemble the cake, spread 1/3 of the sour cream mixture in a 9-inch (23 cm) square pan coated with non-stick vegetable oil spray.

4. Sprinkle on about 1/2 cup of the filling. Repeat layering twice. Bake in a preheated oven at 350°F (180C, gas mark 4) for 30-45 minutes. Cool slightly.

Nutrition: Calories: 224, Fat: 14g, Carbs: 15g, Sugar: 10g, Fiber: 5g, Protein: 12g

328. Crunchy Breakfast Topping

Preparation Time: 10 minutes | **Cooking Time:** 30 minutes | **Servings:** 12

Ingredients:
- 1/4 cup (55 g) unsalted butter
- 1 ¼ cup (140 g) wheat germ
- 1/2 cup packed brown sugar
- 1/2 cup (47 g) ground almonds
- 1 tablespoon grated orange peel
- 1/2 teaspoon cinnamon

Instructions:
1. Melt the butter in a 9 x 13-inch (23 x 33 cm) baking pan into the oven for about 4 minutes.
2. Add the remaining ingredients and mix well. Bake until deep golden brown. Stir.
3. Cool and store in the refrigerator for up to 3 months.

Nutrition: Calories: 178, Fat: 4g, Carbs: 7g, Fiber: 2g, Protein: 27g

329. Veggie Sandwich

Preparation time: 10 minutes | **Cooking time:** 0 minutes | **Serving:** 8

Ingredients:
- Sprouted-grain bread – two slices, toasted
- Avocado – ¼, mashed

- Hummus – one tbsp
- Salt – one pinch
- Cucumber – four slices
- Tomato – two slices
- Carrot – 2 tbsp, shredded
- Clementine – one, peeled

Instructions:
1. Place one slice of bread onto the plate and spread avocado and hummus.
2. Sprinkle with salt.
3. Fill the sandwich with carrot, tomato, and cucumber.
4. Cut in half and serve with Clementine.

Nutrition: Calories; 315, Fat; 10.1g, Carbs; 48.6g, Protein; 11.4g, Fiber; 12.5g

330. Date-Sweetened Banana Bread

Preparation Time: 20 minutes | **Cooking Time:** 50 minutes | **Servings:** 8

Ingredients:
- Two flax eggs (2 tablespoons flax meal + 6 tablespoons water)
- 2 cups gluten-free oat flour
- 2 teaspoon cinnamon
- 2 teaspoon baking powder
- 1/2 teaspoon baking soda
- ½ teaspoon salt
- 1 large ripe & spotty bananas, mashed (about 1 1/2 cups)
- + 1 banana to top, sliced it in half lengthwise (optional)
- 1 cup pitted Medjool date, packed
- ½ cup unsweetened non-dairy milk
- 1 ½ –2 teaspoons of pure vanilla extract (I used 2)
- One teaspoon of apple cider vinegar

Instructions:
1. Preheat the oven to 350°F and line or lightly grease a 9-inch bread pan with parchment paper.
2. Stir together the flax meal and the water. Set aside for about 15 minutes to thicken.

3. Combine the oat flour, baking soda, baking powder, salt, cinnamon, and if using in a large mixing basin. Set aside after thoroughly mixing.
4. Combine the dates, almond milk, vanilla essence, and apple cider vinegar in a food processor.
5. Process until smooth, then use a spoon to incorporate the mashed banana and flax egg.
6. Stir the date and banana mixture into the dry ingredients until a batter forms.
7. Pour the batter into the prepared loaf pan and top with the optional banana, sliced side up, if preferred (refer to photos in post).
8. Bake for 50-60 minutes, or until a toothpick inserted into the center comes out clean.
9. Remove from the oven and set aside to cool fully before slicing.

Nutrition: Calories: 429, Carbs: 19g, Protein: 13g, Fat: 27g, Cholesterol: 10 mg

331. Cobb Salad

Preparation time: 10 minutes | **Cooking time:** 0 minutes | **Serving:** 1

Ingredients:

- Iceberg lettuce – three cups, chopped
- Chicken thighs – one, diced, roasted
- Celery – one stalk, diced
- Carrot – one, diced
- Egg – one, hard-boiled, diced
- Blue cheese – one tbsp, crumbled
- Honey and mustard vinaigrette – 2 tbsp

Instructions:

1. Place blue cheese, egg, carrot, celery, chicken, and lettuce into the salad bowl.
2. Drizzle with dressing.

Nutrition: Calories; 481, Fat; 16.7g, Carbs; 67.6g, Protein; 17.3g, Fiber; 13.4g

332. Pumpkin Pie Butter

Preparation Time: 10 minutes | **Cooking Time:** 50 minutes | **Servings:** 2

Ingredients:

- 2 1/2 cups packed freshly roasted pumpkin (see below for instructions - can also use canned if you like)
- 1/2 teaspoons cinnamon
- 1/2 teaspoon ginger
- 1/2 teaspoon nutmeg
- 1/2 teaspoon ground cloves
- 1/4 teaspoon salt
- 2 tablespoon maple syrup (optional - leave out for Whole30)

Instructions:

1. If using fresh pumpkin, chop it into big pieces (skin on) and remove the seeds (keep them roasting!).
2. Rub the flesh with a small amount of neutral oil (I use coconut oil) and roast for 45 minutes to an hour at 375 degrees Fahrenheit or until soft.
3. Toast when the pumpkin is almost done.
4. Melt the butter in a medium pan over medium-low heat. And toast them for 3-6 minutes, stirring regularly, until they begin to brown and become aromatic.
5. Remove from the heat and put aside.
6. Allow the pumpkin to cool for a few minutes before removing the meat from the skin.
7. Then, in a high-powered blender, combine 2 1/2 cups of the flesh (squeeze it into a measuring cup to make sure you pack it in) (I used my Vitamix).
8. Spices, maple syrup (optional), and salt Blend for 1–3 minutes, or until smooth and creamy.
9. If desired, add extra spices or sugar. Refrigerate in a securely sealed glass jar for 2-3 weeks before serving.

Note: Pumpkin butter may be kept in the fridge for 2-3 weeks in a firmly sealed glass jar. It is also possible to freeze it for up to 6 months. For ease of usage, I recommend freezing in serving quantities of 2-3. I adore using fresh pumpkins since the freshly roasted flavor is fantastic, and they are only available for a few months of the year. I recommend choosing sugar or pie pumpkins since they have the greatest flavor and natural sweetness. You'll need a good-sized pumpkin. Avoid using "jack-o-lantern" pumpkins. If you want, you may use canned pumpkin, but it will be less thick.

Nutrition: Calories: 76, Carbs: 27g, Protein: 11g, Fat: 28g, Cholesterol: 36 mg

333. Packed Burrito

Preparation Time: 10 minutes | **Cooking Time:** 10 minutes | **Servings:** 4

Ingredients:
- ½ of medium red onion (chopped)
- Two garlic cloves (minced)
- 12 oz of extra firm tofu (pressed, see notes)
- 2 Tablespoon olive oil
- ¼ tablespoon turmeric
- ¼ tablespoon cumin
- Sea salt & to taste
- ½ cup of black beans
- ½ of avocado (chopped into small pieces)
- 1/3 cup of salsa any of choice (I used pico de gallo)
- Three large whole wheat tortillas

Instructions:
1. Heat the oil in a medium-sized pan over medium heat.
2. Once cooked, add your onions and season with salt and pepper.
3. Cook until the mixture has been cooked down and color gently (about 4-5 minutes).
4. Cook for another minute, frequently stirring, after adding your garlic.
5. Tofu should be added at this point (crumble it with your hands, see picture). Stir in the turmeric, cumin, and another sprinkle of sea salt. Stir until completely mixed.
6. Turn off the heat.

7. To construct your burritos, arrange all of your ingredients (allowing room on both sides, as seen in the photo) and roll up!
8. Enjoy!
9. You may freeze them by placing them in a tight plastic bag.

Nutrition: Calories: 519, Carbs: 17g, Protein: 27g, Fat: 18g, Cholesterol: 251 mg

334. Black Beans and Avocado Toasts

Preparation Time: 5 minutes | **Cooking Time:** 15 minutes | **Servings:** 2

Ingredients:
- 2 slices of bread of your choice
- ½ avocado
- 4 tablespoons boiled black beans
- 2 tablespoon chopped green onions
- ½ lime
- ¼ teaspoon sea salt

Instructions:
1. Mash the avocado and spread it on the bread pieces.
2. Serve with black beans and green onion on top.
3. Sprinkle salt and lemon juice on top of each.
4. Serve as fast as possible!

Nutrition: Calories: 64, Carbs: 0g, Protein: 5g, Fat: 17g, Cholesterol: 20 mg

335. Blood Orange Chia Pudding

Preparation Time: 5 minutes | **Cooking Time:** 5 minutes | **Servings:** 2

Ingredients:
- 3 blood oranges, peeled (400 grams)
- 3/4 cup lite coconut milk
- 1/2 teaspoon cinnamon
- 1/3 cup chia s

Instructions:
1. In a Vita mix, high-powered blender, or food processor, combine the oranges, coconut milk, and cinnamon. About 1

minute, process until smooth and all ingredients are mixed.

2. Transfer to a resealable medium-sized bowl. Stir in the chia seeds until well blended. Cover and place in the refrigerator for 3 hours or overnight.
3. Serve plain or with preferred toppings.
4. Enjoy!

Nutrition: Calories: 127, Carbs: 14g, Protein: 8g, Fat: 12g, Cholesterol: 162 mg

336. Pumpkin Pie Chia Pudding

Preparation Time: 10 minutes | **Cooking Time:** 180 minutes | **Servings:** 2

Ingredients:

- 1/2 cup raw pecans
- 1/2 cups of pumpkin puree (canned or fresh)
- 1/2 cups almond milk
- 2 teaspoon cinnamon
- 1/2 teaspoon ground ginger
- 1/2 teaspoon nutmeg
- pinch of sea salt
- 1/4 cup chia s
- optional toppings: fresh fruit, nut butter, whipped cream, cinnamon

Instructions:

1. Toasted pecans Allow a small skillet to heat up over medium-low heat for about 30 seconds.
2. Toast the nuts for 4-5 minutes, stirring continuously, until golden brown.
3. In a high-powered blender or food processor, combine pecans, pumpkin, almond milk, cinnamon, ginger, nutmeg, and salt.
4. About 1-2 minutes, process until smooth and all ingredients are mixed.
5. Transfer to a resealable medium-sized bowl. Stir in the chia seeds until well combined.
6. Cover and place in the refrigerator for 3 hours or overnight.
7. Serve plain or with preferred toppings. Enjoy!

Nutrition: Calories: 410, Carbs: 27 g, Protein: 38g, Fat: 18g, Cholesterol: 109 mg

337. Lentil Fritters

Preparation Time: 15 minutes | **Cooking Time:** 10 minutes | **Servings:** 2

Ingredients:

- 300g leftover basic lentils
- a handful of chopped coriander
- 2 chopped spring onion
- 50g gram flour
- 2 carrots
- 2 courgettes
- 1 handful of coriander
- ½ tablespoon oil
- juice of 1 lime
- 3 tablespoon rape oil

Instructions:

1. Set aside the remaining lentils with the chopped coriander, spring onion, and gram flour.
2. Cut the carrots and courgettes into long ribbons with a peeler, then mix the coriander in oil and lime juice.
3. In a frying pan, heat the rape oil.
4. Flatten four dollops of the lentil mixture into patties.
5. Fry until golden on each side, then serve with the ribbon salad.

Nutrition: Calories: 162, Carbs: 22 g, Protein: 18 g, Fat: 12g Cholesterol: 137 mg

338. Great Luncheon Salad

Preparation Time: 20 minutes | **Cooking Time:** 5 minutes | **Servings:** 4

Ingredients:

For Salad:

- ½ C. homemade vegetable broth
- ½ C. couscous
- 3 C. canned red kidney beans, rinsed and drained
- 2 large tomatoes, peeled, seeded and chopped
- 5 C. fresh spinach, torn

For Dressing:

- 1 garlic clove, minced
- 2 tbsp. shallots, minced
- 2 tsp. lemon zest, grated finely
- ¼ C. fresh lemon juice
- 2 tbsp. extra-virgin olive oil
- Salt and freshly ground black pepper, to taste

Instructions:

1. In a pan, add the broth over medium heat and bring to a boil.
2. Add the couscous and stir to combine.
3. Cover the pan and immediately remove from the heat.
4. Set aside, covered for about 5-10 minutes or until all the liquid is absorbed.
5. For salad: in a large serving bowl, add the couscous and remaining ingredients and stir to combine.
6. For dressing: in another small bowl, add all the ingredients and beat until well combined.
7. Pour the dressing over salad and gently toss to coat well.
8. Serve immediately.

Nutrition: Calories: 341; Carbs: 53.2g; Protein: 15.7g; Fat: 8.5g; Sugar: 6.6g; Sodium: 670mg; Fiber: 13.5g

339. Bean and Veggie Taco Bowl

Preparation time: 20 minutes | **Cooking time:** 0 minutes | **Serving:** 1

Ingredients:

- Olive oil – one tsp
- Green bell pepper – half, cored, and sliced
- Red onion – half, sliced
- Cooked brown rice – half cup
- Black beans – ¼ cup, rinsed
- Sharp cheddar cheese – ¼ cup, shredded
- Pico de gallo or salsa – ¼ cup
- Cilantro – 2 tbsp

Instructions:

1. Add oil into the skillet and place it over medium flame.
2. Add onion and bell pepper and cook for 5 to 8 minutes.
3. Mound rice and beans into the bowl. Top with cilantro, pico de gallo, cheese, and vegetables.
4. Top with hot sauce and lime wedges.

Nutrition: Calories; 435, fat; 15.5g, Carbs; 59.6g, Protein; 16.4g, Fiber; 9.6g

340. Winter Vegetable & Lentil Soup

Preparation Time: 10 minutes | **Cooking Time:** 30 minutes | **Servings:** 2

Ingredients:

- 85g dried red lentils
- 2 carrots, quartered lengthways then diced
- 3 sticks celery, sliced
- 2 small leeks, sliced
- 2 tablespoon tomato purée
- 2 tablespoon fresh thyme leaves
- 1 large garlic clove, chopped
- 2 tablespoon vegetable bouillon powder
- 2 heaped tablespoon ground coriander

Instructions:

1. Place all of the ingredients in a large pan. Pour in 1½ liters of hot water and stir thoroughly.
2. Cook for 30 minutes, or until the veggies and lentils are soft.
3. Ladle into bowls and serve immediately or blitz a third of the soup with a hand blender or in a food processor if you like a thick texture.

Nutrition: Calories: 152, Carbs: 38g, Protein: 40g, Fat: 53g, Cholesterol: 20 mg

341. High-Fiber Dumplings

Preparation Time: 10 minutes | **Cooking Time:** 10 minutes | **Servings:** 8

Ingredients:

- 200 g cream quark
- 60 g psyllium husks
- 10 g bamboo fibers
- 1 bowl Vegetable broth
- 2 eggs

Instructions:

2. Take a bowl and add the psyllium husks along with the bamboo fibers.
3. Mix well with a spoon.
4. Put the eggs in the same bowl, add the cream curd and vegetable stock. Knead well, it's best done by hand.
5. Alternatively, the kneading hooks of the mixer can be used.
6. Set a large saucepan with water and bring to a boil on the stove.
7. In the meantime, moisten your hands with water and roll the dough into 12 balls.
8. Put the balls in the hot water and cook for 10 minutes, then serve.
9. High-fiber vegetables like beans and matching sauces also taste great.

Nutrition: Calories: 75, Carbs: 0.1g, Protein:13.4g, Fat: 1.7g, Sugar: 0g, Sodium: 253mg

342. Pizza Made with Bamboo Fibers

Preparation Time: 10 minutes | **Cooking Time:** 20 minutes | **Servings:** 4

Ingredients:

- 2 eggs
- 60 g bamboo fibers
- 80 g sour cream
- 40 g olive oil
- 150 g grated Gouda cheese
- Salt and pepper

Instructions:

1. First, preheat the oven to 180°C and cover a baking sheet with baking paper.
2. Take a bowl and beat in the eggs. Whisk briefly with a fork, then add the remaining ingredients and knead everything well.
3. This is best done by hand, but you can also work with the dough hook on the mixer.
4. Finally, flavor with salt and pepper to taste, then place the dough on the baking tray and roll out evenly.
5. If necessary, flour the dough with a little bamboo fiber so that the dough does not stick to the rolling pin.
6. Bake the tray for 10 minutes on the lower rack.
7. The pizza base can now be topped with delicious low-carb foods, depending on your taste.
8. Then bake for another 10 minutes on the lower rack and then enjoy hot.

Nutrition: Calories: 599, Fat: 19g, Carbs: 9g, Sugar: 4g, Fiber: 2g, Protein: 97g, Sodium: 520mg

343. Vegetarian Hamburgers

Preparation Time: 10 minutes | **Cooking Time:** 30 minutes | **Servings:** 4

Ingredients:

- 90 g protein flour
- 120 ml egg white
- 100 g carrots, grated
- 2 tablespoons coconut oil
- 100 g low-fat quark
- 2 eggs
- 6 g baking powder
- 20 g gold linseed (alternatively other nuts and grains)
- Preferred spices (Worcester sauce, soy sauce, salt or chili)
- Preferred topping (tomatoes, cucumbers, radishes, ...)

Instructions:

1. First, preheat the oven to 180°C and line 6-7 muffin tins with paper cases.

2. Take a bowl, add 50 g of flour along with the egg white and carrots, and then stir well.
3. Divide the dough into 6-7 parts and shape a meatball from each one.
4. Now, put 2 tablespoons of coconut oil in a non-stick pan and heat over medium heat until it has melted.
5. Put the meatballs in the hot pan and fry vigorously on both sides.
6. Take a separate bowl, add the remaining flour along with the low-fat quark, eggs, baking powder and gold linseed.
7. Mix well, then pour into the prepared muffin cups.
8. Bake in the oven for 25 minutes, let the finished rolls cool down well.
9. Finally, cut the rolls in half with a sharp knife, top with a meatball of your choice and season.
10. Then, skewer the finished burger with a toothpick and enjoy.

Nutrition: Calories: 178, Fat: 4g, Carbs: 7g, Fiber: 2g, Protein: 27g

344. Pork Steaks with Avocado

Preparation Time: 10 minutes | **Cooking Time:** 30 minutes | **Servings:** 8

Ingredients:

For the salsa:
- 6 limes
- 3 tablespoons fruity olive oil
- 1 ½ dried chili pepper
- Salt and freshly ground pepper
- 2 mangoes (ripe, but still firm)
- 2 shallots
- 2 avocados
- A bunch of coriander

For the steaks:
- 4 pork neck steaks (approximately 150 g each)
- 1 teaspoon ground anise
- 1 teaspoon ground cumin
- Salt
- freshly ground pepper

- 2 tablespoons clarified butter

Instructions:

For the salsa:
1. Halve the limes and squeeze them thoroughly, measure out 10 tablespoons of lime juice. Place in a small bowl.
2. Add olive oil and stir well with a whisker. Crumble the chili pepper and mix into the dressing together with salt and pepper.
3. Now, peel the mangoes with a vegetable peeler, remove the stone and dice the pulp. Finely chop the shallots with a sharp knife.
4. Take a separate bowl, add the mangoes and shallots; stir well.
5. Remove the stone and skin from the avocados, dice the meat and then fill the mango mixture. Immediately, pour the dressing over it so that the avocado doesn't tarnish. Mix gently.
6. Finally, wash the coriander thoroughly under running water and dry it carefully. Remove the tender leaves and also add to the salsa. Mix again.

For the steaks:
7. Preheat the oven to 60°C. Rinse the steaks under running water and dry them carefully with a little kitchen roll. Sprinkle the anise, cumin, salt and pepper over them. Place the clarified butter in a pan and heat over medium heat until melted. Set the steaks in the hot pan and fry briefly while turning for 3 minutes.
8. Put the steaks on a piece of aluminum foil and seal it tightly around the steak. Place in the oven and let rest briefly for 3 minutes.
9. Arrange on a plate with the meat juice and salsa. Enjoy immediately!

Nutrition: Calories: 303, Fat: 14g, Carbs: 15g, Sugar: 10g, Fiber: 2g, Protein: 30g, Sodium: 387mg

345. Chicken with Asparagus Salad

Preparation Time: 10 minutes | **Cooking Time:** 30 minutes | **Servings:** 4

Ingredients:
- 800 g green asparagus

- 1/2 bunch spring onions
- 3 tablespoons white wine vinegar
- Salt
- Pepper
- 1 teaspoon mustard
- 1/2 teaspoon honey
- 8 tablespoons olive oil
- 4 chicken breast fillets (approximately 200 g each)
- 250 g sliced breakfast bacon
- 2 tablespoons clarified butter
- Basil leaves for garnishing

Instructions:

1. First, preheat the oven to 180°C and place baking paper on a baking sheet.
2. Take the asparagus and peel only the bottom stick.
3. Remove the woody ends, then wash thoroughly. Halve the asparagus lengthways and cut so that oblique pieces are created. Now, wash the spring onions and cut them into large pieces.
4. Take a bowl, pour the white wine vinegar into it. Also, attach 2 tablespoons of water along with mustard, honey, salt and pepper. Stir well.
5. Finally, slowly add 6 tablespoons of olive oil, spoon by spoon. Stir.
6. Take the meat, rinse under running water and dry with a little kitchen roll, then season with salt and pepper on both sides.
7. Take the bacon slices and wrap the meat in them.
8. Put the clarified butter in a non-stick pan and heat over medium fire until the fat has melted. Set the chicken breasts in the hot pan, first placing them to the point where the ends of the bacon slice meet. Turn after 2 minutes and fry again briefly for 2 minutes.
9. Remove from the pan and place on the tray so that the meat can cook in the oven for another 15 minutes.
10. In the meantime, set the remaining olive oil in a pan and heat over medium fire. Put the vegetables in the hot oil and fry briefly.

Meanwhile, salt and pepper. After 4 minutes, take the vegetables out of the pan and add them to the vinegar mixture, mix well.

11. Finally, arrange the meat with the asparagus salad on a plate and enjoy immediately.

Nutrition: Calories: 88, Fat: 13g, Carbs: 22g, Sugar: 6g, Fiber: 12g, Protein: 30g, Sodium: 322mg

346. Hot Pepper and Lamb Salmon

Preparation Time: 10 minutes | **Cooking Time:** 20 minutes | **Servings:** 6

Ingredients:

For the Meat:
- 700 g lamb salmon
- 2 garlic cloves
- 1/2 bunch mint
- 2 sprigs rosemary
- 1/2 bunch oregano
- 10 peppercorns
- 4 tablespoons olive oil
- Salt
- Pepper

For the Peperonata:
- 1 small zucchini
- 2 red peppers
- 2 yellow peppers
- 1 onion
- 3 garlic cloves
- 3 tomatoes
- 1 chili pepper
- 3 tablespoon small capers
- 2 tablespoons olive oil
- Salt
- Pepper
- 2 tablespoons chopped parsley

Instructions:

For the Meat:

1. First, rinse the meat under running water and dry it with a little kitchen roll, then carefully remove the tendons and fat. Peel and cut the garlic to make fine slices.

2. Wash the rosemary, oregano and mint, pat dry carefully. Then, chop the leaves and needles (not too fine). Put the peppercorns in the mortar and press lightly. Take a bowl, add the herbs and peppercorns.

3. Attach 2 tablespoons of olive oil and stir well, then rub the meat with the mixture. Finally, wrap it in foil and refrigerate for 4 hours.

4. Preheat the oven to 70°C, placing a baking dish in it that will be used for the meat later.

5. Now, take the meat and remove the marinade with the back of a knife, then season with salt and pepper. Set the remaining oil in a pan and heat over medium fire.

6. Place the meat in the hot oil and fry briefly while turning for 2 minutes. Put it in the pan into the oven and cook for another 40 minutes.

For the Peperonata:

1. Wash the zucchini thoroughly and dice with the skin. Halve and core the peppers, wash them too. Cut so that narrow strips are created. First, peel the onion and garlic then process into fine cubes.

2. Score the tomatoes, pour hot water, at that time peel them and remove the seeds. Cut the pulp into small pieces. Alternatively, canned tomatoes can also be used here. Halve and core the chili pepper, wash it well and cut into small pieces. Finally, rinse the capers in a sieve and let them drain.

3. Now, pour olive oil over the pan and heat over medium fire. Put the onion in the hot oil and fry briefly, then add the peppers, zucchini, garlic and chili. Cook for 5 minutes, stirring evenly. Attach tomatoes and season with salt and pepper.

4. Let everything fry for 10 minutes, stir in the capers and cook for another 5 minutes.

Nutrition: Calories: 599, Fat: 19g, Carbs: 9g, Sugar: 4g, Fiber: 2g, Protein: 97g, Sodium: 520 mg

347. Pork rolls à la Ratatouille

Preparation Time: 10 minutes | **Cooking Time:** 30 minutes | **Servings:** 8

Ingredients:

For the Ratatouille:
- 2 yellow peppers
- 2 red peppers
- 2 small zucchinis
- 2 red onions
- 3 garlic cloves
- 250 g cherry tomatoes
- A bunch of thyme
- 3 tablespoons olive oil
- Salt
- Freshly ground pepper
- 250 ml vegetable stock
- 3 tablespoons tomato paste

For the Pork Rolls:
- 2 bunches basil
- 30 g Parmesan cheese
- 30 g pine nuts
- 5 tablespoons olive oil
- Salt
- Freshly ground pepper
- 75 g sun-dried tomatoes in oil
- 8 small pork schnitzel (approximately 75 g each)

Instructions:

For the Ratatouille:

1. First, preheat the oven to 180°C.

2. Halve and core the peppers, wash thoroughly and cut so that narrow strips are formed.

3. Wash the zucchini as well, then cut into cubes with the skin on. First, peel the onion and garlic then cut into strips. Clean the tomatoes thoroughly, cut them in half.

4. Rinse the thyme under running water and pat dry carefully, remove the leaves. Take a bowl, add the vegetables with the thyme and mix well.

5. Flavor with salt, pepper and olive oil; mix again. Take the frying pan from the oven

149

and distribute the vegetable mixture in it. Bake for 20 minutes.

For the Pork Rolls:

1. Now, rinse the basil with water and shake dry, pluck the leaves and chop finely. Coarsely or finely grate the Parmesan with the grater to taste.
2. Take a small pan, add the pine nuts and briefly toast them without adding any further fat, then put them in the blender. Also, add half of the chopped basil along with the Parmesan and 3 tablespoons of olive oil. Puree everything into a pesto, then season with salt and pepper.
3. Wash the tomatoes and cut them to make strips. Clean the pork as well, dry it with a little kitchen roll and then plate with a meat tenderizer or a saucepan. Sprinkle with salt and pepper, spread some pesto on top.
4. Spread the sun-dried tomatoes and the remaining basil on top, roll into roulades and set. Add the remaining oil to a pan and heat over medium fire, place the rolls in the hot oil and fry on all sides for 5 minutes.
5. Take a small bowl, add the vegetable stock and tomato paste. Stir.
6. Add the cherry tomatoes and the mixture to the cooked vegetables in the oven. Put the meat on it and bake for another 15 minutes. Enjoy served on a plate with the remaining pesto.

Nutrition: Calories: 280, Fat: 16g, Carbs: 5g, Sugar: 1g, Fiber: 0g, Protein: 29g

348. Pepper Fillet with Leek

Preparation Time: 10 minutes | **Cooking Time:** 30 minutes | **Servings:** 8

Ingredients:

For the Vegetables:

- 50 g sun-dried tomatoes
- 100 g pine nuts
- 4 large leeks
- 2 tablespoon raisins
- 2 cups Peppercorns
- 2 tablespoons olive oil
- Salt

- Freshly ground pepper

For the Meat:

- 2 tablespoons black pepper
- 4 tablespoons sesame seeds
- 1 teaspoon salt
- 4 sprigs rosemary
- 4 beef fillet steaks (approximately 180 g each)
- 4 tablespoons sunflower oil

Instructions:

1. Place the tomatoes in a heat-resistant bowl and pour boiling water over them. Let stand for 10 minutes, then take out the tomatoes and chop with a sharp knife.
2. Now, put the pine nuts in a small pan and briefly toast them without adding any further fat, stirring well. Set aside and wash the leek thoroughly and cut so that rings are formed. Rinse the raisins under cold running water.
3. Take a non-stick pan and pour in olive oil. Heat on high and add the leek. Sauté briefly, add tomatoes and raisins over low heat and stir well. Cook for 10 minutes, season with salt and pepper. Add the pine nuts then carefully stir in.
4. At the same time, put the peppercorns in the mortar and coarsely crush them, stir in a small bowl with salt and sesame seeds.
5. Rinse off the rosemary and steaks then dry them with a little paper towel. Place the steaks with the edges in the pepper mixture so that the spices stick to the edges.
6. Now, heat oil in a non-stick pan on a high level and sear the meat on both sides for 3 minutes. Immediately, wrap in a piece of aluminum foil, covering a sprig of rosemary with it.
7. After resting for 5 minutes, remove the steaks and arrange on a plate with the leek vegetables. Garnish with meat juice and enjoy instantly.

Nutrition: Calories: 504, Fat: 39g, Carbs: 10g, Sugar: 1g, Fiber: 2g, Protein: 28g, Sodium: 755 mg

349. Lamb Chops with Beans

Preparation Time: 10 minutes | **Cooking Time:** 50 minutes | **Servings:** 8

Ingredients:

- 1 kg lamb chops
- 2 lemons juice
- Salt
- Pepper
- 150 ml olive oil (approximately)
- 6 garlic cloves
- 6 sprigs rosemary
- 6 sprigs thyme
- 2 onions
- 12 cocktail tomatoes
- 300 g green beans
- 2 shallots
- 70 g bacon
- 2 teaspoons butter
- Savory to taste

Instructions:

1. First, rinse the lamb chops briefly under running water and carefully dry them with a little kitchen roll. Pour the lemon juice into a small bowl, add 100 ml of olive oil, salt and pepper; stir well. Take the garlic and remove the peel. Cut so that thin slices are formed, also add to the lemon marinade.
2. Now, put the marinade together with the chops in a freezer bag, squeeze out the air and seal.
3. Set aside for at least 2 hours and let it soak in.
4. Preheat the oven to 180ºC. Rinse the rosemary, thyme and pat dry. Take a baking dish and grease it with olive oil. Spread the herb sprigs in it.
5. Add the onions and cut into 4 parts, place them in the mold as well. Wash the tomatoes thoroughly and cut in half depending on the size, then add to the onions.
6. Set the meat out of the marinade and place it on top of the vegetables. Spread the soak

and a little olive oil on top. Bake on the middle rack for 40 minutes.

7. In the meantime, take the beans and cut the ends, then wash. Set the water to a boil in a saucepan, season with salt and add the beans. Cook for 8 minutes. Meanwhile, take the shallots and remove the skin, cut into small cubes. Finely dice the bacon as well.
8. Put the butter in a pan and heat over medium fire until it has melted.
9. Place the shallots and bacon in the hot oil and fry until everything takes on a brown color.
10. Add the beans with a little savory, stir well.
11. Salt and pepper, then serve with the lamb and the bed of vegetables. Enjoy hot.

Nutrition: Calories: 413, Fat: 20g, Carbs: 7g, Sugar: 1g, Fiber: 1g, Protein: 50g, Sodium: 358mg

350. Fillet of Beef on Spring Vegetables

Preparation Time: 10 minutes | **Cooking Time:** 30 minutes | **Servings:** 8

Ingredients:

- 500 g green asparagus
- 2 bulbs kohlrabi
- 1 bunch flat-leaf parsley
- 1 bunch tarragon
- Salt
- Pepper
- 4 beef fillet steaks (approximately 150 g each)
- 4 tablespoons olive oil
- 300 ml cream

Instructions:

1. Wash the asparagus, peel only the bottom stick with the vegetable peeler. Divide off the woody ends, then cut the asparagus in half. Now, peel the kohlrabi with the knife, cut so that narrow sticks are formed.
2. Rinse the herbs under running water, dry them carefully and remove the leaves. Finely chop with a sharp knife. Take a

bowl, pour in 2/3 of the herbs, set aside the rest for now.

3. After that, add the vegetables to the herbs in the bowl, season with salt and pepper and mix well. Put the mixture in a roasting tube (must be closed on one side).
4. Take a large saucepan, pour water up to 1/3 full. Set on the stove and bring to a boil.
5. In the meantime, rinse the steaks with water and dry them carefully with a little kitchen roll.
6. Season with salt and pepper on both sides. Put the oil in a pan and heat over medium fire.
7. Set the meat in the hot oil and fry briefly on all sides for 3 minutes. Place it on the vegetables in the roasting tube.
8. Pour the oil out of the pan and add in the cream. Bring to the boil briefly so that the roasting loosens, then pour over the meat in the roasting tube.
9. Now, close the hose and add it to the boiling water. Cook gently over low heat and cover for 12 minutes.
10. Finally, arrange the meat with the bed of vegetables on a plate and garnish with the remaining herbs.

Nutrition: Calories: 209, Fat: 10g, Carbs: 21g, Sugar: 13g, Fiber: 8g, Protein: 11g, Sodium: 644mg

351. Bolognese with Zucchini Noodles

Preparation Time: 10 minutes | **Cooking Time:** 50 minutes | **Servings:** 4-8

Ingredients:
- 4 zucchini (approximately 200 g each)
- Salt
- 1 onion
- 3 garlic cloves
- 2 tablespoons coconut oil
- 4 tablespoons tomato paste
- 3 tablespoons balsamic vinegar
- 600 g chunky tomatoes (canned)

- 4 sprigs rosemary
- 1 handful basil leaves
- 1/2tbsp. Dried oregano
- 1/4tsp. Dried thyme
- Freshly ground black pepper
- 600 g mixed minced meat
- 2 tablespoons olive oil

Instructions:
1. First, wash the zucchini and cut them into thin, narrow slices.
2. For preparing the Bolognese, peel the onion and garlic; cut into fine cubes. Set the oil in a saucepan and heat over medium fire. Put the onion in the hot oil and fry until it becomes translucent.
3. Stir well and fry briefly before adding the tomato paste. Cook them together again, pour in the balsamic vinegar until the bottom can no longer be seen. Bring to a boil, add the tomatoes.
4. Wash the rosemary, and basil then dry them carefully. Pluck the needles and leaves, chop and add to the Bolognese. Season with the remaining herbs to taste.
5. Reduce the heat and simmer gently for 30 minutes before stirring in the minced meat. Cook for another 15 minutes, then cook over high heat for 5 minutes.
6. At the same time, attach olive oil to the zucchini noodles and mix well.
7. Put the oiled zucchini in a pan and cook only briefly over medium heat without becoming too soft.
8. Arrange with the Bolognese on a plate and enjoy hot.

Nutrition: Calories: 75, Carbs: 0.1g, Protein:13.4g, Fat: 1.7g, Sugar: 0g, Sodium: 253mg

352. Chicken with Chickpeas

Preparation Time: 10 minutes | **Cooking Time:** 30 minutes | **Servings:** 4

Ingredients:
- 12 sun-dried tomatoes in oil
- 2 garlic cloves

- 2 zucchinis
- 500 g chickpeas (canned, drained weight)
- 4 tablespoons olive oil
- 100 ml poultry stock
- 2 bags saffron threads
- Salt
- Freshly ground black pepper
- 1/4 teaspoon ground coriander
- 4 chicken breasts (approximately 200 g each)
- 1 tbsp. Ras el Hanout

Instructions:

1. First, get the sun-dried tomatoes out of the oil and dry them with a little kitchen roll, then cut them so that narrow strips are formed.
2. Take the garlic, remove the skin and cut into slices.
3. Wash the zucchini and cut into cubes with the skin on.
4. Rinse the chickpeas in a colander and drain well.
5. Set a saucepan, add 2 tablespoons of olive oil. Warmth on medium heat, add the tomatoes with garlic to the hot oil. Fry briefly for 1 minute.
6. Place the zucchini with chickpeas, stir well and fry briefly together before deglazing with the broth. Add saffron threads, coriander, salt and pepper. Bring to a boil.
7. Set the heat, cover the saucepan and let the vegetables simmer for 5 minutes.
8. In the meantime, rinse the meat under running water and dry it with a little kitchen roll. Set the remaining oil in a pan and heat over medium fire.
9. For now, sprinkle the meat on both sides with salt, pepper and Ras el Hanout, then add to the hot oil and fry for 7 minutes, turning.
10. Serve the meat with the vegetables on a large plate and enjoy hot.

Nutrition: Calories: 329, Fat: 17g, Carbs: 9g, Sugar: 3g, Fiber: 5g, Protein: 37g, Sodium: 430mg

353. Ham with Chicory

Preparation Time: 10 minutes | **Cooking Time:** 30 minutes | **Servings:** 4-8

Ingredients:

- 4 sprigs chicory (approximately 200 g each)
- 150 g Emmental cheese
- 8 sage leaves
- 40 g butter
- 3 tablespoons orange juice
- Salt
- Pepper
- 8 slices Black Forest ham

Instructions:

1. First, preheat the oven to 200°C.
2. Wash and clean the chicory and cut it lengthways in half. Remove the stalk with a knife.
3. Shred the cheese coarsely or finely with a grater to taste.
4. Rinse the sage leaves under running water and gently shake dry.
5. Put the butter in a pan and heat over medium fire. Extinguish with orange juice and so froth the butter. Add the sage.
6. Place the chicory with the cut side in the hot oil. Reduce the heat and fry for 5 minutes.
7. Remove the chicory, cover with a sage leaf and sprinkle with salt and pepper.
8. Chop the ham and put it on the baking dish. Sprinkle with cheese and drizzle with liquid orange and butter. Bake in the oven for 20 minutes, then serve hot.

Nutrition: Calories: 75, Carbs: 0.1g, Protein:13.4g, Fat: 1.7g, Sugar: 0g, Sodium: 253mg,

354. Pork medallions with asparagus and coconut curry

Preparation Time: 10 minutes | **Cooking Time:** 30 minutes | **Servings:** 4-8

Ingredients:

- 1 kg white asparagus
- 500 g carrots
- 2 onions
- 1 red chili pepper
- 40 g butter
- 3-4 tablespoons curry powder
- 250 ml vegetable stock
- 400 ml coconut milk
- 2–3 tablespoons lime juice
- Salt
- Pepper
- 1 tablespoon chopped coriander
- 4 pork medallions (125 g each)
- 2-3 tablespoons oil

Instructions:

1. First, peel the asparagus and remove the woody ends, wash well and cut into bite-sized pieces. Then, peel the carrots, wash and cut them into slices. Now, take the onions, remove the skin and cut them into cubes. Divide the chili in half, take out the seeds and carefully dice.
2. Put the butter in a pan and heat over medium fire until it has melted.
3. Put the onions and chili in the hot oil and sauté until translucent. Add asparagus, carrots and fry everything for 5 minutes, stirring regularly.
4. Pour the curry over it and fry briefly before adding the broth. Set the heat, cover the saucepan and simmer for 15 minutes.
5. Add in the coconut milk and cook for 3 more minutes. Pour in lime juice, salt and pepper to taste. Sprinkle on 1/2 tablespoon of coriander; stir well.
6. Now, take the meat and season with salt and pepper on both sides. Put the oil in a pan and heat over medium fire.
7. Place the medallions in the hot oil and fry briefly on both sides for about 3-5 minutes.
8. Arrange medallions with curry on a plate, garnish with coriander and serve hot.

Nutrition: Calories: 432, Fat: 12g, Carbs: 12g, Sugar: 5g, Fiber: 3g, Protein: 57g, Sodium: 566mg

355. Lamb with Carrot and Brussels Sprouts Spaghetti

Preparation Time: 10 minutes | **Cooking Time:** 30 minutes | **Servings:** 4-8

Ingredients:

- 250 g Brussels sprouts
- 300 g carrots
- 5 tablespoons sesame oil
- 3 tablespoons soy sauce
- 1 lime juice
- A pinch of sugar
- Salt
- 600 g loosened saddle of lamb
- Pepper
- 2 tablespoons butter
- 2 tablespoons sesame seeds

Instructions:

1. First, preheat the oven to 100°C.
2. Take the Brussels sprouts, wash and clean. Then, cut them into strips.
3. For preparing the marinade, place 3 tablespoons of sesame oil together with soy sauce, sugar, salt and lime juice in a bowl; merge well.
4. Put the vegetable spaghetti in the marinade and let it steep for a moment.
5. In the meantime, flavor the lamb with salt and pepper. Pour the remaining oil into a coated pan and heat on high.
6. Set the meat in the hot oil and sear it on all sides, then put it in the oven and let it cook gently for 10 minutes.
7. After that, melt the butter in the same pan and fry the marinated vegetables for about 3-4 minutes. Arrange on a plate with the sliced lamb and garnish with sesame seeds.

Nutrition: Calories: 270, Fat: 11g, Carbs: 4g, Sugar: 1g, Fiber: 1g, Protein: 39g, Sodium: 664mg

356. Cabbage Wrap

Preparation Time: 10 minutes | **Cooking Time:** 30 minutes | **Servings:** 4-8

Ingredients:

- 1 head white cabbage
- Salt
- 100 ml milk
- 1 roll (from the day before)
- 350 g mixed minced meat
- 1 egg freshly ground pepper
- 2 tablespoons clarified butter
- 250 ml meat stock
- 1 tablespoon flour
- 4 tablespoons cream

Instructions:

1. First, separate the large outer leaves (12-16 pieces) from the cabbage and cut out the strong leaf veins with a knife. Set a saucepan with water and bring to a boil. Salt well and add the large cabbage leaves with the rest of the cabbage. Cook everything for 5-10 minutes.
2. Heat the milk in a saucepan. Put the roll on it and soak for a few minutes.
3. Squeeze out the bun and place in a bowl. Also add the minced meat, egg, pepper and salt. Mix everything well until a batter is formed.
4. Cut the cooked cabbage (not the large leaves) and add to the dough, mix again.
5. Take 3-4 cabbage leaves and stack them on top of each other. Spread some batter on top, then roll the leaves and fix with toothpicks, roulade needles, or kitchen twine.
6. Put the clarified butter in a pan and heat over medium fire until it melts. Then, place the cabbage rolls in the hot oil and fry them lightly brown.
7. Extinguish with the broth, cover the pan and simmer the cabbage rolls over low heat for 25 minutes. Take out the cabbage rolls and briefly keep them warm.
8. Now, stir in the flour in a little cream and add everything to the sauce. Bring to a boil briefly.
9. Arrange on plates with the cabbage rolls.

<u>Nutrition:</u> Calories: 329, Fat: 17g, Carbs: 9g, Sugar: 3g, Fiber: 5g, Protein: 37g

357. Veal with Asparagus

Preparation Time: 10 minutes | **Cooking Time:** 30 minutes | **Servings:** 4-8

Ingredients:

- 800 g green asparagus
- Salt
- 3-4 tablespoons rapeseed oil
- A pinch of sugar
- Pepper
- 1/2 fresh lemon zest, grated
- Oil for frying
- 8 slices veal from the back (60 g each)
- 8 slices Parma ham
- 8 sage leaves
- 125 ml white wine
- 1 tablespoon butter

Instructions:

1. First, peel the lower part of the sticks with a vegetable peeler, then remove the woody ends. Wash the asparagus thoroughly.
2. At the same time, fill a saucepan with water and bring it to a boil. Salt well, add the asparagus, and cook for 8 minutes, they must not become too soft. Drain them and rinse directly with ice water.
3. Place the asparagus on a piece of kitchen roll to dry, then put them in a baking dish.
4. Take a small bowl and add the oil, salt, pepper, sugar 0and lemon zest. Mix everything well and pour over the asparagus stalks. Let sit in the marinade for 25 minutes.
5. Put the oil in a pan and heat over medium fire. Detach the asparagus from the marinade and place them in the hot oil. Fry while turning.

6. Now, pepper the meat and cover it with Parma ham and a sage leaf. Secure everything with a toothpick.
7. Put the oil in a pan, heat it and place the meat in it. Fry briefly on medium heat and turning for 3 minutes.
8. Serve with the asparagus on a plate. Extinguish the now-empty pan with white wine so that the roasting residue dissolves, then stir in the butter and briefly bring to a boil.
9. Pour the sauce over the asparagus and meat. Enjoy hot.

Nutrition: Calories: 599, Fat: 19g, Carbs: 9g, Sugar: 4g, Fiber: 2g, Protein: 97g, Sodium: 520mg

358. Salmon with Sesame Seeds and Mushrooms

Preparation Time: 10 minutes | Cooking Time: 30 minutes | Servings: 4-8

Ingredients:
- 500 g salmon fillet
- 4 tablespoons fish sauce
- 200 g mushrooms
- 400 g fresh spinach leaves
- 2 tablespoons vegetable oil
- 2 tablespoons sesame oil
- 1 tablespoon sesame seeds
- 1 teaspoon sambal oelek

Instructions:
1. First, take the salmon, rinse under running water, dry with a little kitchen roll, and then cut so that strips are formed. Take a bowl, pour in the fish sauce. Soak the salmon in the sauce for 10 minutes.
2. In the meantime, it is best to carefully clean the mushrooms with a brush, cut them to make slices. Rinse and dry the spinach under the tap.
3. Now, take a wok, add the vegetable and sesame oil. Heat on high, add the mushrooms to the hot oil, and fry briefly. Put the spinach in the wok and fry until it collapses.

4. Now, move the vegetables away from the center to the edge of the wok and reduce the heat.
5. Place the salmon on the resulting surface and fry gently while turning.
6. Arrange it with the vegetables on a plate, carefully refine with sambal oelek to taste.

Nutrition: Calories: 599, Fat: 19g, Carbs: 9g, Sugar: 4g, Fiber: 2g, Protein: 97g, Sodium: 520mg

359. Stuffed Trout with Mushrooms

Preparation Time: 10 minutes | Cooking Time: 30 minutes | Servings: 4-8

Ingredients:
- 4 ready-to-cook trout
- 1 lemon juice
- Salt
- Pepper
- 1/2 bunch dill
- 500 g mushrooms
- 2 tablespoons butter
- 2 tablespoons freshly chopped parsley
- 3 tablespoons chopped almonds
- 4 tablespoons oil

Instructions:
1. First, preheat the oven to 220°C.
2. Take the lemon juice and use it to drizzle the trout inside and out. Wash the dill, shake dry and chop.
3. Salt and pepper the trout and refine each with 1 tablespoon of dill. It is best to carefully clean the mushrooms with a brush and cut them into slices.
4. Then, put them in a bowl. Also add the butter, almonds and parsley. Stir everything well.
5. Now, distribute the filling over the trout's abdominal cavities. Fix the abdomen with wooden skewers, wrap the trout well in aluminum foil coated with oil. Let it cook in the oven for 20 minutes.
6. Finally, put the fish on a plate and enjoy hot.

Nutrition: Calories: 413, Fat: 20g, Carbs: 7g, Sugar: 1g, Fiber: 1g, Protein: 50g, Sodium: 358mg

360. Salmon with Basil and Avocado

Preparation Time: 10 minutes | **Cooking Time:** 30 minutes | **Servings:** 4-8

Ingredients:

- 1 avocado
- 1 teaspoon pickled capers
- 3 garlic cloves
- A handful of basil leaves
- 1 tablespoon fresh lemon zest
- 4 salmon fillets (approximately 200 g each)
- Coconut oil for greasing the tray

Instructions:

1. Preheat the oven at 180°C and use a brush to spread coconut oil on a baking sheet.
2. Divide the avocado in half, then remove the core and skin.
3. Mash the pulp with a fork in a small bowl.
4. Put the capers in a colander and drain, chop finely.
5. Peel the garlic cloves and mash them with a press. Alternatively, chop them very finely with a sharp knife.
6. Then, wash the basil and shake it dry, pluck the leaves off and chop them too.
7. Attach everything to the avocado in the bowl, refine with lemon zest and mix well.
8. Wash the salmon, dry with a little kitchen roll, and place on the baking sheet. It is best to spread the avocado mixture over the fish with a spoon.
9. Put the tray in the oven and bake briefly for 10 minutes. Switch on the grill function and bake for another 4 minutes until the avocado takes on a light brown color.
10. Set the salmon fillets on a plate and enjoy hot.

Nutrition: Calories: 209, Fat: 10g, Carbs: 21g, Sugar: 13g, Fiber: 8g, Protein: 11g, Sodium: 644mg

361. Leek Quiche with Olives

Preparation Time: 10 minutes | **Cooking Time:** 30 minutes | **Servings:** 4-8

Ingredients:

- 140 g almonds
- 40 g walnuts
- 25 g coconut oil
- 1 teaspoon salt
- 1 leek
- 50 g spinach
- 2 sprigs rosemary
- 40 g fresh basil
- 30 g pine nuts
- 4 tablespoons extra-virgin olive oil
- 2 tablespoons lime juice
- 1/2 garlic clove
- 50 g pitted black olives
- 1 teaspoon red pepper berries

Instructions:

1. First, coarsely grind the almonds and walnuts in a food processor or blender, then put them in a small bowl together with the coconut oil and 1/2 teaspoon of salt.
2. Merge thoroughly, pour the mixture into a cake springform pan. Press the dough with your fingers at the same time and distribute it in the mold so that a border of 4 cm high is created. Put it in the freezer for 15 minutes.
3. Now, wash the leek, spinach and herbs, then pat dry. Slice the leek and place it in a bowl.
4. Stir in the remaining salt and set aside to draw.
5. Meanwhile, put the basil, pine nuts, olive oil, and lime juice in a blender. Pulse until you have a creamy puree.
6. Alternatively, a large mixing vessel or a hand blender can also be used here.
7. Now, peel the garlic clove and chop half. Remove the needles from the rosemary and also finely chop them.
8. Cut the spinach into narrow strips and halve the olives.

9. Add everything to the leek in the bowl, and then add the basil puree. Mix well.
10. Distribute the mixture to the base of the springform pan, sprinkle the pepper berries over it. Finally, cut the quiche into pieces and enjoy.

Nutrition: Calories: 270, Fat: 11g, Carbs: 4g, Sugar: 1g, Fiber: 1g, Protein: 39g, Sodium: 664mg

362. Fried Egg on Onions with Sage

Preparation Time: 10 minutes | **Cooking Time:** 30 minutes | **Servings:** 4-8

Ingredients:
- 275 g onions
- 1/2 bunch sage
- 3 tablespoons clarified butter
- 1 ½ tablespoon coconut flour
- Salt
- 1 teaspoon sweet paprika powder
- 8 eggs
- Freshly ground black pepper

Instructions:
1. First, remove the skin from the onions, then cut into thin rings.
2. Rinse the sage under running water, pat dry and remove the leaves.
3. Now, put 1 ½ tablespoon of clarified butter in a pan and heat over medium fire until it has melted. Place the sage leaves in the hot oil and fry until they are crispy. Place on kitchen paper to drain.
4. Meanwhile, put the remaining clarified butter in the same pan and heat it, then place the onion rings in it.
5. Scatter the coconut flour on top and fry for 10 minutes, stirring at regular intervals. Sprinkle salt and paprika too.
6. Take the eggs and beat them one by one on the onions in the pan. Let the eggs sink to the bottom of the pan, if necessary, use a wooden spoon to help.

7. Now, cover the pan and fry everything for 10 minutes until the eggs are completely set.
8. Arrange the fried eggs with the onions on flat plates, season with salt and pepper. Garnish with the roasted sage.

Nutrition: Calories: 179, Fat: 13g, Carbs: 6g, Sugar: 3g, Fiber: 1g, Protein: 10g, Sodium: 265mg

363. Quinoa Mushroom Risotto

Preparation Time: 10 minutes | **Cooking Time:** 30 minutes | **Servings:** 4-8

Ingredients:
- 1 garlic clove
- 30 g hazelnuts
- Salt
- 1 fresh lemon zest, grated
- 2 shallots
- 650 g small mushrooms
- 1 bunch flat-leaf parsley
- 70 g quinoa
- 2 tablespoons olive oil
- Pepper
- 100 g baby spinach
- 30 g grated Parmesan cheese
- 20 g butter
- Red pepper to taste
- 500 ml hot water

Instructions:
1. First, peel the garlic clove and put it in a blender. Also add the hazelnuts, lemon zest and a little salt; mix until everything is finely ground. Put aside.
2. Peel the shallots, then cut them into fine cubes. It is best to carefully clean the mushrooms with a brush, chop them so that thin slices are formed.
3. Rinse and dab the parsley under running water, remove the leaves and chop with a sharp knife.
4. Put the quinoa in a colander and wash well under the tap; drain thoroughly.

5. Pour olive oil into a non-stick pan and warmth over medium heat. Put the shallots in it and fry until they turn slightly brown.
6. Add the mushrooms to the shallots and fry them together until they turn brown. Attach the quinoa, but at the same time pour in the hot water. Season with salt and pepper, stir well.
7. Cook over low heat until all the water has boiled away. The quinoa should be soft.
8. Now, add the parsley, spinach, Parmesan and butter; stir thoroughly.
9. Salt and pepper again and set with garlic and the hazelnut mixture.
10. Arrange on a plate and serve garnished with red pepper if necessary.

Nutrition: Calories: 166, Fat: 10g, Carbs: 17g, Sugar: 12g, Fiber: 2g, Protein: 7g, Sodium: 892mg

364. Vegetarian Lentil Stew

Preparation Time: 10 minutes | **Cooking Time:** 30 minutes | **Servings:** 4

Ingredients:
- 50 g carrots
- 30 g parsnip or parsley root
- 30 g celery
- 1 leek
- 1 yellow pepper
- 250 g red lentils
- 1 ½ teaspoon ground cumin
- 3 tablespoons balsamic vinegar
- 3 tablespoons walnut oil
- 2-3 tablespoons maple syrup
- Salt and pepper
- A pinch of cayenne pepper
- 1/2 bunch flat-leaf parsley

Instructions:
1. Measure 1000 ml of water and pour into a saucepan. Warmth on high heat until boil.
2. In the meantime, cut the peppers in half, remove the seeds and wash them together with the leek. Peel the carrots, parsnips and celery.

3. Process everything into fine cubes, only use the white part of the leek.
4. Pour everything into the boiling water and bring to a boil. Then, add the lentils. Cook for 10 minutes, or until they are soft.
5. Ideally, most of the liquid has boiled away, if necessary, drain. Season with cumin, balsamic vinegar, maple syrup, walnut oil, salt and pepper. Add the cayenne pepper to taste.
6. Turn off the stove and set the vegetarian lentils stew aside briefly to steep.
7. In the meantime, rinse the parsley under the tap, pat dry, pluck the leaves off and sprinkle them into the stew.
8. Arrange in deep plates and enjoy hot.

Nutrition: Calories: 413, Fat: 20g, Carbs: 7g, Sugar: 1g, Fiber: 1g, Protein: 50g, Sodium: 358mg

365. Lemon Chicken Soup with Beans

Preparation Time: 10 minutes | **Cooking Time:** 50 minutes | **Servings:** 4

Ingredients:
- 1 onion
- 6 garlic cloves
- 600 g chicken breast
- 3 tablespoons olive oil
- l chicken broth
- 1 fresh lemon
- 250 g cooked white beans (canned)
- Salt
- Pepper
- 120 g Feta
- A bunch of chives

Instructions:
1. First, peel the onion, then the garlic cloves. Divide the onion in half and cut it into thin slices.
2. Rinse the meat under running water and dry it with a little paper towel.
3. Put the olive oil in a large saucepan and heat over medium fire, add the onion and garlic to the hot oil.

4. Fry until everything is soft, deglaze with the chicken stock. Also, add the meat and bring to a boil.

5. In the meantime, wash and dry the lemon, then rub and peel it with a grater, alternatively, you can also use a zester. Add the lemon zest to the broth and cook everything for 40 minutes before adding the beans. Salt and pepper, then cook again for 10 minutes.

6. Now, remove the meat and tear it into small pieces on a plate or board with 2 forks. Put the chicken back into the soup, then crumble the Feta over the soup.

7. Finally, rinse the chives with water, dry and cut them so that small rolls are created. Sprinkle into the soup, stir well and immediately enjoy hot.

Nutrition: Calories: 329, Fat: 17g, Carbs: 9g, Sugar: 3g, Fiber: 5g, Protein: 37g, Sodium: 430mg

366. Blueberry Bircher Pots

Preparation Time: 10 minutes | **Cooking Time:** 25 minutes | **Servings:** 1

Ingredients:
- small apple
- tablespoon whole oats
- tablespoon low-fat natural yogurt
- some blueberries

Instructions:
1. Put 1 small apple, grated, 2 tablespoon whole oats, 2 tablespoons low-fat natural yogurt in a pot, layer with blueberries.

Nutrition: Calories: 222, Carbs: 38g, Protein: 13g, Fat: 20g, Cholesterol: 8 mg

367. Toasted Coconut and Berry Grain

Preparation Time: 10 minutes | **Cooking Time:** 35 minutes | **Servings:** 6

Ingredients:
- 1 cup larger size whole mixed (like Brazil, hazelnut, or)
- 1 cup raw almonds

- 1/2 cup pumpkin s
- 1/4 cup coconut oil
- 1/4 to 1/3 cup maple syrup
- 2 tablespoon vanilla
- 2 tablespoon cinnamon
- 1/2 tablespoon ground ginger
- dash of sea salt
- 2/3 cup unsweetened coconut flakes
- 1 ½ cup to 1 ¼ cup dried berries (blueberry, cranberry, etc.)
- Optional chia s (2 tablespoons)

Instructions:
2. Preheat the oven to 325°F. Preheat the oven to 350°F. Line a baking sheet with parchment paper.

3. Combine your /almonds in a blender or food processor. Pulse approximately 5-8 times until the ingredients are chopped but not ground.

4. Transfer to a large mixing dish and stir in your pumpkins.

5. Combine the coconut oil, extract, and maple syrup in a separate basin. Pour this over the and toss to combine. Then add your spices and stir until evenly covered.

6. Spread the nut mixture equally on the baking sheet and top with a pinch of sea salt. Maybe a quarter teaspoon?

7. Bake for 15 minutes in a preheated oven.

8. Remove from the oven and toss the /s on the tray to turn the sides. Return to the oven for another fifteen minutes of baking.

9. Remove from oven, stir /s, and then put in your coconut. You may place the coconut on the same baking pan as the nuts and syrup or a different baking dish. Just make sure it's evenly distributed on the tray.

10. Continue baking for another five-eight minute, or until the coconut is golden brown.

11. Remove and set aside to cool.

12. After cooling, add the coconut/nut granola to a mixing bowl and stir it around a bit more. Mix in the dried berries and toss everything together.

13. 1Finish with any more spices and optional chia.
14. 1Keep in an airtight container or gift jars.

Nutrition: Calories 200, Carbs 8g, Protein 4g, Fat 13g, Cholesterol 263 mg

368. White Bean Chili

Preparation time: 10 minutes | **Cooking time:** 1 hour | **Serving:** 6

Ingredients:

- Avocado oil or canola oil – ¼ cup
- Anaheim or poblano chilies – 2 cups, seeded and chopped
- Onion – one, chopped
- Garlic – four cloves, minced
- Quinoa – half cup, rinsed
- Dried oregano – four tsp
- Ground cumin – four tsp
- Salt – one tsp
- Ground coriander – half tsp
- Ground pepper – half tsp
- Vegetable broth – four cups, low-sodium
- White beans – 30 ounces, rinsed
- Zucchini – one, diced
- Fresh cilantro – ¼ cup, chopped
- Lime juice – 2 tbsp

Instructions:

1. Add oil into the pot and place it over medium flame.
2. Add garlic, onion, and chilies, and cook for five to seven minutes.
3. Then, add pepper, coriander, salt, cumin, oregano, and quinoa and cook for one minute.
4. Add beans and broth and stir well. Bring to a boil and simmer for twenty minutes.
5. Add zucchini and cook for 10 to 15 minutes.
6. Garnish with lime juice and fresh cilantro leaves.
7. Top with lime wedges.

Nutrition: Calories; 283, Fat; 11.7g, Carbs; 36.7g, Protein; 9.7g, Fiber; 8.4g

369. Chickpea Stew

Preparation time: 10 minutes | **Cooking time:** 30-40 minutes | **Serving:** 8

Ingredients:

- Spinach – 10 ounces
- Canola oil – 1 ½ tbsp
- Onion – one, chopped
- Ginger – one-piece, peeled and minced
- Jalapeno pepper – half, seeded and chopped
- Garlic – three cloves, minced
- Curry powder – one tbsp
- Carrots – three, peeled and thinly sliced
- Cauliflower – half head, broken into bite-size florets
- Chickpeas – 30 ounces, low-sodium, rinsed
- Tomatoes – 28 ounces, drained, diced, salt-free
- Half-and-half – half cup, fat-free
- Coconut milk – 1/3 cup

Instructions:

1. Place spinach into the microwave-safe bowl and then add one tbsp water and cover it. Let microwave it for one to two minutes.
2. Transfer it to the colander and drain it.
3. When cooled, chop it and keep it aside.
4. Add oil into the skillet and heat it.
5. Add onion and cook for eight minutes.
6. Add curry powder, garlic, jalapeno, and ginger and cook for a half-minute. Then, add 2 tbsp water and carrots and cook for ten minutes.
7. Add cauliflower and cook for five to ten minutes more.
8. Add coconut milk, half-and-half, tomatoes, and chickpeas, and stir well. Bring to a boil. Then, lower the heat and simmer for 15 minutes.
9. Then, add reserved spinach and stir well.

Nutrition: Calories; 249, Fat; 6.5g, Carbs; 38.8g, Protein; 11.2g, Fiber; 10g

370. Mexican Enchiladas

Preparation Time: 15 minutes | **Cooking Time:** 20 minutes | **Servings:** 8

Ingredients:

- 1 (14-oz.) can red beans, drained, rinsed and mashed
- 2 C. cheddar cheese, grated
- 2 C. tomato sauce
- ½ C. onion, chopped
- ¼ C. black olives, pitted and sliced
- 2 tsp. garlic salt
- 8 whole-wheat tortillas

Instructions:

1. Preheat the oven to 350 degrees F.
2. In a medium bowl, add the mashed beans, cheese, 1 C. of tomato sauce, onions, olives and garlic salt and mix well.
3. Place about 1/3 C. of the bean mixture along center of each tortilla.
4. Roll up each tortilla and place enchiladas in large baking dish.
5. Place the remaining tomato sauce on top of the filled tortillas.
6. Bake for about 15-20 minutes.
7. Serve warm.

Nutrition: Calories: 358; Carbs: 46.2g; Protein: 20.6g; Fat: 11.2g; Sugar: 4.5g; Sodium: 550mg; Fiber: 10.3g

371. Unique Banana Curry

Preparation Time: 15 minutes | **Cooking Time:** 15 minutes | **Servings:** 3

Ingredients:

- 2 tbsp. olive oil
- 2 yellow onions, chopped
- 8 garlic cloves, minced
- 2 tbsp. curry powder
- 1 tbsp. ground ginger
- 1 tbsp. ground cumin
- 1 tsp. ground turmeric
- 1 tsp. ground cinnamon
- 1 tsp. red chili powder
- Salt and freshly ground black pepper, to taste

- 2/3 C. plain yogurt
- 1 C. tomato puree
- 2 bananas, peeled and sliced
- 3 tomatoes, peeled, seeded and chopped finely

Instructions:

1. In a large pan, heat the oil over medium heat and sauté onion for about 4-5 minutes.
2. Add the garlic, curry powder and spices and sauté for about 1 minute.
3. Add the yogurt and tomato sauce and bring to a gentle boil.
4. Stir in the bananas and simmer for about 3 minutes.
5. Stir in the tomatoes and simmer for about 1-2 minutes.
6. Remove from the heat and serve hot.

Nutrition: Calories: 318; Carbs: 49.7g; Protein: 9g; Fat: 12.2g; Sugar: 24.2g; Sodium: 138mg; Fiber: 9.5g

372. Vegan-Friendly Platter

Preparation Time: 10 minutes | **Cooking Time:** 30 minutes | **Servings:** 4

Ingredients:

- 1 tbsp. olive oil
- 2 small onions, chopped
- 5 garlic cloves, chopped finely
- 1 tsp. of dried oregano
- 1 tsp. ground cumin
- ½ tsp. ground ginger
- Salt and freshly ground black pepper, to taste
- 2 cups tomatoes, peeled, seeded and chopped
- 2 (13½-oz.) cans black beans, rinsed and drained
- ½ C. homemade vegetable broth

Instructions:

1. In a pan, heat the olive oil over medium heat and cook the onion for about 5-7 minutes, stirring frequently.

2. Add the garlic, oregano, spices, salt and black pepper and cook for about 1 minute.
3. Add the tomatoes and cook for about 1-2 minutes.
4. Add in the beans and broth and bring to a boil.
5. Reduce the heat to medium-low and simmer, covered for about 15 minutes.
6. Serve hot.

Nutrition: Calories: 327; Carbs: 54.1g; Protein: 19.1g; Fat: 5.1g; Sugar: 4g; Sodium: 595mg; Fiber: 18.8g

373. Berry Soft Serve & Vanilla Chia Pudding Parfait

Preparation Time: 15 minutes|**Cooking Time:** 630 minutes|**Servings:** 2

Ingredients:

- Vanilla Chia Pudding:
- ¼ cups unsweetened plant milk
- ¼ cup plus 1 tablespoon chia s
- ½ to 2 tablespoons pure maple syrup
- 2 teaspoon pure vanilla extract
- Berry Soft Serve
- 3 cups frozen strawberries
- ½ cup frozen blueberries
- to 2 Medjool dates, pitted (optional to sweeten)
- Topping Ideas:
- coconut flakes
- sliced strawberries
- blueberries

Instructions:
1. Vanilla Chia Pudding:
2. In an airtight jar or container, vigorously mix the plant milk, chia seeds, maple syrup, and vanilla until the chia seeds are evenly dispersed throughout the liquid. To thicken, place in the refrigerator for at least 8 hours or overnight.
3. In the morning, mix the chia pudding thoroughly. If it's too thin, add 1 tablespoon of chia seeds at a time to thicken. If it's too thick, thin with additional plant milk, 1 tablespoon at a time.
4. Soft Serve Berry
5. Just before serving, make the soft serve. Combine the frozen strawberries, sugar, and lemon juice in a food processor. Blueberries, dates (if using) and process until smooth and sorbet-like, stopping to scrape down the sides as required. To start things rolling, you may need to add a very small amount of plant milk. To retain a thick, soft-serve texture, add 1 spoonful at a time and as little as possible.
6. Assemble:
7. Layer the chia pudding and soft berry serve in two jars or parfait glasses, one after the other. Serve immediately after sprinkling with preferred toppings.

Nutrition: Calories: 396, Carbs: 10g, Protein: 20g, Fat: 10g, Cholesterol: 81 mg

374. Raw Granola Clusters, Coconut Whipped Cream, And Dreamy Berry Parfait

Preparation Time: 25 minutes|**Cooking Time:** 5 minutes|**Servings:** 4

Ingredients:

- For the Raw Cinnamon Almond Crumble
- ½ cup raw almonds
- ½ cup pitted Medjool dates
- ½ cup gluten-free rolled oats
- ½ teaspoon cinnamon
- 1/8 teaspoon cardamom
- 2 teaspoon vanilla extract
- For the Coconut Whipped Cream
- 3 cups of coconut cream
- 2 tablespoons of powdered sugar
- one vanilla bean
- Additional Ingredients:
- ½ cup 5-minute vegan caramel sauce
- 2 cups quartered and pitted sweet cherries
- 2 cup raspberries
- 3 cup blueberries
- ½ cup quartered strawberries

Instructions:

1. To Make the Raw Cinnamon Almond Crumble
2. Combine the almonds, dates, oats, cinnamon, cardamom, and vanilla essence in a mixing bowl. Process for 1-2 minutes, or until a crumbly, somewhat sticky substance develops, after pulsing 10 times. Refrigerate until ready to use, covered.
3. To Make the Coconut Whipped Cream
4. Combine the coconut cream, powdered sugar or stevia, and vanilla beans in a medium mixing bowl. Whip the coconut cream for 3-4 minutes on high speed. Or until a thick whipped cream develops, using a hand mixer with whisk attachments. Refrigerate until ready to use, covered.
5. To Assemble
6. Layer the berries in small bowls or jars, then top with the crumble, a spoonful of coconut whipped cream, and a drizzle of the caramel sauce. Repeat once more, then top with fresh berries.
7. Serve right away.
8. Keep any leftovers in the refrigerator.

Nutrition: Calories: 133g, Carbs: 19g, Protein: 22g, Fat: 18g, Cholesterol: 30 mg

375. Cauliflower And Potato Curry Soup

Preparation time: 10 minutes | **Cooking time:** 1 hour **Serving:** 8

Ingredients:

- Ground coriander – 2 tsp
- Ground cumin – 2 tsp
- Ground cinnamon – 1 ½ tsp
- Ground turmeric – 1 ½ tsp
- Salt – 1 ¼ tsp
- Ground pepper – ¾ tsp
- Cayenne pepper – 1/8 tsp
- Cauliflower – six cups, cut into small florets
- Extra-virgin olive oil – 2 tbsp
- Onion – one, chopped
- Carrot – one, diced
- Garlic – three cloves, minced
- Fresh ginger – 1 ½ tsp, grated
- Red chili powder – one, minced
- Tomato sauce – 14 ounces, salt-less
- Vegetable broth – four cups, low-sodium
- Potatoes – three cups, diced, peeled
- Lime zest – two tsp
- Lime juice – 2 tbsp
- Coconut milk – 14 ounces

Instructions:

1. Preheat the oven to 450 degrees Fahrenheit.
2. Mix the cayenne, pepper, salt, turmeric, and cinnamon, cumin, and coriander leaves into the bowl.
3. Toss cauliflower with one tbsp oil into the big bowl. Sprinkle with one tsp spice mixture. Spread onto the rimmed baking sheet.
4. Cook for 15 to 20 minutes. Keep it aside.
5. Meanwhile, add one tbsp oil into the pot and heat it over medium-high flame. Add carrot and onion and cook for three to four minutes.
6. Lower the heat and cook for three to four minutes more.
7. Then, add the remaining spice mixture, chili, garlic, and ginger and cook for one minute more.
8. Add tomato sauce and stir well. Let simmer for one minute.
9. Add lime zest, lime juice, sweet potatoes, and broth, and bring to a boil over high flame.
10. Lower the heat and simmer for 35 to 40 minutes.
11. Add roasted cauliflower and coconut milk and stir well.
12. 1Simmer until cooked well.

Nutrition: Calories; 272, Fat; 14.8g, Carbs; 33.4g, Protein; 5.3g, Fiber; 7.2g

376. Banana-bread muffins

Preparation time: 15 minutes | **Cooking time:** 30 minutes | **Servings:** 12

Ingredients:

- 2 cups oat flour
- 1 teaspoon baking soda
- Pinch sea salt
- 1 tablespoon ground cinnamon
- ½ cup coconut oil
- 3 unripe bananas, mashed
- 2 eggs
- ¾ cup raw sugar
- ¼ cup maple syrup
- ½ teaspoon pure vanilla extract
- ½ cup chopped walnuts or pecans
- ½ cup blueberries

Instructions:

1. Preheat the oven to 325°f. Line a muffin tin with paper liners.
2. Combine the oat flour, baking soda, salt, and cinnamon in a medium bowl. Set aside.
3. In a small microwave-safe bowl, melt the coconut oil in the microwave. Pour it into a large mixing bowl and add the mashed bananas, eggs, sugar, maple syrup, and vanilla. Mix well.
4. Add the dry ingredients to the wet ingredients, and stir until well combined. Gently fold in the walnuts and blueberries.
5. Fill each muffin cup three-quarters full. Bake for 25 to 30 minutes, or until a toothpick inserted into the center of a muffin comes out clean.

Nutrition: Calories: 213; Carbs: 29g; fat: 11g; Protein: 2g; fiber: 2g; sodium: 135mg

377. Berry fruit leathers

Preparation time: 5 minutes | **Cooking time:** 3 hours and 30 minutes | **Servings:** 6

Ingredients:

- 2 cups strawberries
- 2 cups blueberries
- ½ cup maple syrup
- Juice of 1 lemon

Instructions:

1. Preheat the oven to 200°f. Line two baking sheets with parchment paper.
2. Add the strawberries, blueberries, maple syrup, and lemon juice to a blender, and blend until smooth.
3. Divide the mixture between the two small baking sheets and use a rubber spatula to spread it across the sheets in an even layer.
4. Bake for 3 to 3½ hours, or until no longer sticky when you tap it with your finger.
5. Let the berry leather cool for about 30 minutes, then use a pizza cutter or scissors to cut it into 8 strips, each about 1 inch wide and 5 inches long.

Nutrition: Calories: 38; Carbs: 11g; Fat: 0g; Protein: 0.5g; Fiber: 1g; Sodium: 2mg

378. Chocolate-covered banana slices

Preparation time: 10 minutes | **Cooking time:** 5 minutes | **Servings:** 2

Ingredients:

- 1 unripe banana, frozen and sliced
- ½ cup high-quality milk- or dark-chocolate chips

Instructions:

1. Line a baking sheet with parchment paper and place the banana slices on the sheet in a single layer so that they're not touching each other.
2. In a microwave-safe bowl, melt the chocolate in the microwave at 30-second intervals, making sure to stir it between intervals.
3. Pour the chocolate over the banana slices so they're completely covered.
4. Refrigerate for at least 1 hour so the chocolate hardens completely. Transfer to an airtight container and refrigerate for up to 1 week.

Nutrition: Calories: 333; Carbs: 46g; fat: 20g; protein: 5g; fiber: 6g; sodium: 1mg

379. Coconut macaroons

Preparation time: 10 minutes | **Cooking time:** 15 minutes | **Servings:** 12

Ingredients:
- 6 egg whites
- Pinch sea salt
- ½ cup maple syrup
- 1 tablespoon vanilla extract
- 3 cups unsweetened shredded coconut

Instructions:
1. Preheat the oven to 350°f. Line two baking sheets with parchment paper.
2. In a small bowl, add the egg whites and salt. Using an electric mixer on high speed, whisk the eggs until firm peaks form, 5 to 6 minutes.
3. Using a rubber spatula, gently fold in the maple syrup, vanilla, and coconut until well combined.
4. Drop 1 rounded tablespoon of batter at a time on the baking sheet, leaving about 2 inches between each macaroon.
5. Bake for 12 to 15 minutes, or until lightly browned.

Nutrition: Calories: 156; Carbs: 13g; fat: 10g; protein: 3g; fiber: 2g; sodium: 42mg

380. Banana ice cream

Preparation time: 5 minutes | **Cooking time:** 0 minutes | **Servings:** 2

Ingredients:
- 2 frozen bananas
- 2 tablespoons cocoa powder
- 2 tablespoons peanut butter
- 1 teaspoon maple syrup
- ½ teaspoon vanilla extract

Instructions:
1. Put the frozen bananas, cocoa powder, peanut butter, maple syrup, and vanilla in a blender, and blend until smooth.
2. Serve immediately or freeze in an airtight, freezer-safe container.

Nutrition: Calories: 111; Carbs: 18g; Fat: 5g; Protein: 3g; Fiber: 3g; Sodium: 38mg

381. Berry berry sorbet

Preparation time: 30 minutes | **Cooking time:** 0 minutes | **Servings:** 2

Ingredients:
- 1 cup halved strawberries
- 1 cup blueberries
- Juice of 1 lemon
- 1/3 cup maple syrup

Instructions:
1. In a blender, add the strawberries, blueberries, lemon juice, and maple syrup. Blend until the mixture has a smooth and even texture.
2. Pour the mixture into an ice cream maker and freeze the sorbet according to the manufacturer's instructions. It takes about 25 minutes.
3. Transfer the sorbet into an airtight, freezer-safe container and let freeze for at least 2 hours before serving.

Nutrition: Calories: 104; Carbs: 26g; Fat: 0g; Protein: 1g; Fiber: 2g; Sodium: 5mg

382. Oatmeal semisweet chocolate-chip cookies

Preparation time: 15 minutes | **Cooking time:** 11 minutes | **Servings:** 12

Ingredients:
- 2½ cups oat flour
- 1 teaspoon baking soda
- Pinch sea salt, plus extra for garnish
- ½ cup coconut oil
- 2/3 cup dark brown sugar
- 1 egg
- 1 teaspoon vanilla extract
- ½ cup semisweet chocolate chips

Instructions:
1. Preheat the oven to 350°f. Line two baking sheets with parchment paper.
2. In a medium bowl, combine the oat flour, baking soda, and salt. Set aside.

3. In a microwave-safe bowl, melt the coconut oil in a microwave, then pour it into a large mixing bowl.
4. To this large bowl, add the sugar, egg, and vanilla. Mix until well combined.
5. Add the dry ingredients to the wet ingredients and mix well.
6. Fold in the chocolate chips until just combined.
7. Put tablespoon-size scoops of batter on the baking sheets, leaving about 2 inches between each cookie. Bake for about 11 minutes, or until golden brown.
8. As soon as the cookies come out of the oven, sprinkle them with a little salt. Let the cookies cool on the pan for about 2 minutes, then transfer them to a wire rack to cool completely.

Nutrition: Calories: 93; Carbs: 9g; Fat: 6g; Protein: 1g; Fiber: 1g; Sodium: 67mg

383. Coconut-lemon bars

Preparation time: 40 minutes | **Cooking time:** 32 minutes | **Servings:** 12

Ingredients:

- For the crust
- Nonstick cooking spray
- 1½ cups old-fashioned oats
- ½ cup unsweetened shredded coconut
- ¼ cup raw sugar
- Pinch sea salt
- ¼ cup coconut oil
- For the filling
- 2 eggs
- ½ cup raw sugar
- 5 tablespoons freshly squeezed lemon juice
- 1 tablespoon freshly grated lemon zest
- 1 teaspoon vanilla extract
- 2 tablespoons cornstarch
- For the topping
- 1/3 cup raw sugar
- ¼ cup freshly squeezed lemon juice
- ¼ cup water
- 2 tablespoons cornstarch

- ¼ cup unsweetened shredded coconut

Instructions:

1. To make the crust
2. Preheat the oven to 350°f. Spray an 8-by-8-inch baking pan with the cooking spray.
3. In a food processor, add the oats, coconut, and sugar. Process until they're combined and ground to a fine texture.
4. In a microwave-safe bowl, melt the coconut oil in a microwave. Add the melted coconut oil to the food processor, and pulse until it's combined with the oat mixture.
5. Transfer the mixture to the baking pan and press it down with the back of a spoon until it covers the bottom of the pan in an even layer.
6. Bake for about 14 minutes, or until golden brown. Set aside to cool for at least 20 minutes.
7. To make the filling
8. While the crust is cooling, add the eggs to the bowl of a stand mixer. Beat on medium-high speed for 2 to 3 minutes, until the eggs are light and foamy.
9. Add the sugar, lemon juice, lemon zest, and vanilla, and continue mixing until completely combined, about 1 minute.
10. Put ¼ cup of the egg mixture in a small bowl and whisk in the cornstarch. Add that back into the bowl of the stand mixer, and whisk well until fully incorporated.
11. Pour the filling into the cooled crust. Bake for 18 minutes, or until the top is no longer wet.
12. To make the topping
13. While the filling and crust are baking, in a small saucepan over medium heat, add the sugar, lemon juice, water, and cornstarch. Heat, stirring frequently, until the mixture thickens, 2 to 3 minutes. Stir in the coconut and remove the pan from the heat.
14. Pour the topping over the baked lemon bars and gently spread it across into an even layer.
15. Chill the pan in the refrigerator for at least 1 hour before slicing.

Nutrition: Calories: 251; Carbs: 30g; Fat: 14g; Protein: 3g; Fiber: 3g; Sodium: 37mg

384. Flourless chocolate cake with berry sauce

Preparation time: 20 minutes | **Cooking time:** 30 minutes | **Servings:** 10

Ingredients:

- For the cake
- ½ cup (or 1 stick) unsalted butter, chopped, plus additional for greasing the pan
- 6 ounces dark chocolate, chopped
- 2 egg whites
- ¾ cup white sugar
- 3 eggs
- ½ cup high-quality unsweetened cocoa powder, sifted
- For the berry sauce
- 2 cups frozen strawberries
- 2 cups blueberries
- 1/3 cup maple syrup
- 2 tablespoons freshly squeezed lemon juice

Instructions:

1. To make the cake
2. Preheat the oven to 350°f.
3. Grease the bottom and sides of a 9-inch round cake pan with butter, line the bottom of the pan with parchment paper, and grease the top of the paper with more butter.
4. Using a double boiler or a heatproof bowl nestled over a pot of boiling water, melt the chocolate and ½ cup of butter until smooth, stirring frequently. Remove from the heat and set aside.
5. Using an electric mixer, beat the egg whites on medium-high speed until soft peaks form, about 3 minutes. With the mixer running, slowly add the sugar, and mix until just combined.
6. In a large bowl, whisk together the eggs and cocoa powder until just combined.
7. Pour the melted-chocolate mixture into the egg mixture and stir to combine. Then gently fold the egg whites into the batter until just combined, making sure not to overmix. Pour the batter into the cake pan.
8. Bake for about 30 minutes, rotating the pan once after 15 minutes. The cake is ready once it's set in the center and begins to pull away from the sides of the pan. Let the cake cool completely before removing it from the pan.
9. To make the berry sauce
10. Put the strawberries, blueberries, maple syrup, and lemon juice in a medium saucepan over medium-high heat. Use the back of a spoon to break down the berries into smaller pieces as they heat. Constantly stir the sauce until it begins to bubble and thicken, 2 to 3 minutes.
11. Remove the saucepan from the heat and let the sauce cool before serving.

Nutrition: Calories: 296; Carbs: 42g; Fat: 16g; Protein: 5g; Fiber: 4g; Sodium: 37mg

385. Baked parsnip chips

Preparation time: 5 minutes | **Cooking time:** 30 minutes | **Servings:** 4

Ingredients:

- 3 parsnips
- ½ teaspoon extra-virgin olive oil
- Pinch sea salt
- Freshly ground black pepper

Instructions:

1. Preheat the oven to 375°f. Line a baking sheet with parchment paper.
2. Using the slicing blade of a food processor (or a mandolin slicer), thinly slice the parsnips, leaving the skin on.
3. In a large bowl, gently mix the sliced parsnips, olive oil, salt, and pepper, until the slices are coated on both sides.
4. Place the parsnip slices in an even layer on the baking sheet, making sure they don't overlap. Bake for 15 minutes, flip over the chips, and bake for 15 minutes more, or until golden brown and crispy.

Nutrition: Calories: 79; Carbs: 18g; Fat: 1g; Protein: 1g; Fiber: 5g; Sodium: 49mg

386. Lemon ricotta cake (crepe cake recipe)

Preparation Time: 20 minutes | **Cooking Time:** 25 minutes | **Total time:** 45 minutes | **Servings:** 16

Ingredients:

For the ricotta cream filling

- 1/4 cups heavy cream
- 1/2 cup granulated sugar
- Teaspoon vanilla extract
- 32 oz ricotta cheese

For the strawberry sauce

- 3 cups fresh strawberries, hulled and divided
- 1/3 cup strawberry jam
- Pinch salt
- Chopped pistachios, optional garnish

For the crepe batter

- Tablespoons melted butter
- 2/3 cups whole milk
- 1/4 cups water
- 2 1/2 cups all-purpose flour
- 3 tablespoons granulated sugar
- 1/2 teaspoons salt
- 5 large eggs
- Zest of 1 lemon + 1 tablespoon juice

Instructions:

For the ricotta cream filling

1. In a mixing bowl, combine the ricotta cheese. Fill a vita-mix blender container halfway with heavy cream, sugar, and vanilla extract.
2. Cover and push the "start" button at level 1. Increase the speed of the machine to level 10 by turning it on. For gentle peaks, blend for 10-15 seconds.
3. Don't over mix, or you'll end up with churned butter!
4. Scoop the whipped cream from the blender jar and mix it gently into the ricotta cheese with a spatula. (if you put the ricotta in the blender, it will crumble.) Place in the refrigerator until ready to use.

For the strawberry sauce

1. Rinse the blender jar well.

2. To the jar, add 2 cups cut strawberries, strawberry jam, and a sprinkle of salt: blend and cover.
3. Begin with level 1 and gradually increase the speed until the strawberries are dissolved.
4. Refrigerate the strawberry sauce in a small jar until ready to serve.

For the crepe batter

1. Rinse the blender jar well. Combine the flour, sugar, salt, eggs, milk, water, melted butter, 1 lemon zest, and 1 tablespoon lemon juice in a mixing bowl. Cover and mix for 5 seconds on level 1. Then, gradually raise the speed to level 10, until the mixture is foamy. If there are visible flour clumps, scrape the jar's edges. Then, cover and mix for another 5-10 seconds.
2. Over medium heat, heat a 9- to 10-inch flat nonstick crepe pan. Once the pan is heated, spoon batter into the center of the crepe pan with a 1/4-cup scoop. Lift and swirl the pan quickly to form a thin 9-inch circle of batter. Return the pan to the stovetop. If you're having problems forming uniform circles, use a spatula to transfer the batter to the pan's sparse spots swiftly.
3. Cook for 30-40 seconds on each side, turning with a broad flat spatula. The first side should have a light golden hue with golden speckles, and the second side should be lighter. Turn the heat up to medium-high if your crepes are taking longer than 90 seconds total per crepe.
4. Repeat with the remaining crepes on a baking sheet (or plate) coated with parchment paper. The crepes will be brittle at first, but they will soften in a matter of minutes. You should have 20-24 crepes. It is ok to stack them on the sheet. They will not cling together if they are thoroughly cooked.
5. Before proceeding, allow the crepes to cool fully. To expedite the chilling process, place the baking sheet in the refrigerator.

To assemble

1. Begin building the cake after the crepes have completely cooled.

2. One crepe should be placed on a cake stand. Spread 1/4 cup ricotta filling in a thin circle over the crepe, leaving a 1/2-inch ring around the edges without cream.

3. Repeat with the remaining crepes. Spread ricotta cream and stack crepes until all of the ricotta filling and/or crepes are used.

4. To level out the layers, use a flat plate or baking sheet to push down on the top of the cake. Cover loosely with plastic wrap and keep refrigerated until ready to serve.

To serve

1. Slice the remaining 1 cup fresh strawberries and put them on top of the cake.

2. Pour some of the strawberry sauce over the strawberries, allowing it to drip down the edges.

3. The leftover sauce should be reserved for pouring over individual slices of cake. If desired, decorate the top of the cake with chopped pistachios.

4. When it's time to cut the cake, use a serrated knife and make nice, even slices with a gently sawing motion.

5. Serve with more strawberry sauce.

Nutrition: Calories 349, Carbs 53g, Protein 48g, Fat 2g, Cholesterol 284 mg

387. Sweet fried plantains

Preparation Time: 5 minutes | **Cooking Time:** 5 minutes | **Total time:** 10 minutes | **Servings:** 6

Ingredients:

- 3 very ripe plantains yellow with lots of blacks
- 6 tablespoons butter
- Clove garlic smashed
- Salt

Instructions:

1. Remove the plantain tips. Peel the plantains and cut them into 12 inch thick ovals at an angle.

2. Preheat a big sauté pan or cast iron skillet to medium heat. Then, on the side, place a "holding plate" lined with paper towels.

3. Melt the butter in the pan. Once the butter has melted, add the crushed garlic clove and plantain pieces in a single layer to the pan. (depending on the size of your pan, you may need to do this in two batches.) Fry the plantains until golden brown, about 2-3 minutes per side.

4. When the plantains are golden and crisp, transfer them to a holding plate with a slotted spoon. Season generously with salt. If necessary, repeat with the remaining plantains.

5. Remove the garlic clove. Warm it up with your favorite mexican or caribbean dishes!

Notes: be careful to use plenty of ripe plantains... They should be dark or have big black dots if they are fully ripe. When eaten immediately after being fried, fried plantains offer the finest texture and flavor. However, when they've cooled, you may store leftover plantains in an airtight jar in the fridge for up to 3 days. Reheat in the oven, toaster, or on the stovetop. I do not advocate freezing fried sweet plantains.

Nutrition: Calories 210, Carbs 29g, Protein 17g, Fat 22g, Cholesterol 187 mg

388. French chocolate silk pie recipe

Preparation Time: 30 minutes | **Cooking Time:** 15 minutes | **Total time:** 45 minutes | **Servings:** 10

Ingredients:

- Unbaked pie crust, store-bought or homemade
- 6 oz bittersweet chocolate + extra for shavings
- 1/2 cups of heavy cream
- One cup of unsalted butter softened (2 sticks)
- One cup of granulated sugar, divided
- ½ teaspoons of vanilla extract
- 1/2 teaspoon of salt
- Large pasteurized eggs

Instructions:

1. Preheat the oven to 375 degrees fahrenheit. Fill a large 9-inch pie pan halfway with pie dough. The edges should be crimped.
2. Then, cover the pie shell with parchment paper and fill it with dry beans or ceramic pie weights.
3. Cook for 15-20 minutes, or until the edges are golden brown. Allow the pie crust to cool fully after removing the parchment containing the weights.
4. Meanwhile, in a double boiler, melt 6 oz of chocolate.
5. When the chocolate has melted, remove it from the heat and let it cool to room temperature.
6. In the bowl of an electric mixer, combine the heavy cream and 1/4 cup sugar. Whip the cream on high with a whip attachment until it forms firm peaks.
7. Place the whipped cream in a separate dish and set aside until ready to use.
8. Using the same mixer bowl and a paddle attachment, beat the butter and 3/4 cup sugar on high for at least 3 minutes, or until light and fluffy.
9. Turn the heat to low and gradually add the cooled chocolate to the butter mixture, vanilla, and salt.
10. Scrape down the mixer bowl and continue to beat until smooth.
11. Increase the speed of the mixer to high. Add 1 egg at a time, allowing the mixer to beat the egg for at least 3 minutes before adding the next egg. This results in a super-smooth texture.
12. After 12 minutes on high, switch off the mixer. Using a spatula, gently fold in 1/3 of the whipped cream.
13. Fold until the mixture is smooth.
14. Fill the cooled pie shell with the chocolate mixture.
15. Serve with the remaining whipped cream on top. Then, using a vegetable peeler, shave chocolate over the top.
16. Refrigerate for at least 3 hours, or until the chocolate filling has firmed up.

Nutrition: Calories 549, Carbs 30g, Protein 54g, Fat 28g, Cholesterol 197 mg

389. Peanut butter oatmeal chocolate chip cookies (monster cookie recipe)

Preparation Time: 15 minutes | **Cooking Time:** 15 minutes | **Total time:** 30 minutes | **Servings:** 55

Ingredients:

- 5 ½ cups rolled oats (gluten free)
- 5 large eggs
- ¼ cup water
- 2 tablespoons of vanilla extract
- One cup of unsalted butter, softened (2 sticks)
- ¾ cups peanut butter, crunchy or creamy
- ½ cups granulated sugar
- ½ cups light brown sugar, packed
- ½ cup all-purpose flour (or gf baking flour)
- 4 tablespoon baking powder
- 1 teaspoon salt
- 12 ounce semi-sweet chocolate chips
- 12 ounce m&ms

Instructions:

1. Preheat the oven to 350 degrees fahrenheit. Set aside several baking sheets lined with parchment paper.
2. Measure out the oats in a large mixing basin. Then, crack the eggs into the oats and stir in the water and vanilla extract. Allow the liquid to soak the oats before stirring to coat.
3. Add the butter to the bowl of an electric stand mixer. To soften, beat for 1 minute. After that, stir in the peanut butter and both sugars. To break down the sugar crystals, beat on high for 3-5 minutes.
4. Scrape down the sides of the bowl with a spatula and beat again to incorporate.
5. Mix in the flour, baking powder, and salt with the mixer on low. Begin adding the oat mixture once everything has been thoroughly combined.

6. Scrape the bowl one more, then mix in the chocolate chips on low.
7. Finally, using a spatula, fold the m&ms into the dough.
8. To distribute the cookie dough onto the prepared baking sheets, use a big 3 tablespoon cookie scoop. Place the cookies 2 inches apart on a baking sheet.
9. Bake for 15-17 minutes each batch, or until the edges are just starting to turn golden brown. Cool for 3 minutes on the baking sheets before transferring.

Nutrition: Calories 230, Carbs 26g, Protein 4g, Fat 7g, Cholesterol 18 mg

390. Green Beans Greek Style

Preparation Time: 5 minutes | **Cooking Time:** 8 minutes | **Servings:** 1

Ingredients:
- 1 cup - Tomato Bouillon Soup
- 2 cups - green beans
- 8 ounces - Water
- 1 teaspoon - Onion powder
- 1 teaspoon - Oregano
- 1 teaspoon - Garlic powder
- Parsley dash

Instructions:
1. In a large saucepan, pour water.
2. Add tomato soup into the water.
3. Now add all the ingredients into the saucepan.
4. Cover the pan and cook for about 15 minutes until the beans become tender.
5. Serve hot as a side dish.

Nutrition: Calories 134, Fat 2g, Carbs 32g, Protein 12g, Sodium 309 mg

391. Marinated Mushrooms

Preparation Time: 10 minutes | **Cooking Time:** 15 minutes | **Servings:** 1

Ingredients:
- 1 cup - Beef soup
- 1 teaspoon - Parsley flakes
- 1 pound - Mushrooms
- Ingredients from kitchen store:
- 1 teaspoon – Onion powder
- 8 ounces – Water
- 1 teaspoon – Garlic powder
- ¼ teaspoon – Salt

Instructions:
1. In a medium bowl, dissolve the beef soup in water
2. Put all the remaining ingredients in the soup and water mix. Cover it and boil in low-medium heat at least for 2 hours.

Nutrition: Calories 186, Fat 2g, Carbs 31g, Protein 8g, Sodium 155 mg

392. Moch Mashed Potatoes

Preparation Time: 5 minutes | **Cooking Time:** 18 minutes | **Servings:** 1

Ingredients:
- 1 cup - Tomato chicken soup
- 4 ounces – Frozen cauliflower
- ¼ teaspoon - Salt
- 6 cup – Water

Instructions:
1. Cook cauliflower for about 15 minutes in a small saucepan by adding the salt until it becomes soft.
2. Drain excess water after cooking.
3. Mash the cooked cauliflower. Add the chicken soup into the masked cauliflower and heat the mix for 2 minutes. Serve hot.

Nutrition: Calories 165, Fat 3g, Carbs 33g, Protein 12g, Sodium 318 mg

393. Quinoa Chickpea Salad with Roasted Red Pepper Hummus Dressing

Preparation Time: 10 minutes | **Cooking Time:** 0 minutes | **Servings:** 1

Ingredients:

- 2 tablespoons hummus
- 1 tablespoon lemon juice
- 1 tablespoon chopped and roasted red pepper
- 2 cups mixed salad greens
- 1/2 cup cooked quinoa
- 1/2 cup chickpeas, rinsed
- 1 tablespoon unsalted sunflower seeds
- 1 tablespoon chopped fresh parsley
- A pinch of salt
- A pinch of ground pepper

Instructions:

1. In a small bowl, combine hummus, red peppers and lemon extract. To achieve the desired consistency, add enough water to thin.
2. In a large dish, place chickpeas, greens and quinoa.
3. Flavor with salt and pepper to taste and garnish with parsley and sunflower seeds.
4. Serve with dressing.

Nutrition: Calories: 379, Saturated Fat: 1g, Sodium: 607 mg, Fiber: 13g, Cholesterol: 0g, Sugar: 3g, Protein: 16g, Fat: 10g, Carbs: 59g

394. Rainbow Buddha Bowl with Cashew Tahini Sauce

Preparation Time: 10 minutes | **Cooking Time:** 0 minutes | **Servings:** 2

Ingredients:

- 3/4 cup unsalted cashews
- 1/2 cup water
- 1/4 cup packed parsley leaves
- 1 tablespoon lemon juice or cider vinegar
- 1 tablespoon extra-virgin olive oil
- 1/2 teaspoon reduced-sodium tamari or soy sauce
- 1/4 teaspoon salt
- 1/2 cup cooked lentils
- 1/2 cup cooked quinoa
- 1/2 cup shredded red cabbage
- 1/4 cup grated raw beet
- 1/4 cup chopped bell pepper
- 1/4 cup grated carrot
- 1/4 cup sliced cucumber
- Toasted chopped cashews for garnishing (optional)

Instructions:

1. In a blender, mix soy sauce or tamari, cashews, salt, water, oil, lemon juice or vinegar, and parsley until smooth.
2. In the middle of a serving bowl, put in quinoa and lentils; add cucumber, cabbage, carrot, pepper, and beet on top. Ladle 2 tablespoons of cashew sauce over the vegetables; reserve the extra sauce for future use. If desired, add cashews on top.

Nutrition: Calories: 361, Fat: 10g, Saturated Fat: 2g, Cholesterol: 0g, Sodium: 139 mg, Fiber: 14g, Carbs: 54g, Sugar: 9g, Protein: 17g

395. Rice Bean Freezer Burritos

Preparation Time: 10 minutes | **Cooking Time:** 0 minutes | **Servings:** 8

Ingredients:

- 2 (15 ounces) cans low-sodium black or pinto beans, rinsed
- 4 teaspoons chili powder
- 1 teaspoon ground cumin
- 2 cups shredded sharp Cheddar cheese
- 1 cup chopped grape tomatoes
- 4 scallions, chopped
- 1/4 cup chopped pickled jalapeños
- 2 tablespoons chopped fresh cilantro
- 8 (8 inches) whole-wheat tortillas, at room temperature
- 2 cups cooked brown rice

Instructions:

1. In a big bowl, mash the beans with cumin and chili powder until it becomes almost smooth.
2. Stir in cilantro, jalapeños, scallions, tomatoes and cheese then mix to blend.
2. On the bottom of every tortilla, put about 1/2 cup of the filling then spread, and put about 1/4 cup of rice on top.
3. Roll it up snugly and tuck the ends as you go. Use a foil to wrap each burrito. You can freeze it for up to 3 months.

Note: To warm your frozen burritos unwrap the foil and put it on a microwave-safe plate. Use a paper towel to cover it and heat for 1-2 minutes on high, until it becomes steaming hot.

Nutrition: Calories: 401, Fat: 13g, Saturated Fat: 6g, Cholesterol: 28g, Sodium: 646 mg, Fiber: 8g, Carbs: 53g, Sugar: 4g, Protein: 17g

396. Roasted Veggie Hummus Pita Pockets

Preparation Time: 10 minutes | **Cooking Time:** 0 minutes | **Servings:** 1

Ingredients:

- 1 (6 ½ inches) whole-wheat pita bread
- 4 tablespoons hummus
- 1/2 cup mixed salad greens
- 1/2 cup Sheet-Pan Roasted Root Vegetables, roughly chopped (see associated recipe)
- 1 tablespoon crumbled Feta cheese

Instructions:

1. Halve the pita bread. Set the inside of each half of the pita pocket with 2 tablespoons of hummus.
2. Stuff with Feta, roasted vegetables and greens on each pita pocket.

Nutrition: Calories: 357, Sodium: 768 mg, Cholesterol: 8g, Carbs: 54g, Sugar: 5g, Protein:14g, Saturated Fat: 3g, Fiber: 10g, Fat:12g

397. Salmon Sushi Buddha Bowl

Preparation Time: 10 minutes | **Cooking Time:** 0 minutes | **Servings:** 1

Ingredients:

- 1/2 teaspoon rice vinegar
- 1/2 teaspoon honey
- 1/2 cup cooked short-grain brown rice
- 3 ounces sliced smoked salmon
- 1/2 avocado, sliced
- 1/2 cup cucumber
- 1 teaspoon reduced-sodium tamari or soy sauce
- 1 teaspoon toasted sesame oil
- 1/4 teaspoon wasabi paste
- Sesame seeds for garnishing (optional)

Instructions:

1. In a small-size bowl, mix honey and rice vinegar. Mix rice in. Into a shallow serving bowl, put the rice.
2. Place the smoked salmon, cucumber and avocado on top.
3. In a small-size bowl, mix sesame oil, wasabi and soy sauce or tamari; sprinkle on top of all. If wished, put sesame seeds on top.

Nutrition: Calories: 432, Sugar: 4g, Fiber: 9g, Saturated Fat: 4g, Sodium: 772 mg, Cholesterol: 20g, Carbs: 37g, Protein: 20g, Fat:24g

398. Sausage Peppers Baked Ziti

Preparation Time: 10 minutes | **Cooking Time:** 30 minutes | **Servings:** 4

Ingredients:

- 8 ounces whole-wheat penne or ziti pasta
- 1 (16 ounces) bag frozen pepper and onion mix
- 6 ounces turkey sausage crumbled
- 2 (8 ounces) cans no-salt-added tomato sauce
- 1 teaspoon garlic powder
- 1 teaspoon dried oregano
- 1/4 teaspoon salt
- 1/2 cup reduced-fat Cottage cheese
- 3/4 cup Italian blend shredded cheese

Instructions:

1. Following the package instructions, cook the pasta properly in a pot of boiling water. Strain.
2. Meanwhile, place a large ovenproof skillet on medium-high heat.
3. Put in the sausage and frozen vegetables; cook while stirring occasionally for 10-15 minutes, till most of the liquid from the vegetables is evaporated.
4. Set a rack in the upper third of the oven; preheat the broiler.
5. Combine salt, oregano, garlic powder and tomato sauce into the skillet.
6. Set the heat down to medium-low; mix in the pasta and Cottage cheese.
7. Cook while stirring for around 2 minutes, till heated through.
8. Place shredded cheese on top.
9. Place the skillet under the preheated broiler; brown the cheese for 1-2 minutes.

Nutrition: Calories: 408, Fat: 10g, Sodium: 702mg, Fiber: 11g, Cholesterol: 48g, Carbs: 58g, Sugar: 9g, Saturated Fat: 4g, Protein: 27g

399. Sauteed Butternut Squash

Preparation Time: 10 minutes | **Cooking Time:** 15 minutes | **Servings:** 7

Ingredients:

- 1 large butternut squash (2-3 pounds), peeled, seeded and cubed
- 1 tablespoon extra-virgin olive oil

Instructions:

1. In a big saucepan, heat oil on moderate fire.
2. Put in the squash and cook for 15 minutes while stirring often, until brown slightly and soften.

Nutrition: Calories: 75, Sugar: 3g, Protein: 1g, Fat: 2g, Saturated Fat: 0g, Sodium: 5 mg, Fiber: 3g, Cholesterol: 0g, Carbs: 15g

400. Seared Salmon with Pesto Fettuccine

Preparation Time: 10 minutes | **Cooking Time:** 20 minutes | **Servings:** 4

Ingredients:

- 8 ounces whole-wheat Fettuccine
- 2/3 cup pesto
- 1 ¼ pound wild salmon, skinned and cut into 4 portions
- 1/4 teaspoon salt
- 1/4 teaspoon ground pepper
- 1 tablespoon extra-virgin olive oil

Instructions:

1. Boil a large pot of water. Include in the Fettuccine; cook for around 9 minutes, or till just tender.
2. Strain; transfer into a large bowl. Toss with pesto.
2. Meanwhile, season with pepper and salt on salmon. Set a large, non-stick, or cast-iron skillet on medium-high heat, heat oil.
3. Include in the salmon; cook for 2-4 minutes per side, or till just opaque in the center, turning once.
4. Serve the salmon accompanied with the pasta.

Nutrition: Calories: 603, Protein: 44g, Fat: 28g, Saturated Fat: 7g, Sodium: 537 mg, Fiber: 8g, Cholesterol: 80g, Carbs: 45g, Sugar: 1g

401. Sesame Ginger Chicken Salad

Preparation Time: 10 minutes | **Cooking Time:** 0 minutes | **Servings:** 1

Ingredients:

- 4 cups chopped romaine lettuce
- 3 ounces shredded cooked chicken breast
- 1/2 cup fresh spinach
- 1/4 cup shredded carrot
- 1/4 cup sliced radishes
- 1 scallion, sliced
- 3 tablespoons prepared sesame-ginger dressing

Instructions:

1. In a medium bowl, mix scallion, radishes, carrot, spinach, chicken and lettuce, then put in the dressing and toss to coat well.

Nutrition: Calories: 331, Fat: 17g, Saturated Fat: 3g, Cholesterol: 72g, Carbs: 16g, Protein: 30g, Sodium: 378 mg, Fiber: 6g, Sugar: 7g

402. Skillet Gnocchi with Chard White Beans

Preparation Time: 10 minutes | **Cooking Time:** 30 minutes | **Servings:** 6

Ingredients:

- 1 tablespoon extra-virgin olive oil
- 1 (16 ounces) package shelf-stable gnocchi
- 1 teaspoon extra-virgin olive oil
- 1 medium yellow onion, thinly sliced
- 4 garlic cloves, minced
- 1/2 cup water
- 6 cups chopped chard leaves or spinach
- 1 can diced tomatoes with Italian seasonings
- 1 (15 ounces) can white beans, rinsed
- 1/4 teaspoon freshly ground pepper
- 1/2 cup shredded part-skim Mozzarella cheese
- 1/4 cup finely shredded Parmesan cheese

Instructions:

1. On medium heat, heat 1 tablespoon of oil in a big non-stick pan. Add and cook the gnocchi while stirring frequently for 5-7 minutes until it begins to brown and plump; move to a bowl.
2. Add the onion and the remaining teaspoon of oil into the pan.
3. On medium heat, cook and stir for 2 minutes.
4. Mix in water and garlic; cover.
5. Cook for 4-6 minutes until the onion is soft; put the chard or spinach in. Cook and stir for 1-2 minutes until it begins to wilt.
6. Mix in pepper, beans, and tomatoes; simmer.
7. Combine in the gnocchi then scatter Parmesan and Mozzarella, cover.
8. Cook for about 3 minutes until the sauce bubbles and the cheese melts.

Nutrition: Calories: 259, Sodium: 505 mg, Carbs: 29.5g, Cholesterol: 23g, Protein: 9.7g, Fat: 11.1g

403. Spaghetti Genovese

Preparation Time: 10 minutes | **Cooking Time:** 20 minutes | **Servings:** 5

Ingredients:

- 2 cups packed baby spinach
- 8 ounces whole-wheat spaghetti
- 1 cup thinly sliced new or baby potatoes (about 4 ounces)
- 1-pound green beans
- 1/2 cup prepared pesto
- 1 teaspoon freshly ground pepper
- 1/2 teaspoon salt

Instructions:

1. Boil a big pot of water on medium-high heat. Put in the spinach and cook for about 45 seconds, just until it wilts.
2. Move the spinach to a blender using a fine sieve or a slotted spoon.
3. Bring the water back to a boil and put in potatoes and spaghetti.
4. Cook for 6-7 minutes until they are almost soft, only stirring 1-2 times.
5. Put in green beans and cook for another 3-4 minutes until they become soft.
6. When the vegetables and spaghetti are almost cooked, carefully take out 1 cup of the cooking liquid.
7. Pour 1/2 cup of the liquid into the blender: place in salt, pepper, and pesto. Merge until smooth, stop to scrape down the sides if you want.
8. Strain the vegetables and the spaghetti, set back to the pot; add the pesto mixture and stir. Set the heat and cook while gently stirring the pasta for 1-2 minutes until it is hot, and the sauce is thickened. If you want a thinner sauce, you can add in more cooking liquid.

Nutrition: Calories: 333, Saturated Fat: 3g, Cholesterol: 8g, Fat: 12g, Carbs: 47g, Sugar: 3g, Protein: 14g, Sodium: 438 mg, Fiber: 10g

404. Spiced Sweet Potato Wedges

Preparation Time: 10 minutes | **Cooking Time:** 25-30 minutes | **Servings:** 4

Ingredients:

- 2 (20 ounces) sweet potatoes, scrubbed
- 1 tablespoon olive oil
- 1 teaspoon packed brown sugar
- 1/4 teaspoon kosher salt
- 1/4 teaspoon smoked paprika
- 1/4 teaspoon black pepper
- 1/4 teaspoon pumpkin pie spice
- 1/4 teaspoon hot chili powder

Instructions:

1. Set an oven to preheat at 425°F.
2. Put a baking tray in the oven to preheat.
2. Halve each sweet potato lengthwise into 8 wedges or 16 wedges in total.
3. Drizzle olive oil on sweet potato wedges in a big bowl, then toss to coat well.
4. Stir the chili powder, pumpkin pie spice, pepper, smoked paprika, kosher salt, and brown sugar in a small bowl.
5. Sprinkle sweet potatoes with the spice mixture then toss to coat well.
6. On the hot baking tray, lay out the wedges in one layer.
7. Roast until it turns brown and soft, or for 25-30 minutes, flipping the wedges once halfway through the roasting time.

Nutrition: Calories: 124, Cholesterol: 0g, Saturated Fat: 0g, Fiber: 3g, Carbs: 22g, Sugar:5g, Protein: 2g, Fat: 3g, Sodium: 184 mg

405. Stetson Chopped Salad

Preparation Time: 10 minutes | **Cooking Time:** 10 minutes | **Servings:** 1

Ingredients:

- 3/4 cup water
- 1/2 cup Israeli couscous
- 6 cups baby arugula
- 1 cup fresh corn kernels
- 1 cup halved or quartered cherry tomatoes
- 1 firm-ripe avocado, diced
- 1/4 cup toasted pepitas
- 1/4 cup dried currants
- 1/2 cup chopped fresh basil
- 1/4 cup buttermilk
- 1/4 cup mayonnaise
- 1 tablespoon lemon juice
- 1 small clove garlic, peeled
- 1/4 teaspoon salt
- 1/4 teaspoon ground pepper

Instructions:

1. In a small saucepan, set water to a boil.
2. Put in couscous and lower heat to keep a gentle simmer, then cover and cook for 8-10 minutes, until water is absorbed.
2. Move to a fine-mesh sieve and rinse under cold water, then drain well.
3. On a serving plate, spread the arugula.
4. Put the arugula over the currants, pepitas, avocado, tomatoes, corn and couscous in decorative lines.
5. In a blender or mini food processor, mix pepper, salt, garlic, lemon juice, mayonnaise, buttermilk and basil, then pulse until smooth.
6. Right before serving, drizzle the salad with the dressing.

Nutrition: Calories: 376, Carbs: 39g, Sugar: 11g, Saturated Fat: 4g, Fiber: 7g, Protein: 9g, Fat: 23g, Sodium: 266 mg, Cholesterol: 7g

406. Stuffed Sweet Potato with Hummus Dressing

Preparation Time: 10 minutes | **Cooking Time:** 15 minutes | **Servings:** 1

Ingredients:

- 1 large, sweet potato, scrubbed
- 3/4 cup chopped kale
- 1 cup canned black beans, rinsed
- 1/4 cup hummus
- 2 tablespoons water

Instructions:

1. Using a fork, stab the sweet potato all over then microwave on high for 7-10 minutes until completely cooked.

2. Rinse and drain the kale, let the water hold to the leaves. On medium-high heat, cook the kale in a medium saucepan, covered, until it wilts; stir 1-2 times.
3. Put in beans; pour 1-2 tablespoons of water if the pot dries.
4. Cook and stir occasionally without cover for 1-2 minutes until the mixture is steaming.
5. Break and open the sweet potato; add the beans and the kale mixture on top.
6. In a small dish, mix 2 tablespoons of water and hummus. If needed, pour in more water to reach the preferred thickness.
7. Spread the hummus dressing on top of the sweet potato.

Nutrition: Calories: 472, Fiber: 22g, Cholesterol: 0g, Carbs: 85g, Sugar: 20g, Sodium: 489 mg, Protein: 21g, Fat: 7g, Saturated Fat: 1g

407. Summer Squash White Bean Sauté

Preparation Time: 10 minutes | **Cooking Time:** 20 minutes | **Servings:** 4

Ingredients:

- 1 tablespoon olive oil
- 1 medium onion, halved and sliced
- 2 garlic cloves, minced
- 1 medium zucchini, halved lengthwise and sliced
- 1 medium yellow summer squash, halved lengthwise and sliced
- 1 tablespoon chopped fresh oregano
- 1/4 teaspoon salt
- 1/4 teaspoon ground pepper
- 1 (15-19 ounces) can cannellini or great northern beans, rinsed
- 2 medium tomatoes
- 1 tablespoon red-wine vinegar
- 1/3 cup finely shredded Parmesan cheese

Instructions:

1. In a big non-stick skillet, heat oil over medium heat. Add garlic and onion. Cook

while stirring for 3 minutes until starting to get tender.
2. Add pepper, salt, oregano, summer squash, and zucchini; mix to blend.
3. Lower the heat to low; put a cover on and cook for 3-5 minutes until the vegetables are tender-crisp, stirring 1 time.
4. Mix in vinegar, tomatoes, and beans; raise the heat to medium and cook for 2 minutes until heated through.
5. Take away from the heat and sprinkle Parmesan cheese.

Nutrition: Calories: 193, Cholesterol: 5g, Protein: 10g, Fat: 6g, Saturated Fat: 2g, Sugar: 7g, Sodium: 599 mg, Fiber: 7g, Carbs: 25g

408. Sweet Savory Hummus Plate

Preparation Time: 10 minutes | **Cooking Time:** 0 minutes | **Servings:** 4

Ingredients:

- 3/4 cup white bean dip
- 1 cup green beans, stem ends trimmed
- 8 mini bell peppers
- 20 Castelvetrano olives
- 8 small watermelon wedges or 2 cups cubed watermelon
- 1 cup red grapes
- 20 gluten-free crackers
- 1/2 cup salted roasted pepitas
- 8 coconut-date balls

Instructions:

1. Separate the items equally into 4 plates.
2. Serve with hard cider if desired.

Nutrition: Calories: 654, Cholesterol: 0g, Protein: 14g, Fat: 30g, Fiber: 11g, Sugar: 39g, Saturated Fat: 3g, Sodium: 568 mg, Carbs: 84mg

409. Sweet Potato Black Bean Chili for Two

Preparation Time: 10 minutes | **Cooking Time:** 20 minutes | **Servings:** 2

Ingredients:

- 2 teaspoons virgin olive oil

- 1 small onion
- 1 small, sweet potato
- 2 garlic cloves
- 1 tablespoon chili powder
- 2 teaspoons ground cumin
- 1/4 teaspoon ground chipotle Chile
- 1/8 teaspoon salt, or to taste
- 1 1/3 cup water
- 1 (15 ounces) can black beans, rinsed
- 1 cup canned diced tomatoes
- 2 teaspoons lime juice
- 2 tablespoons chopped fresh cilantro

Instructions:

1. Heat a big pan with oil over medium-high heat, add potato and onion, then cook, stirring frequently, until the onion becomes slightly soft, roughly 4 minutes.
2. Add salt, chipotle, cumin, chili powder, and garlic, then cook, continuously stirring, for around 30 seconds until aromatic.
3. Attach the water and bring to a simmer, cover, turn the heat down to keep it gently simmering.
4. Cook until the potato becomes tender, around 10-12 minutes.
5. Add lime juice, tomatoes, and beans, then turn the heat up to high and simmer, stirring frequently.
6. Turn the heat down to keep at a simmer and cook until the mixture reduces slightly, roughly 4 minutes.

Nutrition: Calories: 365, Fat: 7g, Sodium: 629mg, Carbs: 67g, Sugar: 16g, Protein: 14g, Saturated Fat: 1g, Fiber: 18g, Cholesterol: 0g

410. Tabbouleh, Hummus Pita Plate

Preparation Time: 10 minutes | **Cooking Time:** 0 minutes | **Servings:** 4

Ingredients:

- 2 cups tabbouleh
- 1 cup beet hummus
- 1 cup sugar snap peas, stem ends snapped off
- 4 radishes
- 1 cup mixed olives
- 1 cup raspberries
- 1 cup blackberries
- 4 whole-wheat pita bread
- 2/3 cup unsalted dry-roasted pistachios
- 4 vegan cookies

Instructions:

1. Distribute all the ingredients among 4 serving plates.

Nutrition: Calories: 537, Fat: 31g, Sugar: 12g, Protein: 13g, Saturated Fat: 5g, Sodium: 655g, Fiber: 14g, Cholesterol: 0g, Carbs: 55g

411. Tex Mex Bean Tostadas

Preparation Time: 10 minutes | **Cooking Time:** 10 minutes | **Servings:** 1

Ingredients:

- 4 tostada shells
- 1 can pinto beans, rinsed and drained
- 1/2 cup prepared salsa
- 1/2 teaspoon salt-free Southwest chipotle seasoning blend
- 1/2 cup shredded reduced-fat Cheddar cheese, plus 1/4 for garnishing
- 1 ½ cup shredded iceberg lettuce
- 1 cup chopped tomato (1 large)
- Lime wedges (optional)

Instructions:

1. Start preheating the oven at 350°F.
2. Arrange tostada shells on a baking sheet.
3. Bake until warm, about 3-5 minutes.
4. In the meantime, in a medium bowl, mix the seasoning blend, salsa, and beans.
5. Coarsely mash the mixture, using a potato masher or fork.
6. Separate the bean mixture among tostada shells, spreading evenly.
7. Spread on top with 1/2 cup of cheese.
8. Bake until cheese is melted, about 5 minutes. Spread on top of the tostadas with the remaining 1/4 cup of cheese (if

wanted), chopped tomato, and shredded lettuce.
9. Serve with lime wedges.

Nutrition: Calories: 230, Sodium: 660 mg, Sugar: 2g, Cholesterol: 10g, Carbs: 33g, Protein: 12g, Fat: 6g, Fat: 3g, Fiber: 8g

412. Tomato Artichoke Gnocchi

Preparation Time: 10 minutes | **Cooking Time:** 20 minutes | **Servings:** 4

Ingredients:

- 2 tablespoons extra-virgin olive oil
- 1 (16 ounces) package shelf-stable gnocchi
- 1 small onion, sliced
- 1 small red bell pepper
- 4 large garlic cloves
- 1 tablespoon chopped fresh oregano
- 1 (15 ounces) can chickpeas
- 1 (14 ounces) can no-salt-added diced tomatoes
- 1 (9 ounces) box frozen artichoke hearts
- 8 pitted Kalamata olives, sliced
- 1 tablespoon red-wine vinegar
- 1/4 teaspoon ground pepper

Instructions:

1. In a non-stick skillet, heat 1 tablespoon of oil over medium-high heat.
2. Put in the gnocchi; cook and stir often for about 5 minutes, until plumped and beginning to brown.
3. Place them in a bowl and cover
4. -up to keep warm.
5. Lower heat to medium. Attach in the onion and the remaining tablespoon of oil.
6. Cook for 2-3 minutes, stirring occasionally, until beginning to brown.
7. Add in bell pepper; cook for about 3 minutes, stirring occasionally, until crisp-tender.
8. Put in the oregano and garlic; cook for half a minute, stirring.

9. Set in artichokes, tomatoes and chickpeas; cook for about 3 minutes, stirring, until hot.
10. Mix in the gnocchi, pepper, vinegar and olives.
11. Sprinkle oregano on top, if desired.

Nutrition: Calories: 427, Fat: 11g, Sugar: 5g, Protein: 12g, Carbs: 71g, Saturated Fat: 1g, Sodium: 615 mg, Fiber: 10g, Cholesterol: 0g

413. Vegan Buddha Bowl

Preparation Time: 10 minutes | **Cooking Time:** 20 minutes | **Servings:** 4

Ingredients:

- 1 medium sweet potato
- 3 tablespoons extra-virgin olive oil
- 1/2 teaspoon salt
- 1/2 teaspoon ground pepper
- 2 tablespoons tahini
- 2 tablespoons water
- 1 tablespoon lemon juice
- 1 small clove garlic
- 2 cups cooked quinoa
- 1 (15 ounces) can chickpeas, rinsed
- 1 firm-ripe avocado, diced
- 1/4 cup cilantro or parsley

Instructions:

1. Set the oven temperature to 425°F to preheat.
2. In a medium bowl, mix the sweet potato with 1/4 teaspoon each of salt and pepper plus 1 tablespoon of oil.
3. Move to a rimmed baking sheet. For 15-18 minutes, roast, stir once, until tender.
4. In a small bowl, mix the leftover 2 tablespoons of oil, lemon juice, tahini, garlic, water, and the leftover 1/4 teaspoon each of salt and pepper.
5. Split the quinoa among 4 bowls to serve.
6. Garnish with equal amounts of chickpeas, sweet potato and avocado.
7. Drizzle with the tahini sauce.
8. Top with parsley or cilantro.

Nutrition: Calories: 455, Fat: 25g, Sodium: 472mg, Sugar: 3g, Protein: 11g, Carbs: 51g, Saturated Fat: 3g, Fiber: 11g, Cholesterol: 0g

414. Vegan Cauliflower Fried Rice

Preparation Time: 10 minutes | **Cooking Time:** 15 minutes | **Servings:** 4

Ingredients:
- 3 tablespoons peanut oil, divided
- 3 scallions, sliced
- 1 tablespoon grated fresh ginger
- 1 tablespoon minced garlic
- 1/2 cup diced red bell pepper
- 1 cup trimmed and halved snow peas
- 1 cup shredded carrots
- 1 cup frozen shelled edamame, thawed
- 4 cups riced cauliflower
- 1/3 cup unsalted roasted cashews
- 3 tablespoons tamari or soy sauce
- 1 teaspoon toasted sesame oil

Instructions:
1. In a cooking pan or wok, heat 1 tablespoon of peanut oil over high heat.
2. Cook and stir the ginger, garlic, and scallions in the hot oil for 30-40 seconds until scallions have softened.
3. Add the snow peas, bell pepper, edamame, and carrots then cook while stirring for 2-4 minutes until just tender.
4. Move everything to a dish or plate.
5. Set the remaining 2 tablespoons of peanut oil into the pan.
6. Stir the cauliflower in the oil for about 2 minutes until it's mostly softened.
7. Put the vegetables back in the pan; add tamari or soy sauce, cashews and sesame oil.
8. Stir together until blended properly.

Nutrition: Calories: 287, Fat: 19g, Saturated Fat: 3g, Fiber: 6g, Cholesterol: 0g, Carbs: 18g, Sodium: 451 mg, Sugar: 6g, Protein: 10g

415. Oatmeal Bread to Live for

Preparation Time: 10 minutes | **Cooking Time:** 30 minutes | **Servings:** 12

Ingredients:
- 1 ¼ cup (295 ml) water
- 2 teaspoons (10 ml) canola oil
- 1 tablespoon (15 g) brown sugar
- 1 cup (80 g) quick-cooking oats
- 2 ¼ cups whole-wheat flour, divided
- 1 tablespoon vital wheat gluten
- 1 ¼ teaspoon yeast
- 1 tablespoon shelled sunflower seeds

Instructions:
1. Put water, oil, and sugar in the bread machine.
2. Add the oats and let them sit for 5 minutes.
3. Pour 2 cups (240 g) of flour and the gluten.
4. Set a well in the middle of the flour for the yeast.
5. Turn on the bread machine. (Use a setting for 1 ½-pound [680 g] loaf, dark if you have it). If the dough seems too sticky, attach additional flour as required.
6. Add the sunflower seeds to the beep.

Nutrition: Calories: 287, Fat: 19g, Saturated Fat: 3g, Fiber: 6g, Cholesterol: 0g, Carbs: 18g

416. Vermicelli Puttanesca

Preparation Time: 10 minutes | **Cooking Time:** 15 minutes | **Servings:** 6

Ingredients:
- 4 large tomatoes
- 1/4 cup chopped flat-leaf parsley
- 16 large black olives
- 3 tablespoons capers
- 4 anchovy fillets
- 2 tablespoons olive oil
- 3 large garlic cloves
- 1/2 teaspoon ground pepper
- 1-pound whole-wheat vermicelli, or spaghettini
- 1/4 cup freshly grated Pecorino Romano

Instructions:

1. Combine pepper, garlic, oil, anchovies, capers, olives, parsley, and tomatoes in a large pasta serving bowl.
2. In the meantime, in a pot of boiling salted water, cook pasta for 8-10 minutes, until just tender, or following the package Instructions.
3. Drain the pasta and put it into the bowl with the sauce.
4. Next, toss well to combine.
5. Then taste and adjust seasonings.
6. Dust with cheese and immediately serve.

Nutrition: Calories: 379, Saturated Fat: 2g, Sodium: 379 mg, Fiber: 11g, Sugar: 6g, Fat: 10g, Cholesterol: 5g, Carbs: 64g, Protein: 14g

417. Cucumber Almond Gazpacho

Prep time: 20 minutes | **Cooking time:** 0 minutes | **Chill time:** 2 hours | **Serving:** 5

Ingredients:

- English cucumbers – two
- Yellow bell pepper – two cups, chopped
- Whole wheat bread – 2 cups
- Unsweetened almond milk – 1 ½ cups
- Almonds – ½ cup, toasted, slivered
- Olive oil – five tsp
- White-wine vinegar – 2 tsp
- Garlic – one clove
- Salt – half tsp

Instructions:

1. Dice unpeeled cucumber and mix with half a cup bell pepper.
2. Peel the remaining cucumbers and cut them into chunks.
3. Add remaining bell pepper, peeled cucumber, salt, garlic, vinegar, oil, six tbsp of almonds, almond milk, and bread into the blender and blend until smooth. Let chill for two hours.
4. Garnish with the remaining 2 tbsp almonds.
5. Drizzle with oil.

Nutrition: Calories; 201, Fat; 11.8g, Carbs; 19g, Protein; 6.3g, Fiber; 4.3g

418. Pea and Spinach Carbonara

Preparation time: 5 minutes | **Cooking time:** 15 minutes | **Serving:** 4

Ingredients:

- Extra-virgin olive oil – 1 ½ tbsp
- Panko breadcrumbs (whole-wheat) – half cup
- Garlic – one clove, minced
- Parmesan cheese – eight tbsp, grated
- Fresh parsley – three tbsp, chopped
- Egg yolks – three
- Egg – one
- Ground pepper – half tsp
- Salt – ¼ tsp
- Tagliatelle or linguine – 9 ounces
- Baby spinach – eight cups
- Peas – one cup

Instructions:

1. Add ten cups of water into the pot and boil it over high flame.
2. During this, add oil into the skillet and cook over medium-high flame.
3. Add garlic and breadcrumbs and cook for two minutes until toasted.
4. Transfer it to the small bowl. Add parsley and two tbsp parmesan cheese and keep it aside.
5. Whisk the salt, pepper, egg, egg yolks, and six tbsp parmesan cheese into the bowl.
6. Add pasta to the boiling water and cook for one minute.
7. Add spinach and peas and cook for one minute more until tender.
8. Save ¼ cup of the cooking water for your next use. Drain it and place it into the bowl.
9. Whisk the reserved cooking water into the egg mixture, add to the pasta, and toss to combine.
10. Top with breadcrumb mixture and serve!

Nutrition: Calories; 430, Crabs; 54.1g, protein; 20.2g, fat; 14.5g, fiber; 8.2g

419. Fish Tacos

Preparation time: 10 minutes | **Cooking time:** 15 minutes | **Serving:** 4

Ingredients:

- Tilapia fillets – 1lb
- Extra-virgin olive oil – 2 tsp
- Chipotle seasoning blend – 2 tsp
- Coleslaw mix – 2 cups
- Salad dressing – 2 tbsp, ranch
- Whole wheat tortillas – eight
- Avocado – half, thinly sliced
- Cilantro leaves – ¼ cup
- Lime – one, quartered

Instructions:

1. Preheat the oven to 450 degrees Fahrenheit.
2. Place fillets onto the baking dish and brush the fish with oil.
3. Sprinkle with seasoning.
4. Bake for four to six minutes.
5. Meanwhile, mix the dressing and coleslaw into a bowl. Keep it aside.
6. Flake the fish into big chunks and place them into the tortillas.
7. Top with lime, cilantro, avocado, and coleslaw mixture.

Nutrition: Calories; 341, Fat; 12g, Carbs; 30.5g, Protein; 29.5g, Fiber; 21.2g

420. Raspberry Jam Bites

Preparation Time: 5 minutes | **Cooking Time:** 35 minutes | **Servings:** 10

Ingredients:

- For The Bites:
- Raspberries 2 cups
- Raw honey 1 tbsp
- Raisins 1 1/2 cups
- Medjool dates 15-20
- Shredded coconut 1/2 cup
- For The Coating:
- Shredded coconut 1/3 cup
- Freeze-dried 1/3 cup raspberry powder

Instructions:

1. Reserve the raspberries, which have been mashed with raw honey.

2. Combine the raisins, dates and coconut in a food processor. Process until the mixture is smooth and homogeneous.
3. To create the balls, wet your hands and scoop a large spoonful of the mixture into the palm of your hand.
4. To form a cup, lift up the sides and add 1/2 teaspoon of the raspberry mixture inside, being careful not to let any of the raspberry juice drip out.
5. Gently close the ball between the palms of your hands and mold it.
6. Roll it in the raspberry or coconut powder.
7. Repeat with the rest of the mixture.
8. The easiest way to keep these bites fresh is to store them in the refrigerator.

Nutrition : Calories : 350, Fats : 15 g, Proteins : 12g, Carbs : 34 g

421. Spinach and Artichoke Dip Pasta

Preparation time: 5 minutes | **Cooking time:** 15 minutes | **Serving:** 4

Ingredients:

- Whole-wheat rotini – eight ounces
- Baby spinach – five ounces, chopped
- Cream cheese – four ounces, low-fat, cut into chunks
- Milk – ¾ cup, low-fat
- Parmesan cheese – half cup, grated
- Garlic powder – two tsp
- Ground pepper – ¼ tsp
- Artichoke hearts – 14 ounces, rinsed, squeezed dry and chopped

Instructions:

1. Add water into the saucepan and boil it. Add pasta and cook it. Then, drain it.
2. Mix the one tbsp water and spinach into the saucepan and cook over medium flame. Cook for two minutes until wilted.
3. Transfer it to the bowl. Add milk and cream to the pan and whisk it well.
4. Add pepper, garlic powder, and parmesan cheese and cook until thickened. Drain

spinach and add to the sauce with pasta and artichoke. Cook it well.

5. Then, serve and enjoy!

Nutrition: Calories; 371, Carbs; 56.1g, Protein; 16.6g, Fat; 9.1g, Fiber; 7.9g

422. Grilled Eggplant

Preparation time: 5 minutes | **Cooking time:** 40 minutes | **Serving:** 4

Ingredients:

- Water – four cups
- Cornmeal – one cup
- Butter – one tbsp
- Salt – half tsp
- Plum tomatoes – 1lb, chopped
- Extra-virgin olive oil – four tbsp
- Fresh oregano – two tsp, chopped
- Garlic – one clove, grated
- Ground pepper – half tsp
- Crushed red pepper – ¼ tsp
- Eggplant – 1 ½ lbs., cut into half-inch-thick slices
- Feta cheese – ¼ cup, crumbled
- Fresh basil – half cup, chopped

Instructions:

1. Add water into the saucepan and boil it over high flame.
2. Add cornmeal and whisk it well. Then, lower the heat and cook for thirty-five minutes until tender.
3. When done, remove from the flame. Add salt and butter and stir well.
4. During this, preheat the grill over medium-high heat.
5. Add salt, crushed red pepper, pepper, garlic, oregano, three tbsp oil, and tomatoes into the bowl and toss to combine.
6. Rub eggplant with one tbsp oil and place onto the grill and cook for four minutes per side. Let cool it for ten minutes.
7. Let chop it and add to the tomatoes.
8. Sprinkle with fresh basil leaves.
9. Place vegetable mixture over the polenta and top with cheese.

Nutrition: Calories; 354, Carbs; 39g, Protein; 6.8g, Fat; 20.6g, Fiber; 8.4g

423. Chicken Sandwiches

Preparation time: 5 minutes | **Cooking time:** 30 minutes | **Serving:** 4

Ingredients:

- Red onion – four slices
- Red sweet pepper – one, seeded and quartered
- Chicken breast – six ounces, boneless, cut in half, horizontally
- Multi-grain sandwich round – four, split
- Basil pesto – 2 tbsp
- Kalamata olives – 2 tbsp, pitted and chopped
- Mozzarella cheese – 1/3 cup, shredded
- Feta cheese – ¼ cup, low-fat, crumbled

Instructions:

1. Heat the skillet over medium flame.
2. Let coat with pepper and red onion with non-stick cooking spray.
3. Add it to the pan and cook for six to eight minutes.
4. Remove from the skillet. Let coat the chicken with non-stick cooking spray.
5. Add chicken to the grill pan and cook for three to five minutes.
6. Remove from the skillet.
7. Pull chicken into shreds. Cut pepper into strips.
8. To assemble the sandwiches: Spread the pesto onto the sandwich and sprinkle with olives. Place grilled onion slices. Top with pepper strips.
9. Place chicken over it. Sprinkle with feta cheese and mozzarella cheese.
10. Then, place skillet over medium-low flame.
11. Place the sandwich into the skillet and cook for three to four minutes.
12. Flip and cook for three to four minutes.
13. Serve!

Nutrition: Calories; 296, Fat; 10g, Carbs; 27.7g, Protein; 25.8g, Fiber; 6.2g

424. Tex-Mex Bean Tostadas

Preparation time: 10 minutes | **Cooking time:** 15 minutes | **Serving:** 4

Ingredients:

- Tostada shells – four
- Pinto beans – 16 ounces, rinsed and drained
- Salsa – half cup, prepared
- Chipotle seasoning – ½ tsp
- Cheddar cheese – ½ cup, shredded
- Iceberg lettuce – 1 ½ cups
- Tomato – one cup, chopped
- Lime wedges – one

Instructions:

1. Preheat the oven to 350 degrees Fahrenheit.
2. Place tostada shells onto the baking sheet and bake for three to five minutes.
3. Meanwhile, mix the seasoning, salsa, and bean into the bowl.
4. Mash the mixture with a potato masher.
5. Then, divide the bean mixture between tostada shells.
6. Top with half of the cheese. Bake for five minutes.
7. Top with chopped tomato and shredded lettuce.
8. Then, place the remaining cheese and lime wedges.

Nutrition: Calories; 230, Fat; 6g, Carbs; 33g, Protein; 12g, Fiber; 6g

425. Turkey Meatballs

Preparation time: 15 minutes | **Cooking time:** 25 minutes | **Serving:** 4

Ingredients:

- Olive oil – one tsp
- Button mushrooms – three cups, sliced
- Egg – one, beaten
- Quick-cooking rolled oats – 1/3 cup
- Parmesan cheese – 1/3 cup, grated
- Garlic – three cloves, minced
- Dried Italian seasoning – two tsp, crushed
- Salt – half tsp
- Ground pepper – ¼ tsp
- Lean ground turkey – 1 ¼ lbs.

Instructions:

1. Preheat the oven to 400 degrees Fahrenheit.
2. Line a baking pan with foil and coat it with cooking spray.
3. Add oil into the skillet and cook over medium flame.
4. Add mushroom and cook for eight to ten minutes.
5. Transfer it to the blender and blend until chopped.
6. Mix the pepper, salt, Italian seasoning, garlic, parmesan cheese, oats, and egg into the bowl. Add chopped mushrooms and turkey and combine well.
7. Place meat mixture onto the cutting board and cut into thirty squared.
8. Roll each square into the ball, place it onto the pan, and bake for twelve to fifteen minutes.
9. Serve and enjoy!

Nutrition: Calories; 467, Carbs; 49.2g, protein; 36.3g, fat; 16.1g, fiber; 7.6g

426. Sweet Potato and Black Bean Chili

Preparation time: 10 minutes | **Cooking time:** 30 minutes | **Serving:** 4

Ingredients:

- Extra-virgin olive oil – 1 tbsp plus 2 tsp
- Sweet potato – one, peeled and diced
- Onion – one, diced
- Garlic – four cloves, minced
- Chili powder – two tbsp
- Ground cumin – four tsp
- Chipotle chili – ½ tsp, ground
- Salt – ¼ tsp
- Water – 2 ½ cups
- Black beans – 30 ounces, rinsed
- Tomatoes – 14 ounces, diced
- Lime juice – 4 tsp
- Fresh cilantro – half cup, chopped

Instructions:

1. Add oil into the Dutch oven and place it over medium-high flame.
2. Add onion and sweet potatoes and cook for four minutes until softened.
3. Add salt, chipotle, cumin, chili powder, and garlic and cook for a half-minute.
4. Add water and bring to a simmer. Lower the heat and cook for 10 to 12 minutes.
5. Add lime juice, tomatoes, and beans and simmer over high heat.
6. Lower the heat and simmer for five minutes more.
7. Remove from the flame.
8. Garnish with fresh cilantro leaves.

Nutrition: Calories; 323, Fat; 7.6g, Carbs; 54.7g, Protein; 12.5g, Fiber; 15.6g

SAUCE

427. Turkey Parsley Soup (FAST)

Preparation Time: 5 Minutes | **Cooking Time:** 20 Minutes | **Servings:** 2

Ingredients:

- 6 mugs turkey stock
- Table salt and black pepper to the taste
- 1/4 mug parsley, sliced off
- 3 mugs baked spaghetti squash, sliced off
- 3 celery stalks, sliced off
- 1 yellow onion, sliced off
- 1 tablespoon ghee
- 3 mugs turkey, prepared and shredded

Instructions:

1. Warm up a pot with the ghee over moderate immense heat, insert celery and onion, shake and prepare for 5 minutes.
2. Insert parsley, stock, turkey meat, table salt and pepper, shake and prepare for 20 minutes.
3. Insert spaghetti squash, shake and prepare turkey soup for 10 minutes more.
4. Distribute into pots and serve.

Nutrition: Calories: 213, Carbs: 9g, Fat: 5g, Sodium: 213mg

428. Gooseberry Sauce (FAST)

Preparation Time: 30 minutes | **Cooking Time:** 5 minutes | **Servings:** 4

Ingredients

- 5 cups gooseberries, rinsed, topped and tailed
- 5 garlic cloves, crushed
- 1 cup fresh dill, rinsed, stems removed
- Salt to taste

Instructions:

1. Combine gooseberries and dill in a blender and pulse until smooth.
2. Add garlic and salt.
3. Let stand for 30 minutes, covered.

Nutrition: Calories 35, Carbs 8g, Fat 2g, Protein 1g

429. Fresh Tomato Vinaigrette (FAST)

Preparation Time: 5 minutes | **Cooking Time:** 0 minutes | **Serving:** 5

Ingredients:

- 1 fresh tomato, chopped
- ¾ cup olive oil
- ¼ cup apple cider vinegar
- 1 clove of garlic, chopped
- ½ tsp dried oregano
- Salt and pepper to taste

Instructions:

1. Place all ingredients in a food processor and pulse until a smooth paste is formed.
2. Place in containers and store in the fridge until ready to use.

Nutrition: Calories 298, Fat 32g, Carbs 2g, Protein 0.2g, Fiber 0.4g, Sodium 3mg, Potassium 75mg

430. Cabbage & Beet Stew (FAST)

Preparation Time: 20 minutes | **Cooking Time:** 10 minutes | **Servings:** 4

Ingredients:

- 2 Tablespoons Olive Oil
- 3 Cups Vegetable Broth
- 2 Tablespoons Lemon Juice, Fresh
- ½ Teaspoon Garlic Powder
- ½ Cup Carrots, Shredded
- 2 Cups Cabbage, Shredded
- 1 Cup Beets, Shredded
- Dill for Garnish
- ½ Teaspoon Onion Powder
- Sea Salt & Black Pepper to Taste

Instructions:
1. Heat oil in a pot, and then sauté your vegetables.
2. Pour your broth in, mixing in your seasoning.
3. Simmer until it's cooked through, and then top with dill.

Nutrition: Calories 263, Carbs 8g, Protein 20g, Fat 24g

431. Root Vegetable Soup (FAST)

Preparation Time: 5 Minutes | **Cooking Time:** 15 Minutes | b6

Ingredients:
- 1/4 cup olive oil
- 2 medium onions, peeled and chopped
- 6 cloves garlic, peeled and minced
- 1 small butternut squash, divided, seeded, and cubed
- 3 large carrots, peeled and sliced
- 1 medium rutabaga, peeled and chopped
- 5 cups Basic Vegetable Stock
- 1 teaspoon dried marjoram leaves
- 1 teaspoon dried thyme leaves
- 1 teaspoon salt
- 1/4 teaspoon ground black pepper

Instructions:
1. In large soup pot or Dutch oven, heat olive oil over medium heat. Add onions and garlic; cook and stir for 4 minutes.
2. Add squash, carrots, and rutabaga; cook and stir for about 10 minutes or until vegetables start to brown.

3. Add stock, marjoram, thyme, salt, and black pepper and bring to a simmer. Set heat to low, cover, and simmer for 45-55 minutes or until vegetables are tender.
4. Correct seasoning if needed, and serve.

Nutrition: Calories: 205, Carbs: 30g, Fat: 10g, Sugar: 11g, Fiber: 8g, Protein: 3g, Sodium: 476mg

432. Chunky Tomato Sauce (FAST)

Preparation Time: 5 minutes | **Cooking Time:** 15 minutes | **Serving:** 6

Ingredients:
- ¼ cup extra virgin olive oil
- 2 onions, chopped
- 5 cloves of garlic, minced
- 2 red bell peppers, chopped
- ½ cup sliced Portobello mushrooms
- 3 cups diced tomatoes
- 1 tsp dried oregano
- 2 tsps. honey
- 2 tsps. balsamic vinegar
- 1 tsp dried basil
- ½ cup fresh spinach, chopped

Instructions:
1. In a heavy pan, heat oil over medium flame.
2. Stir in the onions, garlic, and bell pepper until fragrant.
3. Add in the mushrooms, tomatoes, oregano, honey, balsamic vinegar, and basil. Season with salt and pepper to taste.
4. Close the lid and bring to a simmer for 10 mins until the tomatoes have wilted.
5. Add in the spinach last and cook for another 5 mins.
6. Place in containers and store in the fridge until ready to use.

Nutrition: Calories 86, Fat 4g, Carbs 11g, Protein 2g, Fiber 2g, Sodium 88mg, Potassium 358mg

433. Homemade Tzatziki Sauce (FAST)

Preparation Time: 20 minutes | **Cooking Time:** 0 minutes | **Servings:** 1

Ingredients:

- 2 ounces (57 g) raw, unsalted cashews (about ½ cup)
- 2 tablespoons lemon juice
- 1/3 cup water
- 1 small clove garlic
- 1 cup chopped cucumber, peeled
- 2 tablespoons fresh dill

Instructions:

1. In a blender, add the cashews, lemon juice, water, and garlic. Keep it aside for at least 15 minutes to soften the cashews.
2. Blend the ingredients until smooth. Stir in the chopped cucumber and dill, and continue to blend until it reaches your desired consistency. It doesn't need to be totally smooth. Feel free to add more water if you like a thinner consistency.
3. Transfer to an airtight container and chill for at least 30 minutes for best flavors.
4. Bring the sauce to room temperature and shake well before serving.

Nutrition: Calories: 208, Fat: 13.5g, Carbs: 15.0g, Protein: 6.7g, Fiber: 2.8g

434. Lemon Celery Soup with Herb Oil (FAST)

Preparation Time: 5 Minutes | **Cooking Time:** 15 Minutes | **Servings:** 4

Ingredients:

- 1/2 of a head cauliflower, cored and broken into florets
- 1/4 mug packed Italian (flat leaf) parsley
- 1/4 mug packed basil leaves
- 1/4 mug olive oil
- 1 tablespoon fresh lemon juice
- 1 tablespoon olive oil
- 1 leek, sliced
- 4 mugs Chicken Bone Broth
- 1/2 of a moderate celery root (about 10 ounces), peeled and slice into 1-inch cubes
- 1/4 tsp. black pepper

Instructions:

1. In an exceedingly large sauce dish heat the one tablespoon olive oil over moderate heat.
2. Insert leek; prepare for four to 5 minutes or till tender.
3. Insert Chicken Bone Broth, celery root, and cauliflower.
4. Bring to boiling; reduce heat. Wrap up and simmer for 20 to twenty-five minutes or till vegetables are tender.
5. Remove from heat; cool slightly.
6. Meanwhile, for herb oil, in a food processor or blender combine the parsley, basil, and also the 1/4 mug olive oil.
7. Wrap up and method or blend till well combined and herbs are in very little items.
8. Set oil through a fine-mesh strainer into a small pot, pressing herbs with the back of a spoon to extract as abundant oil as possible.
9. Remove herbs; set herb oil aside. Shift half of the celery root combine to the food processor or blender.
10. Wrap up and process or blend till sleek.
11. Pour into a large pot.
12. Repeat with remaining celery root mix. Return all of the combine back to the sauce dish.
13. Shake in lemon juice and pepper, heat through. Ladle soup into pots.
14. Drizzle with herb oil.

Nutrition: Calories: 143, Carbs: 6g Fat: 8g Fiber: 4g, Protein: 3g Sodium: 58 mg

435. Tangy Orange Shrimp (FAST)

Preparation Time: 15 minutes | **Cooking Time:** 15 minutes | **Servings:** 4

Ingredients:

- ½ cup of freshly squeezed orange juice
- ½ tsp of cornstarch
- ¼ tsp of freshly grated orange zest

- 1 tsp of olive oil
- 12 ounces (26/30 count) of shrimp, peeled and deveined, tails left on
- 1 cup of broccoli florets
- 1 tsp of unsalted butter
- ½ cup of orange segments
- Freshly ground black pepper

Instructions:

1. In a small bowl, whisk together the orange juice, cornstarch, and orange zest and set aside.
2. In a large skillet over medium-high heat, heat the olive oil.
3. Add the shrimp and sauté until just cooked through and opaque, about 5 mins.
4. Transfer the cooked shrimp to a plate. Add the broccoli and sauté until tender, about 4 mins.
5. Transfer to the plate with the shrimp.
6. Pour the orange juice mixture into the skillet, and whisk until the sauce has thickened and is glossy about 3 mins.
7. Whisk in the butter, and add the orange segments, shrimp, and broccoli to the skillet.
8. Toss to combine and season with pepper. Serve immediately.

Nutrition: Calories 140, Fat 3g, Sodium 132mg Carbs 8g, Fiber 1g, Phosphorus 196mg Potassium 329mg Protein 18g

436. Salmon and Cauliflower (FAST)

Preparation Time: 10 minutes | **Cooking Time:** 20 minutes | **Servings:** 4

Ingredients:

- 4 boneless salmon fillets
- 2 tbsp Coconut aminos
- 1 sliced big red onion
- ¼ cup coconut sugar
- 1 head separated cauliflower florets
- 2 tbsp Olive oil

Instructions:

1. In a smaller bowl, mix sugar with coconut aminos and whisk.

2. Heat up a pan with half the oil over medium-high heat, add cauliflower and onion, stir and cook for 10 mins.
3. Put the salmon inside baking dish, drizzle the remainder inside oil, add coconut aminos, toss somewhat, season with black pepper, introduce within the oven and bake at 400 0F for 10 mins.
4. Divide the salmon along using the cauliflower mix between plates and serve.

Nutrition: Calories 227, Fat 3g, Sodium 96mg, Carbs 12g, Fiber 1g, Phosphorus 151mg, Potassium 242g, Protein 9g

437. Sirloin Carrot Soup

Preparation Time: 30 minutes | **Cooking Time:** 20 minutes | **Servings:** 4

Ingredients:

- 1 lb. chopped carrots and celery mix
- 32 oz. low-Sodium beef stock
- 1/3 cup whole-wheat flour
- 1 lb. ground beef sirloin
- 1 tbsp olive oil
- 1 chopped yellow onion

Instructions:

1. Heat up the olive oil in a saucepan over medium-high flame; add the beef and the flour.
2. Stir well and cook to brown for 4-5 mins.
3. Add the celery, onion, carrots, and stock; stir and bring to a simmer.
4. Turn down the heat to low and cook for 12-15 mins.
5. Serve warm.

Nutrition: Calories 140, Fat 4g, Carbs 17g, Protein 9g, Sugar: 12g, Fiber 3g, Sodium 86mg, Potassium 184mg

438. Vegetable Lentil Soup (FAST)

Preparation Time: 10 minutes | **Cooking Time:** 25 minutes | **Servings:** 4

Ingredients:

189

- 1 tbsp of extra-virgin olive oil
- ½ sweet onion, diced
- 2 carrots, diced
- 2 celery stalks, diced
- ½ cup of lentils
- 5 cups of Simple Chicken Broth or low-Sodium store-bought chicken stock
- 2 cups of sliced chard leaves
- Freshly ground black pepper
- 1 lemon

Instructions:

1. In a medium stockpot over medium-high heat, heat the olive oil.

2. Add the onion and stir until softened, about 3 to 5 mins.

3. Add the carrots, celery, lentils, and broth.

4. Bring to a boil, reduce the heat, and simmer, uncovered, for 15 mins, until the lentils are tender.

5. Add the chard and cook for 3 additional mins, until wilted—season with the pepper and lemon juice.

Nutrition: Calories 19, Fat 6g, Carbs 25g, Protein 13g, Phosphorus 228mg, Potassium 707mg, Sodium 157mg

439. Tender Beef and Cabbage Soup (FAST)

Preparation Time: 5 Minutes | **Cooking Time:** 20 Minutes | **Servings:** 14

Ingredients:

- 1 pound 85% lean ground beef
- 1 small head cabbage, cored and chopped
- 2 green onions
- 1 medium red bell pepper
- 1 medium bunch celery, chopped
- 1 cup chopped carrots
- 4 cups Basic Vegetable Stock
- 4 cups water
- 3 cloves garlic, peeled and minced
- 1/4 teaspoon crushed red pepper flakes
- 1/4 teaspoon dried basil
- 1/4 teaspoon dried oregano
- 1/4 teaspoon dried thyme
- 1/4 teaspoon onion powder

Instructions:

1. Heat a large skillet over medium-high heat. Add beef and cook, breaking up the lumps, until the meat is cooked through and just beginning to brown, 8–10 minutes.

2. Drain excess fat.

3. Place beef, cabbage, green onions, bell pepper, celery, and carrots in a 6-quart slow cooker.

4. Pour in stock and water.

5. Stir in garlic, pepper flakes, basil, oregano, thyme, and onion powder. Secure and cook on low for 8-10 hours.

Nutrition: Calories: 107 Carbs: 8g, Fat: 5g, Sugar: 4g, Fiber: 3g, Protein: 8g, Sodium: 69mg

30 DAY MEAL PLAN

Days	Breakfast	Lunch	Dinner	Snacks
1	Creamy Cherry Smoothie	Shrimp And Mango Salsa Lettuce Wraps	Italian Styled Stuffed Zucchini Boats	Papaya-Mango Smoothie
2	Lemon Baked Eggs	Bacon-Wrapped Asparagus	Chicken Cutlets	Cantaloupe Smoothie
3	Banana Pancakes	Zucchini Pasta with Shrimp	Slow Cooker Salsa Turkey	Cantaloupe-Mix Smoothie
4	Deviled Egg	Sweet Potato Buns Sandwich	Sriracha Lime Chicken and Apple Salad	Applesauce-Avocado Smoothie
5	Basil Zoodle Frittata	Shrimp, Sausage and Veggie Skillet	Pan-Seared Scallops with Lemon-Ginger Vinaigrette	Pina Colada Smoothie
6	Pear And Muesli Muffins	Sea Scallops with Spinach and Bacon	Roasted Salmon and Asparagus	Diced Fruits
7	Green Omelet with Portobello Fries	Liver With Onion and Parsley One	Orange And Maple-Glazed Salmon	Avocado Dip
8	Shakshuka	Egg And Avocado Wraps	Cod With Ginger and Black Beans	Homemade Hummus
9	Salmon Fritter	Creamy Sweet Potato Pasta with Pancetta	Halibut Curry	Tofu
10	Vanilla Almond Hot Chocolate	Roasted Beet Pasta with Kale and Pesto	Chicken Cacciatore	Almond Butter Sandwich
11	Banana And Pear Pita Pockets	Veggies And Apple with Orange Sauce	Chicken And Bell Pepper Sauté	Gluten-Free Muffins
12	Strawberry Overnight Oats	Healthier Apple Juice	Chicken Bone Broth	Roasted Carrot Sticks in A Honey Garlic Marinade
13	Ginger Peach Smoothie	Citrus Apple Juice	Homemade Beef Stock	Apple And Pistachio Salad on Spinach
14	Strawberry Banana Peanut Butter Smoothie	Richly Fruity Juice	Three-Ingredient Sugar-Free Gelatin	Tomato Cashew Pesto
15	Granola	Delish Grape Juice	Cranberry-Kombucha Jell-O	Sweet Potato Aioli
16	Persimmon Smoothie	Lemony Grape Juice	Strawberry Gummies	Eggplant Paste
17	Cranberry Smoothie	Holiday Special Juice	Fruity Jell-O Stars	Catalan Style Spinach
18	Kale Apple Smoothie	Vitamin C Rich Juice	Sugar-Free Cinnamon Jelly	Energy Balls
19	Glowing Skin Smoothie	Incredible Fresh Juice	Homey Clear Chicken Broth	Larabar Snack Bar
20	Cranberry Sauce	Favorite Summer Lemonade	Oxtail Bone Broth	Kulfi Indian Ice Cream
21	Chocolate Tahini Pumpkin Smoothie	Ultimate Fruity Punch	Chicken Bone Broth with Ginger and Lemon	Easy No-Bake Key Lime Pie Recipe
22	Cherry Spinach Smoothie	High-Fiber Dumplings	Quinoa Chickpea Salad	Banana-Bread Muffins
23	Banana Cacao Smoothie	Pizza Made with Bamboo Fibers	Rainbow Buddha Bowl with Cashew Tahini Sauce	Berry Fruit Leathers
24	Spinach And Egg Scramble with Raspberries	Vegetarian Hamburgers	Rice Bean Freezer Burritos	Chocolate-Covered Banana Slices
25	Blackberry Smoothie	Pork Steaks with Avocado	Roasted Veggie Hummus Pita Pockets	Coconut Macaroons
26	Veggie Frittata	Chicken With Asparagus Salad	Salmon Sushi Buddha Bowl	Banana Ice Cream
27	Chocolate Banana Protein Smoothie	Hot Pepper and Lamb Salmon	Sausage Peppers Baked Ziti	Berry Sorbet
28	Cocoa Almond French Toast	Pork Rolls À La Ratatouille	Sauteed Butternut Squash	Oatmeal Semisweet Chocolate-Chip Cookies
29	Muesli With Raspberries	Pepper Fillet with Leek	Seared Salmon with Pesto Fettuccine	Coconut-Lemon Bars
30	Mocha Overnight Oats	Lamb Chops with Beans	Sesame Ginger Chicken Salad	Flourless Chocolate Cake with Berry Sauce

CONCLUSION

Diverticular disease is common in developed countries, where diets are high in processed carbohydrates and low in fiber. It is more widespread in the United States, England, and Australia than in Asia or Africa, where diets are higher in fiber. Diverticular disease affects more than half of people over 60 in the United States. In approximately 10% to 25% of people with diverticular disease, a diverticulum will become inflamed, resulting in infection (diverticulitis). A variety of factors can cause diverticulitis. Both genetic and environmental triggers have been suggested in recent studies

Diverticular disease affects a large number of people who have no symptoms. However, bloating, abdominal cramping, abdominal swelling, rectal pain, and diarrhea are among the symptoms experienced by about 20% of affected. Extreme diverticulitis (infection of the diverticulum), a collection of pus in the pelvis because of rupture of the diverticulum, widespread infection of the abdominal cavity- also called bacterial peritonitis, colonic obstruction, and bleeding into the colon are all serious complications of diverticular disease. Low-fiber diets result in hard stools and a longer "transit time" (the amount of time it takes for stool to pass through the colon), which increases pressure.

Additionally, straining during bowel movements raises blood pressure. Blood pressure medications, "water pills" (diuretics), and narcotic pain relievers, for example, can cause constipation and increase colon pressure. Diverticula can form due to any of these causes of increased pressure. Diets low in fiber cause stool to be more difficult to pass, resulting in constipation. Constipation could indeed cause repeated straining during bowel movements, as well as an increase in colon pressure, which can lead to diverticula formation.

Fiber-rich diets can help prevent constipation and straining and lower the risk of diverticula formation. To keep stool soft and prevent constipation, two types of dietary fiber are required. Soluble fiber dissolves in water in the digestive tract and forms a soft gel-like substance. Insoluble fiber passes almost unaltered through the digestive tract and can act as a laxative, assisting stool passage. Vegetables and fruit, whole grains, and legumes like beans and lentils are all good sources of fiber. If a person has severe diverticulitis symptoms, the doctor may recommend a liquid diverticulitis diet, which includes water, fruit juices, broth, and ice pops as part of the treatment. Then, you can gradually return to a regular diet. Before introducing high-fiber foods, the doctor may recommend you to start with low-fiber foods like white meat, white bread, poultry, fish, eggs, and dairy products. Fiber softens and bulks up stools, allowing them to pass through the colon more easily. It also aids in the relief of intestinal pressure.

Under 51-year-old women should consume 25 grams of fiber every day. For men under the age of 51, 38 grams of fiber per day is recommended. Over the age of 51, women should ingest 21 grams of calcium each day. Men over 51 should consume 30 grams of protein each day. Fiber-rich foods include pasta, whole-grain bread, cereals, kidney and black beans, fresh fruits such as apples, pears, and prunes, as well as vegetables such as squash, potatoes, peas, spinach, and other veggies. As a result, you should include these foods in your diet to assist you overcome Diverticulitis.